# You'll Never Nanny in This Town Again!

## The Adventures and Misadventures of a Hollywood Nanny

# YOU'LL NEVER NANNY IN THIS TOWN AGAIN!

## The Adventures and Misadventures of a Hollywood Nanny

Suzanne Hansen

RUBY SKY
PUBLISHING

# "You'll Never Nanny in This Town Again!"
## The Adventures and Misadventures of a Hollywood Nanny

Copyright ©2003 by Suzanne Hansen

Ruby Sky Publishing
16055 SW Walker Rd. #225
Beaverton, OR 97006-4942
www.rubyskypublishing.com

Distributed by: IPG – Independent Publishers Group
www.ipgbook.com

ISBN 0-9727612-3-3
LCCN 2003090272

First edition: August 2003
Printed and bound in the United States of America
All rights reserved.

Author Photo by Ted Evans
Children's Photo by Marta Shely
Cover Design by Cathy Bowman
Cover Illustrations by E. Vokurka 2003
Sketch Illustrations by Elizabeth Cheek
Text Design and Layout by Anita Jones, Another Jones Graphics

Ruby Sky Books are available at special quantity discounts for bulk purchases,
sales promotions and fundraising.

Ruby Sky's mission is to support parents
in raising healthy, educated and self-confident children.
A portion of all proceeds will be donated to charities that support our ideals.
For more information please visit our website at
**www.rubyskypublishing.com**

*To Dianna,*

*Who is the True Nanny to the Stars*

# OPENING CREDITS

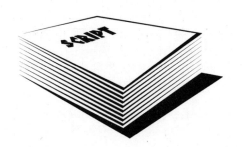

# PREVIEW OF UPCOMING ATTRACTIONS

## OPENING CREDITS

## QUIET ON THE SET....
## CAMERAS ROLLING!

      Making the Cut
      Big Girl on Campus
      What Exactly Do They Teach You in Nanny School?
      Never Have an Affair with Your Boss

      My Interview with a Rat Dog
      Take Two Ritalin and *Don't* Call Me in the Morning
      Do I Look Like Mary Poppins?

## LIGHTS! CAMERA! ACTION!

      Nanny Initiation
      Don't Judge the Art by it's Cover
      I Guess George Clooney was Off That Day
      The LAPD Almost Stopped Me From Getting to *90210*
      Struck by the Stars
      Guess Who's Coming to Dinner?
      Spago for Two

# TAKE TWO!

## "I Need Hair and Makeup Now!"

## FINAL TAKE

## THAT'S A WRAP

## THE OUTTAKES

# Director's Commentary

The decision to write this book—essentially the memoirs of a Hollywood Nanny—wasn't an easy one to make. I agonized over whether this was MY story to tell, especially since the children I loved and cared for are at the heart of it. I have used selective pseudonyms in order to be exceedingly candid in my observations of the families I worked for. I began and ended this writing process with the clear intention of NOT sharing ALL that I observed. That was the balance and compromise that felt best in my heart.

It's been several years since I've been in the nanny business. Since that time I've become a mother myself. I wrote this book, in part, to illustrate how the memories of the children I cared for still continue to inspire me to be the hands-on mother that I am today.

I decided against using a major publishing house so I could tell my story without pressure to reveal personal details that would make this a more marketable "tell-all" book. I was inundated with agents wanting me to sign contracts, but I was determined to tell My Story My Way. Of course, my husband is a little concerned about my judgment since I have completely overextended our credit lines in order to publish my nanny adventures. I'm sure he is a tad concerned about My Way at this point and is thinking "an advance," of any kind, would have been pretty nice.

Although this is a story about my personal experiences, it is far from unique. Nannies don't have a union, but we do chat. I assure you that similar scenes to the ones I describe are playing out in the homes of the wealthy and powerful all across America. Nannies are often kept out of public view; their constancy is disregarded, their nurturing is undervalued and they are often regarded as no more than necessary evils. The amateur psychologist in me speculates that the devaluation of child-care providers has much to do with parents' guilt about putting business lunches, movie premieres and ironically, childrens' charity benefits before time spent with their children.

Finally, I am hoping that this book will provide a little humor for all the mothers out there who have ever wondered why they can't do it all — the way the rich and famous do. It is my hope that everyone will see that none of these women are born with superior multi-tasking genes, they just have one hell of a *secret* support system. It can be a real morale-destroyer for those of us in the diaper trenches to think; if only we were better at juggling responsibilities, we too could have great bodies and flawless skin while keeping up with a busy family. The hard-working moms of America need to know what really goes on behind Hollywood's doors.

*Dear Oprah,*

*Of course you don't know me. I've never even been in the studio audience at one of your tapings. You've never heard the "You go, girl!" I shout to the TV from the privacy of my own kitchen. Nonetheless, you helped provide the inspiration for this book.*

*Over the years, I've seen you interview celebrities and explore the subject of "doing it all." Modestly confessing to being only a mother of puppies yourself, you unfailingly ask these movie star moms what kind of help they require to raise a family while maintaining an Oscar-level career.*

*Sadly, few of your guests share your humility. There have been many afternoons that I have stood in the debris of my kitchen, watching your show from my 4 inch black & white baby video monitor/TV, as I am attempting to throw together a dinner before I race my haggard self out the door to my daughter's ballet lesson. I have heard these Hollywood moms reduce the "help" they have in their lives to nearly nothing. I don't know whether I want to scream, laugh or cry when I see them smile graciously; subtly letting us know it's a tough world for the well-known, but they somehow manage to juggle a glamorous career, home, and family life all by themselves.*

*I know better.*

*After seeing these beautiful, powerful women continually erase the nannies behind them who are wiping up tears and devoting their days to loving and comforting their kids, I decided to speak up and be the voice for the unseen nanny and the children she cares for.*

*So, thank you Oprah, for continuing to let your light shine. I hope you will keep asking the beautiful women of the silver screen how they manage to do it all. You go, girl!*

*With much love and appreciation,*

*Suzanne Hansen*
(A Mommy that is NOT doing it all by herself)

# The Producers of this Book would like to Thank...

I have been dreaming about writing this page since I was about seven. So, this is going to take awhile. If reading about all the family and friends that have been patiently waiting for me to finish this enormous project, bores you to tears, please feel free to skip ahead. I won't be offended in the least and that will allow me not to feel rushed as I go on and on about the people I love in my life.

I love reading the gratitude page of every book. I will flip back and forth between the notes of gratitude and the author's picture. This way, I can accurately make up a story about what I think the author's everyday life is *really* like. If you are like me, I will give you a head start on the story you might be conjuring up about me. First off, I don't look like my author photo every day. So any childhood dreams I ever had of being "recognized" are pretty much zero to none. In reality, most of the time I am wandering the book aisles of Barnes and Noble, un-showered and wearing my husband's baseball cap while explaining to my son why we can't take home the *Real* Thomas the Tank Engine. You know, come to think of it I have yet to really pull this Mommy thing all together....but that is another book. Enough about me, on to my supporting cast.

**Thank you to........**
...My forever girlfriends that know all my secrets, Amy, Christine, Kristi and Missy. I am so grateful we have shared so many years together. I love you all very much.
...Jason, you are the definition of a loyal friend. My life would not be as complete without you in it. Thank you for all you give to me.
...My sister Cindy, my business partner, for all your work (well, the money was nice too) I know it was no easy task trying to keep me within budget (that must have come from all your years of playing CEO instead of Barbies). Your belief in me gave me the wings I needed to fly. I will be forever grateful. To my brother in-law, Mark, for being my *Beverly Hillbillies* expert, and giving so much of yourself for this book.

…My sister Traci, I am so proud to call you my sister. I love you with all my heart.

…My parents, for your **never-ending** love and encouragement. Thank you for always believing in me and my dreams.

…Cassie and Yuki, I feel so blessed to have you both in my family.

…My cousins Jill, Lynn and David and their wonderful partners, thank you for all the love and laughs throughout my entire life.

…Dianna and Mandie Ludlam, you are my family. My life has been greatly enriched by both of you being a part of it.

…Nicole, thank you for all you have brought to my life. You know how much I love you.

…My 'Mommy girlfriends,' Danette, Kristine, Julie and Dawn, thank you for your friendships, even when I was on 'book exile' and couldn't take your phone calls.

…CarolAnn, for being such an enormous blessing in our life.

…Susan Beekman, for being my angel and helping me piece my story together, while giving so much of yourself.

…Candi, still smiling as I made so many tiny changes in the manuscript.

…Robert, for beginning this journey with me. So what, if you are not the descendent of the good guy, you will always be my *Braveheart*.

…Tim, for seeing my plan and changing it. I am grateful every day of my life, for your love.

…All my friends that are labor and delivery nurses at Sacred Heart and St Vincent's hospital. Thank you *ALL* for the years of laughter, and friendship, I miss sharing my life with you everyday.

…Toby and Brandon Matlock, for loving my little ones so much!

…My High School graduating class, for your friendships and wonderful memories of the years we had growing up together.

…Stacy Bellwood, for sending me on the greatest journey of my life and supporting me all the way. Thank you for the gift of, you.

…Tim O'Kelley, for being the most charismatic man I know. Thank you! Mackenzie is so fortunate to have you as her father.

…Ernestine, still working on getting you to the White House for a visit.

…My Team #368, WLS #77 and PLD #8 I love each and every one of you and can never thank you enough for all you have shared with me. Because of you, I am the Mommy I always dreamed of being.

…My precious Jadyn and Parker. You two teach me how to live in the moment. I am grateful every single day that I was chosen to be blessed with your little souls. I love you both more than you can ever imagine. I am honored to be your Mommy.

…Wes, for being the most loving and caring father on the planet. You bless my life. Thank you for believing in me with your whole heart. Your ability to give of yourself still amazes me. I don't have big enough words to describe how much I love and cherish you. Yes, I know you are thinking, "Well you could *SHOW* me how great you think I am by letting me go play 18 with Carl, Jay and Russell"……OK, go get your clubs and get out the door before I change my mind!

# The Movie Trailer

# The Movie Trailer

It was the first actual adult movie my husband Wes and I had seen in ages. My mother was kind enough to drive three hours to watch the kids, since I was sure there was no teenager on the planet that could properly care for my two precious little ones. I was so excited that I ordered the popcorn tub, an extra large Sprite, and my favorite cinema candy, Sweet Tarts. Wes, loyal and supportive sidekick that he is, carried the popcorn and held my hand as we walked into the theater.

The theater was almost empty since it was a weeknight. We were seated just in time to watch the psychedelic roller coaster ride reminding less prepared movie-goers about all the goodies for sale at the refreshment stand. The minute the previews of coming attractions rolled, we started whispering. As exhausted new parents, we had almost no time to talk, and we were completely oblivious to what was new in the world of entertainment. So we were fascinated...so much had been happening while we'd been changing diapers!

"The film industry calls these trailers. Why is that, since they come out *before* the film?" I whispered. "The only thing that word brings to my mind is a house with metal siding on wheels. I don't get the connection."

"I don't know. I doubt anyone who makes the decisions about these productions has actually seen the kind of trailer that you're talking about," Wes commented.

"And why is the sound ten times louder? Seems like they pack the *entire* movie into the preview," I complained.

"No kidding. I think I just figured out the plot to *that* movie," Wes remarked.

"Oh well. Now we don't need to spend our precious child-free hours to see it in the theater," I whispered back.

We were silent for a moment watching scenes from an upcoming romantic comedy. Fortunately we had the entire section of the theater to ourselves so there were no neighbors to shush us. I wasn't about to lose my chance to talk about something besides *Dora the Explorer*.

"Honey, if we made a trailer for our lives, what would it look like?"

"Suzanne, give me a break. Who'd want to watch us go to the grocery store and mow the lawn?"

"I don't know. I could make it interesting. I could start with our blind date and then how you sent me a dozen roses, to profess your undying love for me, when I was in Hawaii working," I smiled, remembering our own personal romantic comedy.

"Okay dear, whatever you think" Wes said dismissively.

The main feature began while I continued my running commentary. As the credits appeared on screen, I took it upon myself to remark on each name.

*Producer*— "Met him."

*Co-producer*— "Went to his house."

*Director*— "Talked to him at a party."

*Cinematographer*— "He stayed the night at our house."

*Scriptwriter*—"His kids came to play when we were at the beach house."

"Jeez, Suzanne. You can't possibly know *everyone* in Hollywood."

"Maybe not, but I'll bet you couldn't name ten Hollywood players that I didn't have some contact with while I was there. You know, kind of like that 6 degrees of Kevin Bacon thing," I explained.

"Hey! I just got an idea! Maybe what you should do is make a movie about all the stuff that happened to you there. That way you wouldn't be answering the same question, every time we go to a party and people ask you the same ole..., 'What was it *like* working for those people." He was doing a *perfect impression* of the same annoying question I always got.

I could hardly concentrate on the movie after his casual suggestion. Maybe I *should* make a movie. Or maybe I could just make a movie trailer that I could run when people asked me about being a nanny. My vivid imagination was starting to write a screenplay.

I could see the rest of my movie trailer now, quick clips in rapid succession; one tacked to the other just enough to suggest the plot. There would be a shot of my blue-collar hometown, my arrival at the mysterious Northwest Nannies Institute, followed by the mansions in Southern California, then shots of family vacations in Aspen and Hawaii. There'd have to be a shot of me scrambling to get my stuff out of the house before sunset, then just glimpses of all that came after that. I'd leave the movie audience wondering what the movie would reveal about the way life REALLY is in Hollywood.

# QUIET ON THE SET... CAMERAS ROLLING!

# The King and I

EXTERIOR - LARGE HOUSE — AFTERNOON

Front door of a large, colonial-style home swings open.
A tattered suitcase comes sailing out, past a large
red steel sculpture on the grass. It opens in mid-
flight. The clothes inside pinwheel out onto the
immaculately maintained lawn. An angry man bursts out
onto the front steps, shaking his fist in the air.

ANGRY MAN

You'll never nanny in this town again! Do you hear
me? Never!

FOREGROUND:

Young woman's head lifts up. Door slams behind her.
The girl picks up her clothes and stuffs them back into
the old suitcase. She is crying. With one hand, she's
picking up her belongings and with the other she's
wiping tears from her cheek.

YOUNG GIRL
(Under her breath)

Jackass!

Okay, so I'm not a screenwriter or a director, but that's the scene I envisioned after I gave Julia Swartz my notice on a Monday night that I didn't want to continue working as the family's nanny. I was afraid she would go to her husband immediately and break the news, at which point he would come pounding down the stairs with my suitcase already packed for me, his arms flailing in righteous indignation.

Only it didn't happen quite that way.

For the next couple of days I walked on eggshells waiting for The King to signal the hooded man to release the heavy blade—nothing. Then Wednesday morning, he approached me calmly and asked me to sit down. I was sure he could see my heart pounding through my T-shirt.

"Julia said that you want to quit." There was a long, awkward pause.

"Suzy, would you please reconsider?" he asked in a soft, nearly pleading voice I'd never heard from him before. *Was the Most Powerful Man in Hollywood actually begging his nanny?* "Can't you just finish out the year?" *Finish out the year? It was mid-January.*

"You know we have the Aspen vacation scheduled for spring break, so how about just hanging on until after that?" I didn't respond. I just put my head down. I was too afraid to answer. I sat there in silence with my shoulders slumped around my chest. I couldn't believe I was about to wimp out again. "You could at least stay until after Julia's week in February at The Golden Door Spa. You know she deserves this vacation." I didn't know if I would ever be able to stand up to this man.

I had told Julia that I would stay for four weeks, and if they found someone to replace me before that, I'd leave earlier. But she didn't seem to be listening to me that night because she was so angry. I wondered what she had told him about my sudden notice.

I knew him well enough to realize that his campaign to have me stay would quickly escalate from two controlled, peaceful questions to a flat demand, and then things would get ugly if he didn't get his way. I steeled myself for his next question.

Instead, he said, "You think about it and then let me know in a few days what you decide."

I told him "Okay, I'll think about it," knowing that there was nothing to think about, knowing I wanted to leave. I just didn't have the nerve to say so.

This had been my home for over a year, and I knew I would dearly miss the three children: Amanda, Joshua and Brandon, for whom I had been pseudo-mother, nurse, playmate, diaper changer, referee, emotional punching bag and chauffeur. I had also become close to the entire household staff, as well as some of Steven's employees at his office. We had been a family within a family, or rather, a little family attached to a family. As for Steven and Julia, well, I wouldn't miss devoting my life to them, but I didn't dislike them. I still wanted the very best for the children's parents.

I had no idea what I was going to do next or where I would go. In less than two years, I had finished high school, graduated with honors from the Northwest Nannies Institute in Portland, Oregon and lived with, and worked fourteen-hour days, and five to seven-day weeks for the man who was said to basically run Hollywood. At the time I was an extremely naive nineteen-year-old (at least by Hollywood standards). My entire life to that point had transpired quite uneventfully in a small, far-away corner of Oregon, where the inhabitants counted as the highlight of the week going to the local BI-MART to see if their membership cards had yielded any big wins on Lucky Number Tuesdays. The best way for you to picture my hometown would be if you imagined a cross between the town of Mayberry and Dodge City in the late 1800s. It was a place where almost every young boy dreamed of owning a four-wheel-drive truck with a rifle in the gun rack, and most of the girls hoped for a boyfriend who fit that description. When we finally got our first fast food restaurant, there was so much excitement that six hundred residents showed up at the local grade school gymnasium to compete for a position that would have them saying "Welcome to McDonalds, would you like to try our value meal today?"

When I was first asked to interview with "a family in the entertainment industry" through the nanny placement agency, I was actually a little disappointed when I didn't recognize the name. I'd imagined someone like Chevy Chase or Bill Murray. I didn't have a clue who Steven Swartz was. The woman at the agency told me only his name and that he was the president of a talent agency. When I first interviewed with his wife Julia in their impressive offices, I was just beginning to get the picture. I soon found out that his agency represented nearly every major Hollywood actor and actress I'd ever heard of, along with some of the biggest directors, writers and musical talent of our time. Eventually, I met most of them. I had no way of knowing when I accepted the position that their frequent dinner parties would be a *Who's Who* of Hollywood.

The first day I went to the office of my future employer stands out in my memory. His company was the Agency of Creative Talent (usually referred to by its well-known acronym ACT) in Century City. I had been sitting in the reception area staring in transfixed awe at the receptionist, who confidently threw around the biggest names in film. Not only was I amazed at the callers, I was also intrigued just watching the receptionists, there were two of them. They both punched the never-ending stream of flicking lights while simultaneously signing for delivery packages and greeting guests. Both of them were extremely poised and professional, both in their attire and their phone etiquette. In those days, Steven Swartz was King; although at that time, I didn't know of what. However, I did know who the movie stars were. When you grow up in a less than thriving metropolis, you consider "The Arts" seeing a movie at the local drive-in. The one in my home town of Cottage Grove could have very well been the last outdoor theater operating in the United States where you still had to hang the metal speaker that produced more static than sound from your partially rolled-down window.

My first interview in this intimidating office was with Julia Swartz. As I was ushered into the dramatic conference room with floor-to-ceiling glass, I was stunned at how beautiful the blonde woman was. She was wearing a butter-colored silk outfit and diamond stud earrings the size of small grapes. Her style and demeanor qualified her immediately, in my mind, for the title of Queen.

"Hello, I'm Julia Swartz. It's nice to meet you," she said as she smiled warmly and extended her hand to welcome me.

During that interview I learned a great deal more about her children. I shared with her my love of children and explained the nanny training program I had just completed. Julia told me that if I "made the cut" I would next meet Mr. Swartz. I was more excited than nervous when I left the office.

## Making the Cut

I must have made it through the first audition because, before I knew it, there I was again, sitting in the luxurious waiting area for the second time in three days, while the receptionist continually answered calls from Academy Award-winning actors. I realized I was in the presence of someone far more important than myself. Obviously this wouldn't have been difficult. I'd gone the first round with his wife, and was there now to meet with Mr. Swartz. I was about to meet someone whose every phone call could mean millions.

Suddenly a door swung open from what I had thought was simply a wall. A beautiful woman dressed in three different shades of beige, wearing a strand of pearls around her neck and carrying a note pad in one hand, said, "Ms. Hansen, please step this way. Mr. Swartz will see you now."

Even the receptionists were dressed in expensive and well-coordinated outfits. I, on the other hand, stood up in my blue dress and white patent leather pumps, humiliated that I was violating the Labor Day white shoe rule by eons. My mom and I had realized in the motel that I looked quite tacky, but I had no other option when I dressed for the interview. Looking down at my fashion faux pas whites, I became even more nervous. I couldn't have felt more out of place if I'd been wearing athletic socks and Birkenstocks.

That's when I felt all the blood drain out of my face and into my hopelessly unfashionable feet. The room began to turn slowly, then more quickly in circles. I did manage to gather myself by grabbing the backs of the chairs and then the receptionist's counter. I steadied myself and focused on not fainting as I followed on the elegant heels of the woman with the pearls. We walked down the corridor, past one movie poster after another, with people bustling by in both directions. I peeked into the busy offices. I saw framed and autographed photos on the desks of Rob Reiner, Dan Ackroyd and Robin Williams. At the end of the hallway, I could see into a spacious office where an attractive man was seated behind a desk the size of two formal dining tables. He was wearing a telephone headset, and reclined back at an angle that must have strained the limits of his ergonomically-correct leather chair. He had short light brown hair, bright eyes and a white shirt, meticulously pressed and starched. He was wearing a conservative plum-colored tie that I noticed matched the colors in a painting on the wall behind him.

My escort paused silently in the doorway and I stood motionless just behind her. As the man said goodbye to his caller, he pulled the headset off and gave me a warm smile. In a very officious manner, befitting the introduction of a visiting diplomat, the woman announced, as if to a large audience, "Mr. Swartz, this is Ms. Hansen to see you, your ten twenty. She has already interviewed with Julia."

On the one hand, I felt honored to receive such an introduction. On the other hand, as his "ten twenty," I was imagining how jam-packed this important man's calendar must be. I wondered if he had a "ten twenty-five" scheduled. He said to the woman, "I need some uninterrupted time here. I don't want to take any calls for fifteen minutes."

The man gestured to a seating arrangement like you might find in an issue of *Architectural Digest*—a leather couch and several low-slung chairs arranged around a modern coffee table at the other end of his huge office. An immense contemporary painting dominated the wall. I had never been in a place quite so intimidating, with perhaps the exception of the principal's office in high school the time I was being grilled over my possible involvement in some prom night shenanigans. (Setting the record straight, I was NOT involved in the now infamous Morning-After-Suspension-from-School. I told Mr. Otton I knew nothing of my dear friends Amy and Christine's involvement that night with some men named Bartles and James.)

Sitting in the magnificent office of Steven Swartz, I was even more petrified. I sat silent. Thinking back now, I realize how ridiculous I must have appeared. Mr. Swartz laughed and said, "You look scared to death, white as chalk. Just relax." *Yeah right, just relax? Every one of the people I've talked to casually mentions that you're the Most Powerful Man in Hollywood. It's just a wee bit intimidating.*

For thirty minutes, he asked questions in the verbal equivalent of italics and exclamation marks, and did not seem much interested in my answers. He included a quick question about my driving record and my ability to drive in the snow, since the family frequently found themselves in Aspen. He didn't seem to care that my answer was not what you would want to hear from a prospective employee, especially one who would be entrusted with the safe transport of your precious children. It seemed to me that he was more interested in what his next question would be. He inquired about nanny school, having never heard of such a thing. He seemed to find the whole idea amusing, and he asked, "What exactly do they teach you in nanny school?" He seemed even more amused that I attempted to answer him. I fumbled for words while he watched, grinning slightly.

Later I came to believe that Steven was most comfortable when others were not. It seemed that he enjoyed seeing people crumble into nervous wrecks in his presence. So my terror during the interview had just made his day. And when he invited me to a follow-up interview at his home, he made mine. His question about nanny school, and my awkwardness in answering him, got me thinking about what had led to this turn of events in my life...

## Big Girl on Campus

I was eighteen and my high school graduation was looming. Some of my friends had been applying to various colleges. I had been at my best friend Kristi's house when she was filling out her application to her father's alma mater, Stanford. I had just hoped to God her parents wouldn't ask me where I was going—I hadn't applied to any colleges. I think they just understood that it was better not to ask, given my lack of interest in academics.

My high school career had unfortunately pinnacled with my election as homecoming princess of the sophomore class. My grades were fine, that wasn't so difficult; and the times I actually lugged any homework home were few and far between. The focus of my high school career was the social life. Keeping updated on who was dating whom, was my greatest motivation to get to school every morning. I was considered the comprehensive resource for all that was socially dish-worthy. I wasn't confident these skills would transfer successfully to college.

The day all the college-bound students in my senior class were scheduled to take the SATs, I was sitting in Mr. McDonald's psychology class. One of the students with a less than stellar grade point average (we called him Smokin' Joe Weed) raised his hand to tell Mr. McDonald that he just remembered he was supposed to leave class to take the test. Though most of the school suspected that Mr. McDonald was tipping the bottle between classes, he was no dummy. Smokin' Joe's chances of needing to take the SATs were about as likely as Spicoli becoming the valedictorian in *Fast Times at Ridgemont High*. He wasn't about to let Joe out of class.

"Mr. Weed, do you have your registration slip?" Mr. McDonald asked, knowing that would immediately settle the matter.

"Uh, I left it at home?" he attempted without conviction.

"I guess you won't be taking the SATs without that slip. Now, Ms. Hansen here, on the other hand," he pointed to me. "I'm sure she's registered and will be leaving soon," he announced to the class at large.

My heart sank. My face became flush. I sat there thinking how wise, my slightly inebriated homeroom teacher was. Why wasn't I taking the test? Until that point, I must admit, I hadn't given much thought as to what I was going to do with my life. I knew that I didn't want to live my adult life in Cottage Grove, but that was as far as I got in my post-graduation planning process.

When everyone started talking about what they were going to do after graduation, I began to search my own reservoir of desires to determine what would be ahead for me. My guidance counselor, fortunately, gave me an application to a nanny-training program in Portland when he saw that I hadn't signed up to take any college entrance exams. I'm sure he was hoping to give me some direction. I was grateful he noticed. I sent in my application, relieved that I'd found a solution. Nanny school seemed perfect: I had been baby-sitting from the age of nine. And I had worked for several families for years. I loved being with children and I knew I'd enjoy working with them as a "profession."

When the day came that classes were being let out for the summer, there was a large piece of butcher paper posted in the hallway, Kristi and I stopped to read it and add our information.

### Seniors, what are your plans after graduation?

| | |
|---|---|
| **Ben Bangs** | *Colorado State* |
| **Craig Jenkins** | *Drink beer all summer, then go to SOSC* |
| **Drew Birdseye** | *Play drums for a heavy metal band* |
| **Shaunna Griggs** | *Pacific University* |
| **Scott Cates** | *Go water–skiing* |
| **Alan Gates** | *Drive the boat that Scott is skiing behind* |
| **Tami Thompson** | *Move as far away from this town as possible* |
| **Jenny Heckman** | *Beauty College* |
| **Amy McCarty** | *Follow Ozzy around on tour* |
| **Suzy Hansen** | *NNI* |

I wasn't sure my fellow classmates would even know what a nanny was, so NNI conveyed the proper sense of dignity and respect. I prayed no one would ask me what that stood for. I was hoping they would think that it was a small college in Northern Nebraska. Or maybe the National Neuropathy Institute?

I don't know why I cared about what other people thought, since my hometown had a low percentage of college-bound seniors, anyway. I guess I didn't want my career plans to seem like a joke because, damn it, I was serious about my professional development.

When the answer to my application arrived in the mailbox, it had a rich gold logo embossed in the upper left corner, which read Northwest Nannies Institute (NNI). I stared at the envelope for a moment. I sounded out the initials in my best upper class British accent—ehn, ehn, eye.

"Greetings," it had begun.

"Congratulations! Your application has been accepted. You have been selected to attend the Northwest Nannies Institute as a fall enrollee."

As I reached my front doorstep, my mind began to drift off, envisioning the stately institute...

CUT TO:

EXTERIOR - BRICK BUILDING ON COLLEGE CAMPUS - DUSK

Scene evokes an Ivy League College campus. An orchestra is playing Pomp and Circumstance. Students are milling and passing with textbooks in hand. A matronly, but professorial looking woman extends her hand...


                    DEAN OF THE SCHOOL
Welcome, Suzanne. We are so pleased and proud that you have chosen NNI. Please come in.

A young woman smiles and extends her hand to the woman.

                    SUZANNE
Thank you, Dean. I am honored to be here.

The two turn together and walk through the massive doorway.

Having only been to a large city like Portland on a couple of visits, I had never seen an *Institute*. Just the thought of attending a school that looked like a University you'd see in Cambridge, Massachusetts intrigued me.

Along with the application, the institute asked for three letters of recommendation, which I easily provided from the families I had worked for. They also requested an essay entitled: *Why I want to be a Nanny*. That was a breeze—I was bursting with lofty aspirations, eager to provide the privileged young people of the world with the most devoted and most loving of attentions. I knew this training program would prepare me properly.

I'd made it through the criminal background check unscathed, save for my dismal driving record, which they were willing to overlook. My rap sheet included four speeding tickets in the two short years I'd been driving. (Okay, actually I had five citations and they removed one from my record because I attended an all-day driver's safety course. That little educational experience, was a bit frightening. Upon sharing introductions in this class of multiple offenders, I realized I was the only one in attendance that did not have a prison record. The moving violation counselor that I was assigned reviewed my poor driving history. She said she had never before counseled a teenage girl who had good grades and was on the rally squad. So unlike the other lead-foots there, my chances for eventual life success was as high as fifty-fifty. But I had to really want to salvage my wayward soul, she warned. I did, I did; I wanted to become a nanny. )

The acceptance letter sealed my excitement about my future career. I could easily visualize myself working for a wealthy family with adorable children. We were big *Dallas* fans in my family when I was very young. We even had a huge lottery going the night we found out who shot JR. So, I just plugged myself into a picture of a home similar to South Fork where the mom would be driving around in a Mercedes convertible just like Pamela Ewing. Perhaps my positive influence could even spare them some of the Ewing family-type grief.

The more images I conjured up in my daydreams, the more I wanted to get on with my new life. I could see myself wearing one of those collegiate cardigan sweaters proudly sporting the gold NNI letters. Besides, the tuition was reasonable and my parents were more than happy to pay for my four months of "higher education."

At the end of the summer, my bags were packed and I bid my parents a tearful goodbye as I waved from my little Toyota. I imagined all my college-bound friends doing the same as they traveled off to exotic places and revered schools. I knew I would miss all of the friends that I had grown up with. Many of the kids in my graduating class had attended nursery school with me. This act of self-direction was a real life milestone.

My heart was pounding, my pulse racing when I saw the green highway sign that read "Portland 50 Miles." Shortly thereafter, the first skyscrapers came into view. It was a magnificent sight. There was so much activity and energy. The city was alive and buzzing, and I was intrigued and excited.

I settled in with the host family, an arrangement that had been made for me by the school. That first night, I barely slept; too filled with anticipation. There were skittish butterflies in my stomach. It felt just like my first day of school in fourth grade, when I had laid out my new school supplies along with my new Wonder Woman lunch pail.

The drive early the next morning took less than twenty minutes. First, I passed through the heart of the financial district with all of its powerful looking, glass-encased buildings, then through a part of town where the buildings quickly became shorter and older, and finally to an area that looked decidedly underwhelming. I began to seriously wonder if I was lost. Perhaps I had to go through this area to get to the pastoral countryside I had envisioned, where the stately institute would be standing. I unfolded the map again, checked the address on the letterhead and continued to scour the numbers on the sides of the buildings. There must be some mistake. Where am I? Where in the middle of all this concrete is the "Institute"?

I reached the cross street I had been given in my directions. I looked out the window, smudged with the residue of car exhaust, slowing down to peer at a strip mall that looked more like a prison block. In the middle of the block was a stucco two-story building, which I can best describe in architectural terms as a long beige box stacked on top of another. There was a 7-Eleven, which looked like it might have been the very first one in the franchise. It shared a wall with a business that had a door that read "*Beauty Parlor*" in peeling vinyl letters. Beside that was a dry cleaner, and further down on the other side of the 7-Eleven was a Chinese takeout place. It didn't look anything like the Harvard campus I'd been dreaming of all summer long.

I thought maybe I'd mixed up the directions. I wondered if I'd read the address correctly. A hundred thoughts raced through my mind, as once again I pulled NNI's letter out of my purse, hoping to find I was on the north*east* side of Portland by mistake, not the north*west*. To my dismay, I read the numbers 2332 Northwest Broadway on the letter, then turned to the tarnished brass numbers on the side of the second story of the building and found they were identical. My hopes for being in the wrong part of town vanished in that moment.

I desperately wanted to turn my car around and drive back home very fast (within the speed limit of course, since I was still one moving violation away from having my license suspended) but a piece of advice that my grandmother had given me years before came into my head:

*When you feel afraid, it's your heart speaking to you,*
*Telling you to use this opportunity to face your fear.*

Did I have a fear of old tarnished buildings in big cities? Um, yes I did, so Grammy's words rallied my courage. I had come this far. The least I could do was investigate a little further. After all, I told myself, I could always go home and go to dental hygiene school. (This had originally been my plan until my mother commented that she thought it would be gross to look in peoples' mouths all day. I had realized that she had a good point, one that hadn't occurred to me before, so I had abandoned the idea. But now, suddenly a career in dental decay was beginning to look appealing.)

As I began to climb the concrete steps, couldn't find the elevator, to the second story a hundred pictures sprang to mind; none of them looked anything like the ivy-covered walls of academia I had previously envisioned. At that moment I could have never imagined that in four short months I would fly to Los Angeles, go on interviews with some of the wealthiest people in the country and become the highest paid nanny to have graduated from NNI.

## What Exactly Do They Teach You in Nanny School?

My desk was a wooden seat with a table top welded together with gray steel tubes, the kind you remember from third grade, the ones that had hearts and initials carved into them. As I sat down that first morning my first thought was *Maybe I have made a wrong turn on my career path: How can I leave without making a scene?*

There were fourteen other girls and women seated in the neat rows of mini-desks. At the front of the room was a large desk with a grown-up sized chair and behind that an enormous blackboard where the following words were written:

**A Professionally Trained Nanny is:**
- **Not a maid**
- **Prepared for the unexpected**
- **Always conducting herself in a professional manner**
- **Truly committed to the profession**

Following the *Nanny Code of Conduct*, there was an outline of some of the material we would be covering:

**Today's Subjects:**
- **Etiquette—Table Manners**
- **Grooming—Hygiene**
- **Family Dynamics—Husband and Wife as Parents**
- **First Aid-CPR**

In the short time between receiving the acceptance letter from NNI and my presence in the classroom, I hadn't given much thought to what other duties the nanny would have. Obviously, I knew my main responsibility was to care for the children, and I already considered myself a professional of sorts in that arena. When I read the chalkboard, I was pleasantly surprised at the scope of material we would be covering. I just never anticipated a lengthy dissertation on personal hygiene.

"Carolyn," I called out after raising my hand like a school child.

"Yes, Ms. Hansen."

"I would like to know whose hygiene you are referring to in your blackboard note and how long could a class on hygiene actually be?"

"That is something we can discuss in private after class today, if you wish to stay," she explained calmly.

I started to feel a little sheepish and concerned about the impression I'd made on my teacher the first day of school.

*But it did look like we needed to talk; surveying this room, there might actually be students who could benefit from some grooming tips.*

During our after-school meeting she explained, "Not all of our students share your privileged background," as if my last name was Kennedy. After our little chat about my insensitivities to my classmates, and having taken stock of the others around me more carefully the next day, I realized that what Carolyn had said was true. Even though I didn't come from the wealthy lineage that Carolyn implied, I did get the gist of what she was saying. I needed to be *less* judgmental of others. *Oh great, just like my mother had always been telling me!*

I've always been kind of an amateur Sigmund Freud. That is to say, rather nosy. I started analyzing people's behavior before the age of ten. This probably led to my mother's continual admonishment, "Suzanne, it's not nice to judge people until you've walked a mile in their shoes."

Carolyn's lesson reminded me of my first baby-sitting job when I was in the fourth grade. I'll never know what possessed my mother to think that I was responsible enough to oversee a child who was only two years younger than me. She'd promised my services to our Avon lady, who wanted me to watch her four children, ages one to seven, for an evening. She told me she had an important date that night. I remember being fascinated by her beaver-like front teeth, and as soon as she left, I started checking out the kids for evidence of their buck-toothed genetic heritage. Setting the stage for my later interest in other people's relationships, I wondered who she was dating, and who was the father to the four she already had. I quickly reminded myself that I wasn't supposed to criticize people unless I'd been wearing their shoes.

When I arrived at her house, the Avon lady informed me that there had been recent reports of a prowler in the area. I should call the police if anything suspicious should happen. I spent the entire night peeping out from behind the curtains in several rooms, with most of the lights in the house turned on. How could anyone let me, a nine-year-old who still played with Barbies and was scared of the witch on *The Wizard of Oz*, take care of her children in the face of such imminent danger? Despite my reluctance and fears, the dollar-an-hour wage convinced me to tough it out. Besides, I was responsible for my young charges, and I wouldn't let a little fear stop me. That night began my baby-sitting career.

I see now that my very first baby-sitting experience was truly an early indication of things to come. All the elements that defined my future were there — my talent as a busybody, my propensity to psychoanalyze people and their relationships, my alternating confidence and self-doubt, and my willingness to push against my personal limits in the interest of child-care excellence.

NNI was one of the first and only nanny schools in the nation. At that time, the whole concept of formal training for nannies was unique. Carolyn and Linda had begun the nanny school a year earlier and like many new businesses, they did it all. Sometimes during our lessons they would have to interrupt class to take phone calls. I will never forget one memorable call. "NNI, may I help you?"—"Yes. Uh, yes."—"No, we don't do pet sitting."—"Well, uh yes, sometimes our nannies do work for families that have pets."—"Uh no, we don't offer a dog walking service."—"Yes, I realize there are similarities between babies and puppies."— "Perhaps your vet would have a referral?"—"No, once again, sir: just human beings, not Schnauzers . . ." The concept of a nanny was still a new one in Oregon.

One of the first things they taught us at Nanny School was the definition of a nanny, to whit: "A nanny's role is to provide support to the family by serving as a loving, nurturing and trustworthy companion to the children. A nanny has special child-care skills and a deep love and understanding of children. A nanny offers the family convenient, high-quality care to meet each child's physical, emotional, social and intellectual needs."

Carolyn continued to add topics to the blackboard...
- **Household management**
- **Health and safety**
- **Physical and cognitive development of children**
- **How to talk so kids will listen**
- **Understanding the complexities of the family unit**
- **Interpersonal relationships—Life skills**
- **Career planning—Employment contracts**
- **Resumes—Interviewing techniques**

The curriculum was beginning to look more thorough than I had imagined, and by the end of the week I had decided to continue my education. At the time, the potential pay for a "live-in" nanny averaged $150-200 per week and included room and board. In my mind, the room and board was the equivalent of another $800 a month. I was looking forward to working for a well-to-do family, caring for their children and possibly traveling, too. The prospect of being paid well for something I loved doing appealed to me. Besides, I was beginning to think of myself as a "professional," and I was looking forward to increasing my knowledge in my new field of study.

## Never Have an Affair with Your Boss

Our lessons continued, with attention given to the scope of a nanny's duties. We were counseled to remember that a nanny isn't a maid or a cook. Carolyn and Linda were experienced enough to know that there would indeed be families that would be looking for a nanny to also perform duties that sounded more like a housekeeper's responsibilities; doing laundry, washing dishes or making dinner. There was even one unusual example, where a family required the nanny to shovel snow from their Chicago doorstep each morning. I didn't pay much attention to those possibilities because it was my goal to work with a family that had hired someone else to do the routine household chores. I didn't want a glorified version of teenage baby-sitting, where I would be doing the dishes and cleaning the house. I had heard too many horror stories of nannies being taken advantage of, right down to having to buy the mother's underwear for her. That wasn't going to be me. I was very clear about that.

Before she gave colorful examples from her case files, Carolyn listed for us a few basic nanny rules, which we wrote in our notebooks:

- **Don't wear suggestive clothing.**
- **When you're out to dinner with the family, don't order the most expensive item on the menu.**
- **Don't smoke in the house.** (**I seriously doubt any families will be providing a *nanny smoking section*.**)
- **Maintain a professional decorum. Don't make your employers your friends.**
- **Do not be the wife's confidante about her troubles with her husband (or in some instances, don't be the mistress' confidante), and of course, above all, don't *become* the mistress.**

My brain really kicked in on this one: *Is this really necessary? Isn't it just assumed that you shouldn't sleep with your boss? Has this actually been a problem in the past?* I couldn't wait to hear this Nanny-from-Hell story.

And there on the board was the cardinal rule, stated and re-stated almost every day:

- **Get a signed contract detailing pay, hours, and rate for overtime, and any other expectations before agreeing to the job.**

In a few weeks time nanny school became relatively routine and I actually began to enjoy the process. I was also becoming less critical of my fellow classmates. A girl named Mandie and I became the closest. I grew very fond of her, although we were vastly different. It could have been my mothering instinct that was drawing me to her, urging me to take her under my wing. She seemed so alone, having driven all the way from Montana by herself. Her father had given her only one piece of advice as she started her journey: "Count to ten before you speak." She explained to me that her father's behest was a result of her tendency to say things she later regretted.

Another teacher, Mary, came in once a week to talk to us about family dynamics and etiquette. An off-handed comment I made when she was lecturing changed my attitude toward my fellow students dramatically. It began with my remark about Mary's sense of fashion. Mandie and I were whispering while Mary was telling the class how important it was to wear clothes that fit well (she meant that we shouldn't wear low-cut tops, mini-skirts or anything suggestive). Being the fashion trendsetter that I was, I asked Mandie, "Does she mean we have to wear clothes like hers? She dresses like our school librarian."

Mandie leaned over and whispered, "I have a blazer exactly like the one that Mary's wearing."

I was mortified, and in that moment, when I couldn't work up an apology or even think of the appropriate words, I realized I was no better than the other students that I was quick to criticize. After all, what had I accomplished in my eighteen less-than-illustrious years? Maybe *I* was the one who should be counting before *I* spoke.

Of course, that didn't stop me from critiquing my fellow students, as the skilled psychoanalyst that I thought I was. I continued in my lifelong habit of viewing people and life through an amateur therapist's microscope. This, of course, was how I dealt with my own frailties and insecurities and kept myself from taking life too seriously when things appeared to be overwhelming.

Later, after I'd been working for Steven and Julia Swartz, I was able to get Mandie a position with one of their friends. I didn't know it when we met, but Mandie would become the only friend I would have in a very foreign land. She would save my sanity.

### Practicum Makes Perfect

**Prac·ti·cum** *n.*(prăk′tĭ-kəm) (n.) activities that emphasize the practical application of theory, or one in which a student gains on-the-job experience in a field of study. An educational course, especially one in a specialized field of study, which is designed to give students, supervised practical application of previously studied theory.

I had to look up the word describing the next segment of our training. Since our field of study was the art and science of nannying (a word I couldn't find in the dictionary, but you get the idea), we would be sent out to work for families in the surrounding area. They became our practicum families. I would later use the references from these families as the bulk of my resume.

Though we weren't expected to cook as nannies, Carolyn and Linda knew there would be exceptions; so in their infinite wisdom, we would be required to prepare a meal, a personal favorite, for one of our practicum families. The whole point of the exercise was to see if we were able to buy the groceries and make the dinner while caring for the kids at the same time. The dish that was my personal favorite at the time was also the ONLY one I knew how to make, unless you count bologna boats. It was a casserole. It had a full complement of chicken, cheddar cheese, a can of Campbell's Cream of Chicken Soup, and mashed potatoes, along with two cubes of butter and a pint of half & half. This was all layered over a couple of pounds of fried hamburger. My grandmother used to make it for me every Sunday night. I felt great nanny guilt for sticking my practicum children in front of the TV (educational programming, of course) while I slaved over the stove. It took me hours to assemble. When it was done, I thought it turned out great. The parents seemed to like it okay, but the six-year-old said it "looked like throw up" and refused to eat it.

A few weeks into class, Mary, the family dynamics teacher, chose me to help take care of her own two girls, as well as the special-needs children she cared for. I loved working for her, usually after school and on the weekends, *and* getting paid the much-welcomed sum of $4 an hour. She told me she had chosen me from all the girls in class, after careful consideration, because of my maturity. I could have told her that. I'd always felt I was the most responsible one in my age group at school. What else could explain the fact that I had been chosen as the head of the fire drill exercises in second grade and the attendance taker in the third grade?

In reality, I probably wasn't chosen as the fire drill guide just for my leadership abilities, but for my then "stocky" frame. Remember the ole "husky" size clothes at JC Penney's? I wore those. My friend, Ben, and I were chosen by Mrs. Meyers since we both looked like we hadn't missed a meal in our lives. She must have thought we would be able to carry fellow seven-year-olds down the ladder to safety during a disaster. The good news is that Ben and I didn't stay the same size throughout our years in school together. My lifelong friend went on to play college football and at times tipped the scales at close to 300 pounds.

However, because of my "leader of potential disaster" assignment, and the fact that my teachers always let me grade papers for them, I began to see myself as one of the most responsible among my peers. When I was older and in high school, I never did get into trouble or do any drugs. At parties, as Jeff Foxworthy always says, I was elected as the spokeswoman when the police came to the door telling us to keep the noise down. My approach had been to tell the officer that I'd been asking them all night to turn that music down.

I'm not saying I didn't have fun. There *was* one time I drove the getaway car at two o'clock in the morning for Missy after she stole one of those green road signs bearing the last name of her latest heartthrob. *Is it really a federal offense to steal a government sign?* But, overall, I was pretty straight. Oh wait; there was the time I got caught blatantly cheating on a History test in Mr. Barrett's class. I always thought that was justifiable since he was so tough that even Eriko Yagi, the most brilliant member of our graduating class (who later graduated from MIT, I might add) barely got an A out of him. I just seemed to be the one that wasn't up for the most extreme teenage fun. I was kind of over-cautious. I saw myself as the mother hen of my group of girlfriends, and I was always trying to keep them out of trouble. All right then, as I think about it, there are a couple more examples of less-than-goody-two-shoe behavior. So let's stay with this summary: I didn't do any illegal drugs, and I thought I was wise beyond my years. The last thing I need is for Craig Jenkins, my seventh grade boyfriend for two whole weeks, to come forward on *The Montel Williams Show* with some incident I've forgotten.

My four months of schooling sped by, and by the end of December I had graduated and was ready to go to work. I'd logged more than 400 hours in classroom and practicum training and passed my certification test with flying colors. I was now a highly qualified child-care professional. I had a clear focus for my future: to take care of children. I figured I could do that well anywhere in the world—children are children, after all. So I set my sights on Southern California, the land of milk, honey, sunshine and money.

That's where I asked the NNI placement department, namely Carolyn and Linda, to send me. To my surprise, within a week they had lined up several interviews through a domestic placement agency in Santa Monica.

There was no doubt in my mind that it was time to leave my little home town for good. I knew that I'd miss my parents, two sisters, and all my friends there, but I had no qualms about moving further away from home for my first job. There was no romance anchoring me there, other than my on-again-off-again relationship with Troy, my high school boyfriend who probably couldn't wait for me to disappear, so he could start dating Gayle Buda, The Homecoming Queen. I was excited to leave Cottage Grove since its only claim to fame was that *Animal House* had been filmed there in the 70's. I was off to the Film Capital of the World.

# Hollywood
# Screen Test

"Sepple—veedah," I tried to sound out the word to my mother. My inflection was on the "veeduh." It was such an odd looking word. "That's where our hotel is, on Sepple-veedah Boulevard," I shouted from my bedroom as I finished packing my suitcase. In just a few hours, she and I would be landing in Los Angeles. I was already excited by the prospect of seeing all the movie stars, their homes, Disneyland and Hollywood.

The first disappointment was our hotel room on Snapple-whatever Boulevard, which was one step below a Motel 6. When the woman at the placement agency said she would find a reasonably priced hotel in the area, I didn't know she was referring to one you could rent by the hour.

Our window faced a congested, dirty and turbulent street somewhere in Los Angeles. By now, thanks to our cab driver who wasted no time correcting my pronunciation through his own foreign dialect, I learned it was Sepulveda Boulevard. Either way you pronounced it, it was an ugly street in an ugly town. This was not the Los Angeles I had pictured. I couldn't imagine any movie stars living within a hundred miles of the area. The street was lined with telephone poles with a morass of wires running in every direction. The exhaust from thousands of passing cars filtered into our room, not to mention the horns honking, and sirens wailing throughout the night.

Everything seemed so flat. I craned my neck out of the only window in the room, scanning above the rooftops of dingy discount liquor stores, laundromats and porn shops to search for the Hollywood sign; which of course wasn't remotely near. Not that I could have seen it with the curtain of smog that hung at our windowsill, fighting the fumes from the street for entry.

I had never seen smog, which I was told was a combination of smoke and fog. Based on the odor that pinched my nose and the sting that made my eyes water, I doubted that there was much fog in the formula.

My mother didn't say a word. I think she sensed my monumental disappointment; she had always been good at making the best of all situations. She never complained about our less than luxurious accommodations. However, when we saw that our bed had one of those coin-operated-make-the-bed-vibrate things attached to the headboard, she did comment, "Oh my, this motel is pretty shady."

We hadn't finished unpacking when the phone rang. It was three in the afternoon on a Thursday and the local placement agency was calling to tell me they had my very first appointment "penciled in." She was ready to "ink me in" if I could make it. The woman said it was in Hollywood. I was excited that I would be interviewing the very next day, in Hollywood! Maybe I'd even be able to see the sign... if it wasn't too smoggy.

My mom was totally supportive. She was happy for me, and never even registered any disapproval at her 18-year-old daughter bouncing up and down on the vibrating bed, yelling, "Hollywood here I come!"

My mature self had already done a fair amount of thinking about what kind of positions I should apply for. In school, I had learned that nannies' jobs come in two main varieties: live-out or live-in. In the live-out situation you work for a couple during their working hours, essentially 9-10 hours a day. These people want consistent care in their own home and want to avoid taking their children out every day to a day care center. Usually, both parents work outside the home. This type of arrangement could also be with a stay-at-home mom who could afford to employ a second pair of hands. The nanny and the mom in this case work together as a team to meet the needs of the children throughout the day.

The second type of nanny job is a live-in position. This had always been my aspiration. I thought this kind of nannying would be ideal because I knew paying for housing in LA would take up my whole paycheck. I liked the idea of working for a family that had a housekeeper to do household chores. This seemed like an essential element, based on Carolyn and Linda's horror stories in which the nanny had gradually become the all-purpose housekeeper/cook/personal assistant.

During our last few weeks at NNI we were asked to think carefully about the kind of position that would work for us. Carolyn had assured us that job satisfaction depended upon a good match. When she interviewed me before placement, she asked whether I wanted live-in or live-out, and what my preferences were regarding ages of children and religious and ethnic background. By then, I had already decided I definitely wanted to go to Southern California and that religion and ethnic background didn't matter much. I was adamant about wanting to work with at least two children, preferably three, and I wanted one of them to be a newborn. I was planning to care for the kids during the day, and be available for extra duty over agreed-upon weekends and evenings when the parents needed me. My thought was that I'd be off-duty two days a week. And when the parents were home and ready to take over, I would be free to come and go.

What I didn't realize as a tender young nanny-in-waiting, was that there are folks who are *never* without hired help for their children. They arrange their lives so there is always a paid caregiver available to them. It never occurred to me that there were people who really didn't want to spend as much time as they could with their children. I soon learned that many parents did not hurry home after work so they could see their children before they went to bed. They paid other people to raise their kids so they could spend their time raising their social status and financial worth. LA was one big ladder, I would soon learn. Nannies were the people who sat at the bottom of the ladder, entertaining the kids, while the parents climbed.

The night before my first interviews, after my mother and I returned from The International House of Pancakes, I spent two hours trying to decide which one of the outfits I'd packed to wear for my interview the next morning. It was late December, and having come from the rain capital of the world, I had only packed clothing that would be appropriate for winter in Oregon. I chose a black knit dress. As luck would have it, Friday was supposed to be one of the hottest December days of the decade in LA. A typical eighteen-year-old, I was far more concerned about what I would look like running around in a thick black dress on a summer like day than I was about physical discomfort. Anyway, my wardrobe choices were limited. At least in the black dress, I would look like a professional; it had clean simple lines, no distracting patterns, and an appropriate hem line. I decided to top it off with two small gold hoop earrings and equally conservative black shoes with two-inch heels. I was ready for my first Hollywood adventure: finding a job.

## My Interview with a Rat Dog

The next morning we opened the Los Angeles street map to find Bellwood Avenue, the home of some famous chef, my first interview. The lady at the placement agency said that this interview was with one of the top ten chefs in Los Angeles and that it took three months to get into his restaurant. Of course, I didn't recognize his name.

Finding an address in Los Angeles is more difficult than fishing the letter Z out of a bowl of Campbell's Alphabet Soup. For one thing, everything is in Spanish. For another, you can't tell if you're actually in Los Angeles, Studio City, Hollywood or half a dozen other cities. Everything runs together, and unlike my hometown, there are no signs that read "You Are Entering the Covered Bridge Capital of America, Population 7,143." To make matters worse, street names are duplicated in every city. So, you might be on Sepulveda in Westchester, or you might be on Sepulveda in Van Nuys, - which is in the Valley (whatever that means) and technically part of LA.

Another problem was the division of cities into their eastern, western, northern and southern parts. There is a North Hollywood, a West Hollywood and just plain Hollywood. I wondered which of them owned the sign, and why there wasn't an East Hollywood to round out the compass points. I wondered where was the Hollywood where all the stars lived? Later I found out not many of the stars even live in Hollywood. They live in Beverly Hills, Bel Air or Malibu. I also found out that not much related to the movies actually goes on in Hollywood. Except perhaps the sidewalks that contain the names of the stars (the Walk of Fame, I think they called it) and the famous sign on the hill, which I still hadn't seen by the time I left.

As it turned out, my interview with the famous chef did lead us into the Hollywood Hills. There were some lovely and stately homes in that area. Some were beautifully restored to their original 1920s architecture. The address I'd been given matched a Mediterranean-style house with a deep green front lawn.

Before going up to the front door, I looked at my mother and said, "Wish me luck. How do I look?"

"Honey, you look beautiful," she said proudly. "Don't be nervous. I know you'll be able to explain to the family how much you love taking care of children."

That was good advice, and it pumped me up. She was right. I wasn't there to interview as a deep space physicist, thank God. I was there to potentially be a caregiver to the chef's children.

A tall woman, about 35-years-old and quite attractive, answered the door. She looked about seven months pregnant. She introduced herself and showed me into the immaculate living room. The minute I sat down, what I call a rat dog (the small, Chihuahua kind that yip non-stop), came bounding into the room yapping. She immediately went for my leg and fastened her small but powerful chattering jaws around my ankle as if I were a fresh hambone, tearing my hose and puncturing my skin.

It happened so quickly I didn't have time to say anything. I winced and put my hand around the little devil's neck; not yet pulling her off, hoping the chef's wife would do or say something. I've never really been a dog person and the little fleabags always seem to know it.

"Oh Mimi, leave the poor girl alone," she said, sitting motionless.

I could see that she had no intention of pulling the dog away or otherwise making any move verbally or physically to stop the assault. I squeezed harder on the pooch's neck; her teeth still attached to my hose. I pulled her up and flung her backward head over heels onto the carpet. This, of course, caused convulsions of near epileptic proportions in the woman. She jumped up, grabbed the dog and hugged it so close to her chest I thought she would suffocate the thing.

At that point, I was ready to excuse myself and leave to join my mother, who was sitting in the rental car across the street; waiting for me to return gleefully with a job as a nanny to some famous chef. I started to get up. The woman, sensing I was leaving, became apologetic.

"I'm sorry. Mimi does get a little aggressive with strangers."

As the dog trotted toward me again, she patted her hand at the air as if making a feeble effort to shoo the dog away.

"Are you all right?" she said in a half sincere way.

I wasn't sure if she was talking to the dog or me.

"Um, yes, I'm fine. There's only a little bit of blood. I'll be okay," I offered, while I tugged at my hose and blotted the wound with a piece of Kleenex I found in my purse. In fact, it hurt a lot. I bit my lip, determined to persevere. Throughout the entire interview, the giant rodent snarled incessantly, while its "mother" did nothing.

"My husband is Jacques LaRiviere, I'm sure you've heard of him." She rolled her eyes and looked heavenward. "He's one of the top ten chefs in Los Angeles."

*Who votes on this top ten stuff?* I doubted the contest was anything like the local chili cook-off in my town, where blue ribbons are awarded by Bill Whiteman, our longtime mayor, after he tastes everyone's home-made entries.

*Yeah, sure, of course, who hasn't heard of Jacques?* At the time, I didn't even know who Wolfgang Puck was. I smiled and nodded, just trying to follow her lead.

"As you can see," she patted her stomach lovingly, "I'm expecting, so, I will need you to take care of little Dominic, our three-year-old. I'm due in March, so of course then I will also expect you to handle Zachary."

*Handle?* I thought, as if she had psychically figured out that her new-born was either going to be a problem child, or some sort of toy.

"And of course I will need you to do the cooking as well." Probably seeing the look of shock on my face, she added, "Don't worry about pleasing my husband. He's never satisfied with any meal he ever eats."

I was bewildered. She wanted ME to cook for one of the foremost chefs in Los Angeles? Yes, I would certainly take care of Dominic and handle Zachary when he came along, but cooking for a chef? *This woman must be out of her hormone-saturated mind.* What would possess her to think that an 18-year-old girl, whose previous cooking experience pretty much consisted of boiling water for Top Ramen noodles, would be capable of pleasing one of the most discriminating palates in all of Los Angeles?

CUT TO:

INTERIOR - RESIDENTIAL KITCHEN - EVENING

Young girl stands in enormous gourmet kitchen wearing a white chef's hat and a white apron. Counter tops are thick granite. Hanging overhead is an array of expen-sive copper pots and pans. Fine German cooking knives are arrayed on the counter.

INTERIOR — FORMAL DINING ROOM — DINNER TIME

               WIFE
       (yelling at full volume)
How much longer before dinner?


           YOUNG GIRL
It will be ready in just a few more minutes, Mrs. LaRiviere.

Girl is in the kitchen whistling while she stirs a pot with a large wooden spoon. Contents appear to be a mixture of mashed potatoes, cream of chicken soup, lots of butter and bits of meat.


           HUSBAND
       (Sarcastically)
Where did you find this one? Was she fired from Denny's?

Girl rests spoon inside pot and approaches dining room door with a big smile on her face.


           YOUNG GIRL
       (Loudly)
Ready or not, here I come. You're just going to love my fried hamburger casserole.

    Mrs. LaRiviere had seemed to be dutifully recording my comments and answers, and maybe even her own observations, on a note pad. I imagined that what she had really been writing on her pad was something close to this:

*Dear Dr. Ludlam,*

    *Mimi has recently been traumatized during a job interview I conducted. I believe this may have set her back in dealing with her trust issues. She may be reluctant to be open and honest with you following this negative encounter. She was just beginning to feel comfortable taking doggie treats from you during your therapy sessions. I hope that she can overcome this emotional trauma; I fear she may regress and begin urinating on our leather sofa again. I know she needs to learn that there will be people in the world that react to her unenthusiastically, like this prospective nanny did. Nevertheless, I want her to know that this says nothing about her character. Dr. Ludlam, I know you can help Mimi realize she is still a wonderful creature that is capable of being loved. It was obvious to me that this girl had deep-seated unresolved issues toward Chihuahuas. If you could continue to support her to share her feelings with others during your counseling appointment on Friday, I would be very appreciative.*

*Sincerely,*
*Mimi's Mommy*

When she was through, she stood up as the dog continued to jump and yip. Looking at her watch, she said, "Can you let yourself out? I must make a phone call. I didn't realize how late it was."

"Yes, Mrs. LaRiviere, of course," I answered.

The house wasn't that large. The living area we had been sitting in was just down the hall from the front door. I smiled, stood up and began to make my exit, the dog still nipping at my heels as I kicked at her in a mildly threatening manner.

Reaching the large heavy front door, I pulled it open. By this time, it was noon and it was stifling outside. As I was about to close the door behind me, the little ankle-biter came bounding out across the front lawn. She was running like an escaped convict who hadn't seen the light of day in forty years. I realized that Mrs. Famous Chef was undoubtedly engrossed in her phone conversation and would not be of immediate help. My first thoughts were that the dog would get away, never to be found again; or worse, would throw her skittering little self in front of an approaching car. Mrs. LaRiviere would be beside herself with grief and anger and would have her famous husband roast my head slowly over hot coals. I would never work in this town again. Come to think of it, I hadn't yet worked in it.

My mother, immediately sensing the gravity of the situation, jumped out of the car and joined me in the chase. She was wearing a dress and heels as well, so it was quite some time before we caught up with the four-legged inmate and were able to herd her, in a manner of speaking, back down the street toward her home.

As I began to cross the lawn, half stooping, cajoling and shooing at the dog, Mrs. LaRiviere came running out the front door screaming "Mimi, Mimi. Where is my Mimi?" Her arms were whirling and flailing in the air, as she looked in all directions for her beloved "baby." I was sure she was going to go into premature labor right then and there on her porch.

Thank God that upon seeing the woman, the dog immediately charged back into the house. As Mrs. LaRiviere glared at me, about to say something, the automatic sprinklers came on. The yard was quite large, and as I turned to look at the car parked nearly fifty feet away, I knew that not even a bolt to the street would save us.

I turned, just as the sprinkler soaked me and calmly put my arm around my mother's shoulder and began a slow, dignified pace back to the car. We laughed all the way back to the motel on S-whatever the heck it is-Boulevard.

I had two more interviews that day and one on the next. A quick blow-dry of my hair and change of winter wear and I would just be able to make the next one. It would still be a few more days before the nanny agency would call and send me out to interview with the Most Powerful Man in Hollywood, or at least with his wife.

Needless to say I didn't take the job as *handler* and chef, though it was offered to me, surprisingly enough.

## Take Two Ritalin and *Don't* Call Me in the Morning

We were off to Studio City, which I'm still not sure is actually a city, or just a part of LA. I was to meet with a wealthy businessman and his wife. The agency didn't tell me what his business was. I was just told that they had one son, the father was a prominent businessman and the wife's family came from famous money. I wasn't thrilled at the prospect of working with only one child. As we parked in the driveway, I was surprised at the size of the house. The information sheet I had on the family referred to it as a bungalow. The agency had specified that this was a live-in position. But, oddly enough, the place looked really tiny.

As I stood on the porch and began to ring the doorbell I saw a small plaque that read "We already gave at the office, so don't bother knocking." Bizarre!

I could hear a women yelling from inside… "Jonathan, stop jumping on the couch. Do you hear me? Stop jumping on the couch!"

The door quickly opened to reveal a haggard looking woman in her early 30's.

"Hello, I'm Julie Foshay. Won't you come in?" she said as the boy continued to jump up and down behind her. The child was about four. He was using the sofa as a trampoline, bouncing and yelling incoherently, oblivious to his mother's admonishments.

"My, what a beautiful (I paused for a second searching for a word)… uh, *cozy* home you have, Mrs. Foshay." I wanted to start out with a compliment.

"Jonathan," she turned to yell at the boy again, "I told you to stop jumping on the couch." I followed her into a dining room just off the living area that was the size of my bedroom at home. We sat.

"So, Susan, it is Susan, isn't it?" she asked, but didn't wait for me to answer. "Tell me all about yourself."

I didn't bother to correct her about my name since I figured this would probably not be the job of my dreams anyway.

I told her about NNI, how I'd scored the highest of my class on my certification tests, how I'd always loved kids, how I'd baby-sat for many families while growing up, but that I wanted to live in a larger city, yada, yada, yada, expecting her to break in at any moment when she'd had enough—only she just kept staring at me, smiling. Every so often she would yell out to Jonathan again, who by now, had been bouncing non-stop for nearly twenty minutes.

When she finally did interrupt me, her first question was "How much?"

I assumed she wanted to know what the going rate was for a nanny. I thought the agency would have given her that information. I said, with as much confidence as I could muster, "Since I'm going to be a live-in nanny, I would like to make $250 a week."

She seemed stunned by this figure. "Oh no, we can't afford that! We're already mortgaged to the hilt with our recent remodel. Besides, I'm not sure where I would put you," as if I was going to be the third car and they only had a two-car garage.

Little Jonathan continued to wail like a banshee and do his jumping jacks. I wanted to wail, too: *"Why are you interviewing me? Why did you call the agency asking for a live-in nanny, for God's sake?"*

I ended our interview by sneaking a peek, on my way out the door, at the stack of library books, Jumpin' Johnny had knocked off the end table:

*The Hyperactive Child; A handbook for Parents*
*Living With Our Hyperactive Children*
*Raising a Hyperactive Child*
*The Hyperactive Child and the Family*
*Allrighty then.......*

When I reported back to the agency, I told them this was definitely not the family for me or for any other live-in nanny unless they were going to bring their own RV with them to work each day.

I won't bore you with the details of my last interview that day. Let's just say the words "toddler twins, a pregnant mother, lots of housework, bedroom shared with a parakeet, $150 a week" and move on.

## Do I Look Like Mary Poppins?

The next day's interview was a real doozie as well. Looking back, perhaps it was the most entertaining of the four.

The agency called early in the morning and gave me the number for a woman named Barbi Benton. Not being a regular follower of the life and loves of Hugh Hefner, I was unacquainted with her claim to fame. But with a name like Barbi, I made a pretty accurate guess as to what she looked like.

Amy, the agency's placement coordinator I had been working with, had instructed me to call their house manager to set up a preliminary interview. If the house manager thought I had potential, then I would meet the family.

"Hello. Is this Ms. Benton's residence?" I asked over the phone.

"Yes, this is Ms. Chambers, the house manager. Who is this?"

"I'm Suzanne Hansen. The nanny agency gave me your number to call for an interview."

"Oh yes. Yes, of course. You are the one from Oregon. When would you like to come up?"

"I'm available today, if that's all right."

"Good. How about two-ish."

"Uh... two-ish would be great," I replied. "Could I please have your address?"

"Just come to the block of Welby in Pasadena, near the Rose Bowl."

Before I replied, I thought, *Okay, but what's the address? This sounds like she lives in a shopping center, the Block of Welby. I don't get it. How would I find it on the Thomas Guide without a number?*

"Uh, Ms. Chambers, could you give me the street number? Is it Welby Street?"

"Yes. It's the block of Welby," she replied, sounding a little agitated that I did not know that the Barbie dollhouse took up one entire city block. There was no need for a number because there were no other homes on that block. I couldn't wait to see this estate.

As my mother drove down one street and up another in Pasadena, the castle-like structure came into view. A black, ornate wrought iron fence nearly fifteen feet tall surrounded it with an entry gate that looked like it belonged at Buckingham Palace. I expected to see a guard standing in the small brick house near the gate, but there was only an intercom box. I had dropped my mother off a few blocks away so I could drive through the gates alone. I got out of the car, pushed the button and a woman's voice said, "Hello. Who's there?"

When I explained who I was, she told me to come ahead. Then the heavy gates creaked and magically opened. I never did get to see the inside of that mansion. It was larger than any building in Cottage Grove by far—even the Rainbow Motel. I was ushered through a lovely rose garden, past the house, and up to the front door of what turned out to be an office; Mrs. Benton's husband's office.

Once inside I met Ms. Chambers, a professional looking woman, who would be interviewing me. Before the interview began, we were interrupted by a pinch-faced, sack-bosomed matronly woman with teeth like rows of Chiclets. She was probably about sixty-five years old with a face seamed with wrinkles like an old soccer ball. She walked into the office complaining, under her breath, about the swelling in her ankles. Without acknowledging me, she retrieved a white envelope from Ms. Chambers and then walked out. Ms. Chambers, noticing the confused look on my face, informed me that the current nanny, "old swollen ankles," who had just hobbled out the door, would be leaving in a couple of weeks.

"You're attractive. That will bother her," Ms. Chambers began the interview. From that remark, I guessed that Barbi was indeed a doll. I wondered what Mr. Benton must look like. She sat looking at some papers on the desk in front of her. I assumed she was waiting for me to respond.

I paused a moment then said, "Thank you. I hope that won't be a problem," all the while I'm thinking, *Jeez, if I could live here I could ugly myself up a little. Maybe not wear any makeup; just wash my hair once a week. I guess she didn't have to cover this part of the interview process with the current Grandma Moses.*

After I had given this woman the short version of the story I'd told Mrs. Foshay the day before, she began to rattle off a litany of rules and quirks that I would have to deal with. For one, there was the issue of the refrigerator. It had a lock on it. It looked like a safe, and in essence, that's what it was. All the goodies that Barbie and Ken did not have the willpower to resist were locked safely inside the colossal, chrome Sub-Zero.

I asked, "Who has the key?" I couldn't believe that two intelligent adults had to keep their own food in solitary confinement.

"The only time it is open is to prepare their meals. They are both very strict about their diet," she continued.

"Does she ever beg the chef to open it in the middle of the night?" I had to know. That question solicited a stern dip of her eyebrows.

"Of course not, what kind of people do you think they are?" she finally responded.

*I don't know, you tell me. Anyone who doesn't trust herself with her own food has got to be just a wee bit odd. Why the hell does she buy things she can't eat anyway? Why not just stock up on lettuce and bottled water and leave the fridge unlocked?*

"Now, back to the issue of your looks," she continued. "You will, of course, be required to wear a uniform. Actually it's quite lovely," she added, as if knowing I would not be caught dead in a nanny habit. At that point, she stood up, crossed the room to a closet, reached in and pulled out a dress that looked like it belonged to Mary Poppins and displayed it to me proudly. Apparently, every member of the household was expected to work in costume. I just about died.

In the middle of our interview, I heard a man's voice announce over the intercom "I am done with my coffee." Ms. Chambers immediately buzzed inside the house to instruct the staff to remove The Mansion Owner's coffee cup from his desk. She rang into several rooms of the mansion, announcing the urgent situation. I know my mouth must have been hanging open as I sat there. The funny part was that she didn't seem to think it was peculiar. She didn't realize that this was just a tad abnormal for about 99.9% of the American population. She just continued on down her checklist after the coffee cup problem was resolved and her attention was back to our conversation.

"Are there any questions so far?" she asked

"Not yet."

"Good. Now about the Rolls, when you travel with the family in the convertible Rolls Royce, you will always ride in the front seat with the driver and be in uniform. It is very important to them that when they are out for a drive, it is clear to onlookers that you are *the help*.

By the way, how is your health?" she asked. *How do you think my health is? I'm only eighteen years old, for God's sake. How bad off could I be? Do you want to know about my menstrual cramps once a month and the fact that I dislocated my knee trying out for the track team in the eighth grade? I mean look at the current nanny. She's 95 and looks like she just emerged from an all night bingo parlor with her portable oxygen in tow— and she managed to work here—how hard could it be?*

After four days of these types of interviews, I felt like I'd been an extra in *One Flew Over The Cuckoo's Nest*, and like Chief Bromden, I was finally walking out into the light of day. I was relieved when I met Julia and Steven Swartz at the Agency of Creative Talent. Julia was strikingly beautiful and intelligent. She and Steven were both charming, but it wouldn't be long before I would discover that they both had their own share of Hollywood eccentricities.

# LIGHTS! CAMERA! ACTION!

# My Big Break

I could tell that Steven had liked me, even though I looked so timid and scared in the interview. I crossed my fingers and hoped for the callbacks. The next day, I received a call from the Human Resources Manager at ACT to arrange for me to go to the Swartz's house on Saturday to meet the children. I realized this was the final round.

While I was waiting, I had done some research, since ACT seemed to wield so much power in Hollywood. I discovered that it was one of the largest talent agency in Hollywood, the Entertainment Mecca of the world. Their clients were the most well known actors, directors, screenwriters, musicians and authors in the industry. As talent agents, they made their livings getting the best deals for their clients, negotiating with studios in exchange for a percentage of the client's earnings. Most of the truly famous names in the industry were with ACT. It was widely known that they had enough pull to get clients the most lucrative contracts. As president of the agency, Steven Swartz could essentially make or break an actor's career.

CUT TO:

INTERIOR - MOVIE STUDIO — DAYTIME

Ten young women are seated in a waiting room. Some are fidgeting some are very poised and calm.

                        PRODUCER
Next, Sue Ann Hayson or is it Hadson, whatever, next.

Nervous girl rises from her chair, drops her portfolio on the floor, quickly stoops down to pick it up
then tightly grips it across her chest, follows man
into large conference room.

INTERIOR - LARGE CONFERENCE ROOM

Eight men and women in business suits are sitting
around a long conference table.

                        PRODUCER
Please have a seat. We are looking for a bubbly, energetic nanny for this role, like a young Goldie Hawn.
Someone who is mature, not star-struck, capable of
interacting with pillars of the community as well as
three small children.

                    EXECUTIVE #1
Please tell us what projects you have worked on recently
that would qualify you for this role.

                    YOUNG WOMAN
Well, um, I've been baby-sitting for the past nine
years. I brought references for you. Um, I just graduated from Northwest Nannies Institute in Oregon,
uhhhh….

Executive #1 takes portfolio from girl.

                    EXECUTIVE #2
We'd like to see a sample of your work. We're going to
bring in three children, and we'll be observing you
during the next five minutes while you entertain them.

Nicely dressed woman brings children and a bag of toys
into the conference room. Young girl tries to sit on
floor gracefully with her dress and high heels as she
begins playing with the children.
Five minutes pass.

EXECUTIVE #3

Now, Miss, we would like to assess your stamina. We've
set up a treadmill in the other room. Please jog on
the treadmill without stopping while we audition the
next girl. The incline level is set on steep and the
pace is set to fast. Please don't adjust the settings.
The timer is set for 20 minutes. After you're finished,
take a seat and we'll call you back in. Please do not
take a break for water or to use the restroom during
your endurance test.

YOUNG GIRL

Yes sir.

The interviewee steps on the moving treadmill. She
trips and flies off the back end of the conveyor belt.
Takes off her high heels and steps on again.

When I pulled up to the curb near the Swartz's driveway, I saw four
luxury cars sitting alongside a very exotic looking black sports car, similar
to the one Christie Brinkley drove in *Vacation*. As I pulled up to the
entrance a man came from the house, apparently the owner of the
futuristic looking car, waved to Julia in the entryway and said "I'll be
at Stallone's house if Steven needs me." I would meet this man several
days later. He was Rick Dyer, one of Steven's partners. Of course I was
immediately impressed with the casual way he referred to the star. I was
just beginning to get the picture of the type of people that Steven
worked with on a daily basis.

I parked and walked to the gate. My hand began to shake as I reached
to the intercom next to the twelve-foot-high wrought iron fence. It was
beginning to sink in that I might actually live in a residence that you had
to ask permission to enter. A far cry from even the most expensive home
in our small logging community. In fact, I don't think most people in my
town even locked their back doors, let alone put iron fences around their
homes. Looking back, the gates were a pretty good indicator of the new
life I was entering. I didn't know it then, but I had passed through a

checkpoint, and would never again be able to walk back into my old life with the same outlook.

But instead, that first day I was so excited and curious about the Swartz' that I was all eyes. The first thing I noticed was that the house, though it was situated on nearly an acre of land, did not look like JR Ewing's Texas mansion at all. A two-story Southern Colonial, it was made of brick and wood with three majestic white columns across the front and two massive black lacquer front doors with shiny brass handles. In the brick-inlaid driveway, a man was busy washing a Jeep, while the three other cars were waiting turns to be bathed and pampered. (This was to be a ritual for the rest of the time I spent with them: the same man would come every Saturday morning and perform what amounted to a full detail of all of the family's vehicles.)

The way I imagine it now, there should have been a play-by-play announcer commenting to the audience that day as I walked through the gate. The whole thing would play like an episode out of the Crocodile Hunter. Steve Irwin would be narrating my adventure into the unknown, "As Suzy approaches the rare female albino croc, a very territorial reptile, the Croc senses her unwelcome presence. She opens her massive jaw and hisses at the intruder. At any moment the crocodile may strike out, in an attempt to protect her nest."

"Whoa, watch out Suz-O. That was a close one! Wow, this is amazing to witness; I have never seen anyone ever get this close to an albino croc in the wild and live to tell about it. Boy, oh boy, will she have a story to tell her grandchildren!"

Okay. How it really happened was that Julia simply greeted me at the side door. She seemed friendly enough, although she was a little aloof.

"Technically this is our *side* front door," she told me as she led me into a family room with an informal dining area. Then she led me to the main entry with the tall black doors and said, "This is our front door." *I've been here two minutes and I'm already confused.*

She glanced back and gestured for me to follow her, "Come on. I'll show you around."

Passing from the kitchen through the formal dining room toward the living room, I stopped dead in my tracks, gawking at photos hanging behind the elaborate wet bar. *My God, my mother would die if she saw this. I think that's Barbra Streisand with Mr. Swartz.* I was feeling every bit my part as a star-struck fan. I stared at one of the many pictures of Steven with various celebrities. There was Steven with Michael Caine, Steven and Julia with Tom Hanks and Steven with Jane Fonda on the set of a movie. My mouth was hanging open in awe.

I remembered the personnel director at Mr. Swartz's office warned me that celebrities such as Paul Newman would be coming over to the house frequently. She asked me if I thought I could maintain my composure.

So I stayed silent, almost stoic, during my tour; acting as if I too grew up in a home where it was commonplace for Charlie Sheen to stop by for dinner.

"Susan, you can follow me this way," Julia's voice snapped me back into the moment, so much for trying to be mature and use my full name, Suzanne. I thought I would be taken more seriously if I didn't have a name that conjured up a ditzy cheerleader, but apparently that wasn't going to work for me.

"Uh, Mrs. Swartz," I said gently touching her arm, "Uh, it's Suzy."

As I followed her from one room to another I noticed that there was art on every wall, with the possible exception of the bathrooms and the kitchen. I had never seen so much art. Julia told me that there was even an art gallery above the family room. I didn't recognize any of the artists' work that was displayed; except there *was* one that I thought might be a Picasso replica. I felt terribly ignorant, or at least uneducated. I just knew that the country bumpkin inside could be heard screaming: *I have never been in a house like this. I'm used to visiting friends that have fake fur covering their toilet seats and blue water in the toilet bowl. Where I grew up, a nice kitchen was one that had plenty of frozen Pizzas, Kool-Aid and Cheetos.*

Suddenly I found myself wishing that my high school had offered a course in Art History.

"As you can probably see, Steven is one of the foremost art collectors in the country" she said. Then picking up one of the small animal ceramics and holding it up to the light she asked, "Suzy, have you ever been to Africa?"

*Oh sure. I'm eighteen. My home town was so small my graduating class was one of the largest in the history of the school with a whopping 186 members. Needless to say, they didn't offer a foreign exchange program to the African Savannah.*

Later I would look back and remember Julia's question as an early warning sign I hadn't heeded. It had been the first evidence that the wealthy and famous, at least this wealthy and famous, didn't have a clue about how the rest of us live. I wanted to say, where I'm from, two of my friends can't even get cable television up their gravel driveways because their houses are too far away from the main road. We don't exactly do a lot of world traveling.

It had never occurred to me that art of this magnitude would be hanging in someone's home. Before this tour, I had thought that all the famous pieces of art hung in galleries or museums. The only art collection I had seen up to that point in my life belonged to Missy's dad, Melvin. His John Wayne collection filled their entire family room. I think Melvin's spittoon even had The Duke's picture on it. I kept wondering if that could be a REAL Picasso hanging on the living room wall.

Moving from one room to another, we passed a young Hispanic woman in a starched white uniform. She and I exchanged smiles, but there was no introduction. Julia told me the entire staff's schedules and that I would have Saturdays and Sundays off. I couldn't believe how many people it took to manage the house.

My guided tour continued as she took me upstairs to show me the room I'd be staying in. Located between the children's room, it had matching twin beds with peach colored bedspreads and was quite spacious. It even had its own bath! At home, my two sisters and I shared one bathroom.

Once I'd received the tour, Mrs. Swartz asked me to sit in the living room to talk. She was dressed in a coordinated casual outfit, and she looked even more perfect than she had before. She began to ask me questions about my family and in particular, my mother, since she knew she had flown into town with me for my interviewing process. In fact, she began to insist upon meeting her. I didn't think that was necessary; I was almost nineteen years old and grown-up enough to make this decision on my own. I don't think there are any other professions where they ask you to bring your mother to the interview. I'm not sure what my mother was doing at the time, probably walking the streets of Brentwood. I had dropped her off somewhere in the neighborhood so I could go to the meeting alone. Then it occurred to me that she probably wanted to gauge me better by viewing my mother. I felt a little like a foal that was being purchased and the buyer wanted to check the teeth of the mare.

After a stilted conversation in which I explained that I *wasn't* going to get my Mommy, I was introduced to the children. Julia ushered me into the room of Brandon, her six-week-old baby. As we walked in, Mr. Swartz was telling his son Joshua to leave the baby alone. Apparently the six-year-old was trying to pick the baby up out of his crib. Next to Steven, was three year old Amanda. *These children could be on magazine covers. They're so gorgeous, just like their mother.*

"Joshua, I'm not going to tell you again. Put the baby down and meet Suzy," Mr. Swartz said. Joshua turned, shot me a disinterested look and once again started to reach into the crib.

"Amanda, this is Suzy. We think she's going to be your new nanny," Mrs. Swartz said. Having just been taken on the grand tour of their home, I was a little surprised that she was still "thinking" about hiring me. I guessed that my final test was to win the approval of the kids.

"Hi, Amanda," I offered. She smiled shyly as she hid halfway behind her mother. "Hello, Amanda," I said peeking around Julia. "It's very nice to meet you."

*Okay, on a scale of one to ten I just scored a five point five... maybe.* My last chance would be with the baby, Brandon, who was only six weeks old. I walked up to the crib and looked down at the most adorable creature I'd ever seen. He was attempting a smile and gurgling pleasantly, despite the fact that his brother had been antagonizing him. I reached down, picked him up and cradled him in my arms. He fit perfectly.

As I cuddled his small being in my arms, I had the immediate sense that I had found my ideal family. This was what I had wanted most, a family with three children. Here was everything I had hoped for in nanny school: a newborn baby to care for, a busy household with three children and a full-time housekeeper.

"He's absolutely adorable," I said as I turned and faced Joshua. "Here, Joshua, sit in the rocking chair. Let me show you how to hold your brother," I said, as I gently put the baby into his arms. "Make sure you always cradle his head like this." I showed him what to do and propped a pillow under the arm that was cradling his youngest sibling.

Steven and Julia seemed pleased. They just stood watching us. Finally, Julia said, "Do you have any questions?"

I have no idea why, but I was uncharacteristically at a loss for words at that moment. I never asked about a contract, how many hours I would work each day, what I would be responsible for, or how I would be compensated for overtime. All of the things that my instructors had drilled into my head about contracts just seemed to evaporate. I didn't even ask if I would be offered health insurance. Looking back now, it's hard to believe I didn't have anything to say. It was pretty bad timing for me to choose that moment to contain my outspoken nature.

Unfortunately, the only words that came into my mind as we left the room was, "How do you feel about spanking?"

There was an awkward moment of silence, and then Steven said in a loud voice, "Oh yeah, I beat them all regularly." Then he let out a quick laugh.

I felt like a complete fool knowing he was trying to make a joke about my awkward question. What I wanted to say was, "It's just that I don't want to work for a family that uses spanking as a punishment. I don't agree with it." I would soon wish that we had talked more about what discipline strategies they **did** use with the children. If any.

They must have thought I was more than a little naïve when that was the only question I could come up with. Looking back, I don't think it was an oversight that a contract was never mentioned. I fit the part they were casting me for perfectly. I was a trusting, small-town girl whose only concern was for the well-being of their children. When you have servants, it's nice to believe that they work for you chiefly out of a desire to devote themselves to your comfort. It removes any pressure for equality or respect. Nannies weren't supposed to care about money or working conditions.

At the end of the interview, Steven said they would like to hire me right away. I told them it would take a few days to organize my life at home. He wanted to know how long I planned on staying with them. I told them I could commit to two years. They seemed pleased, and I was happy to make that commitment. Steven told me he didn't like turnover because of the impact on the kids. He said that their cook had been with them for seven years and he hoped she would stay forever. I was really glad that he realized how hard it must be on his children to have people come in and out of their lives. Hearing that they'd had a loyal employee for that long confirmed that this was the family for me. I didn't stop to think that there might be a bit more to the story of the cook's tenure there.

Steven told me to call the office when I got back home and they would make arrangements for my flight back. I was very grateful for his generous offer, and I looked forward to becoming a great employee and excellent caregiver. I had always thought that the care of children was the most important work in the world. I was thankful that NNI had given me a sound education on meeting children's physical and emotional needs. I felt like a professional with my new knowledge of child development. And now I was going to be the highest paid NNI graduate ever. The placement agency told me that this position paid $300 a week...Little did I know that my biggest education was yet to come.

## Nanny Initiation

I returned to LA a week later to begin my new career. Josh, who worked in the mailroom at ACT, picked me up from the airport. He was a cute guy, just a little older than me. He was really nice and we laughed a lot on the drive to my new home. I even gave a fleeting thought to dating him, but he never asked. I later learned that Josh was Ali McGraw's son. It was surprising to me to find out that even celebrities' children still had to start in the mailroom at Steven's company.

When I'd left home, I had shipped my clothes and other belongings in separate boxes. I had sent them down two days ahead of my flight. I had addressed them to the correct street address, but I had assumed that my new home was Brentwood, not Los Angeles. Evidently, Brentwood was not its own city. As a result, all my earthly possessions were shipped to the wrong city, somewhere else in California. It wasn't until two weeks later that they finally arrived at the house. Looking back, that may have been an omen.

The first day that I finally settled in, unpacked everything and met the staff and the children once again was the last "normal" day I remember having for a very long time. From that point on I lived inside a movie that was filled with everything you would expect from a good comedy/ mystery/love story/tragedy. There would be the thrill of victory and the agony of defeat, and always, always, the unexpected. I would cross a frontier that year, marching through it all, head high, shoulders back, trying to look determined and unafraid; a naïve young soldier led into battle by invisible generals. Okay. That's my idealized version. If you really want the truth I stumbled through challenge after challenge, adventure after adventure, with very mixed results. Often I was brilliant in my role as professional nanny. And just as often, the adventures and misadventures I got myself into would've made for great material for a sequel to the movie *Adventures in Babysitting*.

I didn't get to spend much time with the children the first day, so my first jolt of reality came the second day I was there. I learned quickly that when charming, dimpled, three-year-old Amanda didn't get her way, there would be hell to pay. Temper tantrums were daily and lengthy. Her shrill screams were like air raid sirens. She would stomp and flail her arms, as the tears would begin to roll down her cheeks and the veins in her little neck would become engorged. And through it all, it seemed everyone, including me, was almost completely powerless to stop her. She carried on in this manner like a crazed Energizer bunny, until she just ran out of juice, which took a long, long time.

In all my experiences as a baby sitter, I had never worked with a child with such determination or tonsil power. Usually a stern talk, an ice cream bribe or a timeout in a bedroom would do the trick in short order. I was an avid reader and had read every child development and parenting book that I could get my hands on because I felt that I had to be one step ahead of the child. However, the first time I tried to take Amanda to her room for a timeout, Julia just looked aghast and a little dazed as she walked away. I got the message that disciplining the kids wasn't in my job description - and I didn't have the nerve to ask Julia and Steven how they wanted me to handle problems when they came up. I never did discover any rules regarding the children's behavior, but the Swartz' did have rules about other things in the home.

## Rules of Engagement

For the first few weeks I was at the Swartz', I carried a notebook with my notes from school; to which I added an ever-growing list that I hastily scribbled each time I learned something new about Steven and Julia's preferences, propensities and peculiarities. I was determined to please them in every way.

The first day of my tour of duty I discovered several major rules:

- ✔ **Don't touch the artwork-** This rule had me truly rattled because artwork was everywhere—it seemed there were few places left to touch. I was scared the kids would fall into a million-dollar painting and I would be held responsible. *Oops! Liability —yet another thing I forgot to clarify during my interview.*
- ✔ **Keep the front/side door unlocked-** I guess this was because they had so many employees coming in and out.
- ✔ **Under no circumstances was I to set off the security alarm or**

**motion detectors.** I didn't know exactly what would set them off, so I just decided to tread with caution.

The last rule scared the daylights out of me because I had always had a sleepwalking problem. Throughout my childhood and into my teens my mother would regularly find me wandering about the house in the middle of the night. I had once been found thoroughly washing my Ken and Barbie at 3 am in the bathroom sink. When I was a teenager I would plug in my curling iron and get in the shower at 2 am to get ready for school. My worst sleepwalking incident was when I walked off the top bunk while on vacation with my friend Kristi and her family. I didn't even wake up after I dropped to the floor. My sleepwalking was no joke, at least not to me. So I was completely paranoid about cruising around the house in my PJs in the middle of the night and setting off a three-alarm fire bell. My solution for curtailing my nocturnal jaunts at the Swartz's house was to dutifully lock myself in my room, which I did every night. I wasn't sure that I wouldn't unlock the door in my sleep, but I hoped I wouldn't.

More rules from day one:

- ✔ **Do not feed the kids fast food** - The family followed a strict low fat diet that did not include French Fries. *Are they only supposed to eat fruits and vegetables? How am I going to find new and exciting ways to fix carrot sticks?*
- ✔ **Never interrupt Julia or Steven during their morning work-outs -** *Got it*!
- ✔ **Steven will always take calls from the kids** - This particular rule made me feel great. This was the kind of family I wanted to work for: a family where the emotional well-being of the kids was the overriding concern.

These were just the stated rules. There were many, many other unwritten rules of course, but we'll get to that in due time.

Always striving to be the professional, I struggled from the very beginning to keep in mind the foremost principle that I had learned at nanny school: a nanny should not make her employers her friends. It was very difficult for me, a teen social queen from a small friendly town, to curb my natural tendencies. The first week I was there Julia brought home a couple of magazines and left them by my door. I was so touched. I thanked her several times and studied the magazines thoroughly, wondering if she was trying to pass on some beauty tips. I thought maybe she was taking me, the "small-town girl" under her gilded wing. But it never really happened quite that way. My efforts at connecting with her usually seemed to completely miss the target.

Then I remembered one of the prime directives from my training about the nanny's role: *"The nanny is taking care of part of the family, but she is not a member of the family."* I had a difficult time understanding this when I was in training, and I was having a hard time applying it now that I was on the job. I guess underneath it all I wanted to be treated as *both* a professional and a part of the family. This wasn't realistic, and I knew I wasn't supposed to feel that way, but being away from my own family for the first time, made me want to cling to the family that I lived with. And yet there was so little to cling to. Julia was often gone, and when she was home she seemed distracted, busy or generally unavailable. And I hardly ever saw Steven. He usually left pretty early in the morning and returned about ten or eleven most nights.

Since I knew I had to restrain my natural feelings for the sake of professionalism, and since I wasn't finding my employers particularly receptive either, I found myself becoming attached to the household staff. Maria the cook, immediately became my friend and she gradually became a kind of mother figure. I also became close to Concetta; she was 24 and had already worked for the family for three years. The other employees at Steven's office would become other members of my "little family." They were my sounding boards, my confidantes and occasionally they would offer a shoulder or two to cry on.

It took nearly a village to support the Swartz household. There was me (the nanny), Maria (the live-in cook), Concetta (the live-in housekeeper, relief cook and weekend nanny), Gloria and LaRosa (the weekday house-keepers), a weekly gardener (with whom Maria had an on-again/off-again romantic relationship), as well as the guy who detailed the cars and various people they hired for extra gardening and little household fix-it jobs. It was amazing how good the teamwork was, considering all the players who had a part in keeping up with the Swartz's place.

Steven held high expectations for the appearance of his home. The thing is, he held high expectations for appearances, period. When Gloria began to wear rollers in her hair to do her work in the morning, Steven had Julia speak with her. Even though she wasn't within view of anyone outside the house, the maid who cleaned his bathroom and emptied his trash every day was required to look professional. The housekeepers worked hard every day. The brass door-knocker and the black lacquer doors they adorned had to gleam. The Plexiglas child-safety guards on the stairway were kept clean of children's fingerprints, a totally impossible job, as most parents can attest. The marble floors had to be kept as smooth and clean as poured cream. Each morning LaRosa's first job was to remove all the lint off the dark emerald green carpeting on the stairs. As far as she was concerned, the hand-held vacuum that was used on the stairs was not up to the task. She would stoop down and tweeze each speck of fuzz with her fingers. Steven wanted things to be perfect, and so did LaRosa.

Steven valued the housekeepers' abilities to keep the house perfect, the way he and Julia wanted it, but Maria had the most status with him. She did all the grocery shopping, going out twice a week to an upscale market to get fresh food to stock the Sub-Zero refrigerator. Our nightly three-course dinners would stand up to anything you'd find at a fine restaurant. Although Maria did not live to "serve" dinner guests, she put together artful, sophisticated menus night after night for the family. The food was low fat and truly delicious. Steven prized her for that and she was not shy about using Steven's allegiance to her advantage. She was the grand dame de cuisine, the queen of the kitchen. The rest of the household staff grumbled a little when they were scurrying around the house to get their work done and Maria was reading *Gourmet* in the kitchen. But she wouldn't budge. She knew her job was secure as long as she continued cooking delectable and healthy dinners. Steven paid her a generous salary, but after a time, I found out that every couple of years or so she would get fed up with her live-in status and ask to be able to live-out. Maria owned a home, she had a boyfriend and she wanted to spend time with her family; she wanted a life. But Steven wouldn't hear of it. Her salary and the demands of her job kept her in chains to Steven's expectations. She had her own home, but was only able to stay there two nights a week, on her days off. Maria was convinced that if she left, she would be leaving without a reference. She said she would never be able to get another job that paid as well, if she took that step out the door.

Sometime toward the end of my first week at my new job, I started feeling pretty homesick. One night I opened the drawer beside my bed and pulled out the journal that Kristi's parents had given me as a graduation present. The cover design had flowery script that read "Wishes and Dreams." I opened it up and reread the inscription:

*Suzy – May all your thoughts be happy ones,*
*and all your experiences milestones.*
*We love you — George and MaryAnn*

I was suddenly aware of how enormous the distance was between me and the people who had watched me grow up and who loved me no matter what. Here, I was an unknown. Although I was making friends, I was still lonely. I decided that this was the perfect time to break open my present and start recording my new life. Over the course of my stay with the Swartz', I would go to this book almost nightly to pour out my decidedly mixed batch of thoughts and experiences.

I've been here a week now, and I'm just getting to know everyone, but it's kinda lonely. I miss my friends, my sisters, my mom and dad. Every day is the same basic routine. Well, not exactly. In order to have a beginning you have to have an end. I don't think my day has an end. Here's how it usually goes:

- Rise before 7 with Brandon, feed him, help Maria or Concetta fix the kids breakfast.
- Help Julia get kids dressed for school.
- Maria packs lunches; I intervene in the inevitable debate over its contents with Joshua.
- Help get the kids off to school.
- Care for and entertain Brandon until they return.
- Amanda comes home at 12:30 from preschool, Josh at 3:30 from kindergarten.
- Read with all the kids, play with toys, or succumb to the lures of the VCR.
- Eat dinner with Julia and the kids.
- Bathe all the kids, sometimes with Julia's help.
- Get Brandon ready for bed, help the other two with pajamas, then Julia or I read to them.
- Feed Brandon his bottle, rock him and put him in his crib.
- Nightly ritual: two bottles for Brandon, put them in a huge metal bowl filled with ice and bring it to my room. Take infant monitor to my room and listen for him to wake up.
- In the middle of the night when he cries, traipse down the hall where there is not, thank God, a red beam of light from

the elaborate alarm. I rock and cuddle him as I warm the bottle in the bottle warmer. He drinks the bottle and then at the precise moment he sucks down the last drop, with talented dexterity, I remove the bottle and simultaneously slip the pacifier into his mouth. He's off to la-la-land again.

- Repeat the bottle ritual a couple of hours later.
- Then it's morning and I start all over again.

Nanny school should have mentioned that getting up with infants in the middle of the night was expected! And what about sleep deprivation? I sure could've used some pointers on how to get by on not enough sleep.

It wasn't long before I started to feel more at ease in my new job, mostly because the staff had accepted me and taken me under their wings as the new girl on the block. It was generally much less tense when we had the house to ourselves after Julia took the kids to school, and left for the rest of the day. I loved just hanging out and playing with Brandon, coming up with new activities for him. He didn't have a lot of toys or baby equipment, so most of the time I just carried him around wherever I went. Julia had noticed how much he liked me to carry him and had come home from a shopping trip very excited one day with a front pack. It ended up that I hardly ever used it, because it was so much easier to just carry him on my hip.

Like most other highly-positioned Hollywood families, the Swartz had hired a baby nurse for the first six weeks of Brandon's life. Her job was to take care of his infant needs 24/7. Baby nurses were generally older women who had raised their own families and who were fairly traditional about leaving babies in their cribs and letting them "cry it out." I was his first caretaker after the baby nurse. And I took on the role whole-heartedly.

From the time he was really small, I loved to go on outings with Brandon; we often went to the park and took long walks through the neighborhood. It was on a walk with him when I realized we only lived a block from OJ Simpson's house. We often saw him and his daughter on walks, his little girl loved seeing and talking to the "tiny baby." One morning while I was pushing Brandon in his huge English pram, feeling like a typical English governess minus the gray hair, I began to cross the sidewalk in front of OJ's house when the gates opened. I saw a large white SUV backing out of the driveway at full throttle. I managed to pull Brandon back and narrowly retrieve my own right leg before the four-wheel-drive whisked past us and then screeched to a halt. I recognized Nicole from other times I had driven past the house and we had done the "neighbor wave." She stuck her head out of the window and apologized profusely, and then sped off down Rockingham.

During one of my first weeks on the job, Steven's office assistant, Jason, called the house to leave a message. Steven had given him his seats for a Lakers basketball game that evening. But now he wasn't going to be able to use them because he had too much work to do at the office. He casually suggested that I take them. When I gathered up my courage and followed Jason's suggestion, Steven said, "Sure, why don't you take a friend?" I couldn't believe his generosity or my good fortune. Since I had no friends within a 1000-mile radius at that point. I said, "Can I take Concetta?" Steven and Julia looked perplexed, but they agreed. He handed over the tickets along with a VIP parking pass.

Concetta and I were about as excited as could be as we headed off on our adventure in her old car. We drove right up to the arena and a parking valet appeared at the door, ready to whisk away our carriage; but I didn't have a clue how to handle the protocols of power, LA-style. *So, now, did this guy need a tip? How much? Now or later?* My last experience at a big venue was when Ozzy Osbourne played in Portland. I'd gone with my friend Amy and we had to hike the North 40 between the parking space and the Coliseum because we didn't have enough money to pay for stadium parking. It didn't dampen Amy's excitement. And Concetta had no problem with having fun, either. She got right into the spirit of being a big shot for a night. I felt I'd found a friend. I'd fine-tune parking protocol later.

It got even better when we got inside. We were seated directly behind the visiting team – that night, it was the Seattle Super Sonics. Concetta found the TV cameras right away and settled in for a night of viewing and being viewed. I wasn't used to this kind of media coverage. I remember wondering every time the camera pulled back, whether I was making a splash in Cottage Grove.

Our seats came with our own server, who came by several times to ask if there was anything we wanted. It was fun to have the perks of power, even if they were just borrowed for the evening. I was overwhelmed with all the questions running through my head: *What was my status with the server? If you hold the ticket, do they think you are someone important?* Such are the complexities of modern-day servitude. We never did order anything because we were too embarrassed to ask if it would cost extra, and we only had $8 between us. My short-lived ascension into status that night at the Lakers game turned out to have a lasting benefit. From that time on, I knew the exact location of Steven's seats. Over the years, I would be extremely grateful for that knowledge.

## Don't Judge the Art by it's Cover

Since I grew up in a place where it was customary for most men over the age of 50 to start almost every sentence with "Well, I reckon..." talking about the world of art had not been a big part of my life. My father's idea of art was the bowling trophy that he won back in '66 for bowling a perfect 300 game. It also doubled as our living room clock. My mother's art collection consisted of a snowman that my sisters and I had made her out of one of those yarn things you hook; the kind that's on the squared burlap and you match the yarn with the painted pattern. As for me, I was not a big art collector; unless you consider the framed picture of Jon Bon Jovi that I special ordered through *Teen Magazine* and kept on my dresser.

One Friday afternoon Steven told me, as he was leaving for the office, that some deliverymen would be arriving that day with a large painting from his friend's art gallery in New York. Steven purchased a great deal of art from him. He often came for overnight visits and would stay in the luxurious guest suite that was just off the upstairs gallery.

I was to show the deliverymen into the sitting room and tell them to hang the painting on a particular wall. Julia was going to be gone all day, and it was Maria's day off, so it would be my responsibility to handle this important matter carefully. I had no idea how much the painting was worth. My only frame of reference was one of the small paintings in the family room. Maria had told me it was worth $750,000. I decided this was a responsibility that required my full attention.

Steven must have called six times, nearly every half-hour, that day wanting to know if the painting had arrived. I repeatedly told him it had not. I didn't leave the house all day for fear I'd miss the delivery. Then at 4 pm, a truck appeared and I buzzed them in the front gate. Two men approached the front door carrying a wooden crate that was about six feet long. I could see the butcher-paper-covered package through the wooden slats. Steven's important painting had arrived. I immediately took the men into the living room, where they began pulling the crate apart with claw hammers and then carefully tearing off the paper covering. When they finally pulled all the butcher paper off, there was yet another piece of solid black paper wrapped tightly around the painting.

"Where do you want it, Miss?" one of them asked.

"Over here. See, those two hooks are all ready for it."

At that point, I expected the men to tear off the final cover, but they just lifted it up by the sides and carefully and slowly hung it on the wall. *Why hadn't they uncovered it? Had they been told to leave it that way? Perhaps Steven wanted it to be a surprise at an upcoming dinner party. He must be planning a grand unveiling. He would make a big to-do about pulling off the black cover, at which point he would expound on the virtues of his newest acquisition.*

The suspense was killing me. *Why didn't they unwrap the damn thing?* I went on stewing about that painting for days. Four nights went by and still there was no unveiling. To add to the mystery, Steven had a railing installed in front of it, protruding out about three feet. The intent was to keep people from getting close enough to touch it. I'd heard him telling Maria not to let the *girls* (referring to the housekeepers, all adult women) touch it, dust it or breathe on it; so it bothered me that it remained wrapped. For the life of me I could not figure out why, and, of course, I didn't want to appear the country bumpkin that I was by inquiring.

Finally, one night I overheard Julia and Steven talking about the painting. *How could they be discussing it without seeing it?* It was then that I realized it wasn't being covered by anything. It was just a large black painting! No scene, contrasting colors, no nothing; just a canvas of black. As I looked closer, I discerned that there were three separations, with black fabric wrapped around each panel. This is embarrassing to admit, but I really studied it hard to see if it could possibly be three different 'shades' of black. I figured the "artist/fabric wrapper" who put this piece together must have had some phenomenal talent, imperceptible to all but the very wealthy.

## "I Know You are But What am I?"

After the first few weeks as a nanny, I was pleased with my ability to care for Brandon. He was growing chubby-cheeked and was such a happy baby.

Amanda and I had fun making up stories and we were getting along well, at least when she wasn't having a tantrum. But Joshua wasn't really warming up to me. Then one night I set our "getting to know you" period back by eons. Joshua was in the kitchen all by himself at dinnertime when I walked in to see what he was doing. I found him sitting atop the center island by himself, playing with an entire stick of butter, which was beginning to get very soft. He had dropped the wrapper on the floor. As I picked it up, I scolded him, "Joshua, don't eat that. You can't eat butter all by itself."

"Yes I can," he said loudly.

"No you can't!" I responded, now breaking one of my own rules by getting engaged in a childish shouting match.

"Yes I can."

"No, you can't!"

"Yes, I can." His voice was getting louder and more imperious

*This is crazy. I'm acting like a kid myself. I've gotta do something!*

I put my hand around his wrist and began to wrestle the stick from his hand, forgetting my other rule to always be smarter than the child. When he jerked his hand away yelling "let go of me, you idiot" a big dollop of the greasy stuff flung into the air and stuck to the side of his face.

"I hate you. You gooooot bbbbuuuttter on me!" he screamed as he started crying. Then he threw what was left of the greasy mass at me, and a huge chunk lodged in my hair.

I felt absolutely ridiculous. To make matters worse, Steven's parents Irving and Lillian, were staying at the house for a couple of days while Steven and Julia were out of town. I was already very fond of them both. Grandpa Swartz had a small potbelly and was very quiet, but you could tell the wheels in his brain were always turning. Lillian Swartz was the caricature of a Jewish mother, and she had a heart of gold. She wore sweatshirts with rhinestones and sequins sewn all over them. She talked constantly, which drove Grandpa to his silences. The only time he really seemed to respond to her was when they argued. They would get caught up in this exchange where they would both keep saying the same thing over and over: "Don't start. I'm telling you, don't start with me." I loved watching them interact. They had been married forever, and despite their disagreements you could tell underneath it all they couldn't live without each other.

When Mr. Swartz heard the commotion, he came in and inquired what the ruckus was about. I told Mr. Swartz I had discovered Joshua eating a stick of butter and that he had thrown it at me, to which Joshua piped up, "But Grandpa, she threw it at me first."

One glance easily confirmed Joshua's argument. Mr. Swartz looked at the butter on Joshua's face then turned to see the clump in my hair. *Food Fight* were the first words that popped into my head. I realized that it would be hard to explain my way out of this one. Although Mr. Swartz had a gruff exterior at times, he was a very kind and caring man. I was mortified when he gave me a you-should-know-better look as he used a dishcloth to wipe the butter from Joshua's face. I felt so foolish that the words just wouldn't come to explain that I had not purposely splattered his grandson with fat.

Things were not going well.

I couldn't recall a lecture at NNI entitled "What to Do When You're Accused of Throwing Food at Your Charges." To make matters worse, Mr. Swartz said, "Perhaps you should take a time out, Suzanne. I'll talk with Joshua." My face went flush with his words. *Take a timeout? Could a nanny ever be admonished in a more demeaning manner?* And yet, part of me was glad to take a timeout from this frustrating child. Perhaps that wasn't such bad advice.

By this time it was past eight o'clock at night. I had already put Brandon to bed and I knew that Grandma Swartz would take care of Joshua and Amanda. I went to my room and put on my bathing suit, wrapped myself in a robe and went down to the pool for the first time. The water was always heated to about eighty-five degrees, and I thought it would be a good antidote to my anger. My plan was clear: *I'll swim a little, float in the warm water, relax and rinse the last of the butter out of my hair.*

The pool wasn't a large one but it had a great slide. I decided to take my plunge by sliding down on my stomach headfirst. *Whee-e-e*, the slide was slicker than I had anticipated and I hurled off the end through the short length of the pool like a torpedo launched from a nuclear submarine. I hit the bricks on the other side of the pool deck, at about 50 mph, or so it seemed, and I immediately began to sink like a big hunk of concrete. It's strange what goes through your mind when you think you're dying. Most people would think about their loved ones or an unfulfilled dream. Instead, I remember thinking; *I'm going to die in this pool. My God, what an idiot they'll all think I am. They'll be convinced that the last act of a dying woman was to throw butter at a six-year-old. What an embarrassing demise.*

But of course I wasn't dying. I'd just been stunned, so I continued talking to myself. *I should never have come down here to swim alone. Now I've compounded the trouble with Joshua a thousand fold.* I shook my head a little to get my bearings and then pulled myself out of the pool. I could feel a knot the size of a Ping-Pong ball forming on my forehead. It started to throb. I held my hand to it and then looked at my fingers where the blood was running through down to my wrist and onto my arm. *I'm not going to drown. I'm going to bleed to death.*

I could see the headline tomorrow in the *Los Angeles Times:*
**Nanny Accused of Throwing Butter at Six Year Old - Apparently Commits Suicide to Avoid the Wrath of Super Agent Swartz.**

CUT TO:

INTERIOR — MORTUARY - DAYTIME

A funeral in progress, approximately 100 people are seated facing a casket on the stage. The casket is open. A professionally dressed couple whispers together in the front row.

> JULIA
> Steven, do you really think we should have paid for this?

> STEVEN
> She died in our pool, didn't she?

> JULIA
> What's that got to do with it? Her parents should have taken care of it. After all, she did throw butter at Joshua.

## I Guess George Clooney was Off That Day

The last thing I needed was for Grandma and Grandpa Swartz to see me in this condition, so I slithered quietly up to my room where I got a gander of the gash on my head. It wasn't long, about half an inch, but it was deep, very deep, and the blood would not stop running down between my eyes.

"Suzy, are you all right?" I could hear Grandpa Swartz calling out. He must have seen the trail of blood I left on the marble entry. I knew I had to confess at that point.

"Uh, Mr. Swartz, I'm up here. I bumped my head in the pool," I replied, not wanting him to climb the stairs. Irving Swartz was in his mid-sixties, but in a flash he was up the stairs and in my room.

"Let me see that," he said as he pulled my hand and the towel away from my face.

"Oh my God, that is a nasty one; pretty deep. You'll have to get stitches."

The situation was becoming more convoluted by the minute. Mr. Swartz insisted on driving me to the emergency room to have the cut stitched. *I should have just let Joshua eat the butter. Maybe he wouldn't have gotten sick. Then I wouldn't have gone swimming and I wouldn't have to explain this whole ridiculous affair to my new employers.*

Adding to my embarrassment, poor Mr. Swartz was deeply concerned. He was kind enough to hold my hand the entire time the doctor was suturing my gash. I went back to the house with a huge gauze bandage taped to my forehead to protect the eight stitches.

My own family has always accused me of being overly dramatic. They still think I exaggerate every illness I ever have. So I knew when I called to report my latest injury, they'd all sit around laughing, trying to decide if this cut was as catastrophic as a hangnail or a common cold. But with these stitches, I had proof. Boy, this time I'll show my doubting family. I DID actually have to go to the emergency room and I have real stitches to prove it. Not only that, I'll tell them that while I was there I saw Grandma Horton from *Days of our Lives,* which used to be my mother's favorite soap. So that serves my mom right for calling me a hypochondriac.

I had felt Julia's disapproval of my behavior on several occasions, so I dreaded having them find out about my little incident. Oddly enough, they reacted quite differently than I expected. They both seemed to find the entire story amusing, and they didn't seem angry at all. Julia just said, laughing, "Sounds like Suzy and Josh got in a food fight while we were gone."

I was mortified, I found absolutely no humor in the situation and I tried to explain what really happened, but Julia didn't seem much interested. I think they *must* have had some doubts as to my judgment, at the very least.

 What I have learned today:
    1.  Try to be a responsible role model.
2. Tell my mother that the rule about waiting an hour after you eat to go swimming should be expanded to:
      Never go swimming alone
      Make sure the pool is long enough to go head first off the slide
      Don't go swimming to relax after throwing butter at a child – judgment might be impaired
Note to self: Tell Mom about seeing Grandma Horton.
Call nanny school and find out what you do when you're given a timeout.

## I Didn't Know I Would be Involved in a Needle Exchange Program

"Suzy, you must have hit those bricks pretty hard. I think that you should go see my acupuncturist, just in case," Steven suggested. I didn't see the immediate connection to my gash and an acupuncturist until he added, "You probably jammed your neck pretty good. Better safe than sorry. Have it looked at now so you won't have any back or neck problems later," he explained. That made perfect sense and I told him I appreciated his concern. He even went so far as to have his secretary, Sarah, make an appointment for me the next Saturday.

I'd heard of acupuncture before, but Cottage Grove wasn't exactly the Mecca of alternative health, so I had never seen the procedure done. When I arrived at the office, it looked more like a parlor for a palm reader than a doctor's office. In place of a door to separate the receptionist's area from the examining rooms, there hung strands of jingling, jangling colored beads; a throwback to the 60's. Vanilla incense burned my nose. Dr. Chu Bauschelt was his name. *How do acupuncturists come by the title "doctor" anyway?*

I remembered that movie where people were suspended from the ceiling with needles poked in their bodies. I can't really say that I was totally calm. After filling out the new patient form, I was ushered into a small room with a table that appeared to be a cross between the medieval rack and a barber's chair. Dr. Bauschelt entered, asked me a few questions about how I'd sustained my injuries, and then told me to lie face down on the padded apparatus. After cranking a handle on one side and rotating a wheel on the other, I was elevated to the proper position.

I told him that it was my neck I was concerned about. He nodded and opened a drawer in a cabinet to reveal a variety of short, thin needles.

"This won't hurt a bit," he said as he pulled on a surgical glove and reached into the drawer. He was right; it didn't hurt. I was also surprised that he had inserted five of the needles in my lower back, and the rest on various parts of my body; including my ears, but none of them anywhere near my neck. Then came the disturbing news.

"Aha!" he said. *I never have liked it when a doctor says aha.*

"What?" I demanded.

"Oh, you have weak kidneys," he said, with a matter-of fact tone.

"How do you know that?" I asked.

Without answering the question, he said "It's probably the result of your parents being in conflict at the time of your conception."

I was speechless. Don't get me wrong; I'm very open-minded. In fact, my family has always been into alternative medicine— my grandmother worked for a chiropractor before most people even knew what one was—but the idea of conception conflict causing my compromised kidneys was a little hard to believe. I began to conjure a picture of myself on dialysis, living the rest of my life with a colostomy bag hanging from my belt. I was sure this would greatly decrease my chances of ever finding a husband. And yes, I do know that having a section of your bowel removed doesn't have anything to do with your urinary system, but the connection between the two was all it took to inspire my vivid imagination.

When I left, the receptionist handed me the bill along with a self-addressed envelope, for my convenience. The total was $75. It seemed a fair amount, and a little high for my budget. But then it occurred to me that this was Steven's doctor and that he had suggested I come here. He'd even made the appointment. Maybe he was intending to cover the expense since health insurance was never discussed in the contract non-negotiation. *That would be really nice,* I thought.

When I got back to the house that afternoon, I put the bill with the envelope on the desk downstairs where the mail usually stacked up. I didn't give it another thought, except to thank Steven later and to tell him I felt fine and didn't think I'd have any problems. I didn't share with him, his doctor's observation and the impending doom that I was sure lay ahead as I spent my life wearing Depends. That would be my own private torment.

The next night, as I was in my room getting ready to lock myself in for the evening, I noticed a piece of paper on my dresser. It was the acupuncturist's bill. I thought it odd, but I figured LaRosa, seeing my name on it, had brought it up. The next morning I returned it to Julia's desk. That evening as I was getting ready for bed I noticed it was back on my dresser. Again, I went downstairs and put the bill back on Julia's desk and made a mental note to talk with LaRosa. The next day the bill was back. The bill went back and forth like that four times before I had a chance to tell LaRosa to leave it on Julia's desk.

"But Miss Soozy, I deedint poot any-ting on your dresser," she said. *Ohhhh.* It was then that I realized it was Julia who was putting it in my room. I paid the bill myself, and as with too many other subjects, never brought it up to Julia.

## Wheel-less in a City Built on Wheels

Julia had told me when I interviewed that I could use the family's Jeep Cherokee on my days off. This agreement worked well for me because I didn't want to bring my less-than-reliable transportation with me to LA. Since they also owned a Mercedes, a Jaguar and a Porsche, transportation was never a big issue in their house. The only problem was, ever since I had arrived, Julia had used the Jeep to go to their home in Malibu nearly every weekend. This meant I didn't have a way to get around on my days off in a city where the car is king. When I described the problem to Julia, she shrugged and said she was sorry. She said that she hadn't thought about the weekend car conflict when she'd hired me; and since she didn't like other people driving her Mercedes, that just wouldn't be an option. So, I just stayed at the house most every weekend. In the beginning it didn't really matter because I didn't know a soul in Los Angeles, and I had no social life outside of the house staff.

I'd adjourn to my room on my days off, where I'd read, catch up on my sleep or write in my journal. I still felt uncomfortable socializing with my employers, so when Steven was home and I wasn't on duty I only ventured out of my room to go to the kitchen to eat. A couple of times this modified confinement lasted from Saturday until Monday morning. Steven made it a priority to spend weekends with the family, so if they weren't in Malibu they were usually in and out of the house on Saturday and Sunday. I'd be in my room listening at the door until I thought the family had left the house for an outing, then I would make my way downstairs to visit with the other staff.

I knew that I had to force myself to start going somewhere on the weekends, even if it meant doing it alone. One day when I was reading the LA Times, I noticed an ad for people to audition for a game show in Hollywood on the next Saturday. I called the 800 number and signed up for the audition. It sounded like fun. Maybe I could even win some money, or a new car. Who knows? Maybe I'd be discovered! At the very least, I could call my family and friends and tell them to watch me on television. The only person I had ever known that was on a game show was Tim Taylor's grandma, who was a big winner on *The Price Is Right.*

Maria and Concetta were going to be off that Saturday so I asked LaRosa if I could use her truck to go to the show. She kindly obliged, and I chose a dressy black dress. Basically, my wardrobe was comprised of shorts, T-shirts and this little number. I didn't have a clue how ludicrous I would look until I pulled up to the security gate at the television studios and caught sight of myself in the round security mirror. I was a sight to be seen in LaRosa's faded '73 Chevy pick up, without a front bumper and with a Baja Mexico license plate tied to the grill with bailing wire. The enormous camper shell added a nice touch, since it was secured down with black rope to match my dress.

I reached out the window and handed the guard my confirmation number. My faux diamond bracelet slid to the end of my wrist, which caught his eye. His gaze then traveled up my arm to survey me in all my splendor, in my lovely cocktail dress. My face was framed nicely by the ring of red dingle balls that were tacked all along the headliner, and the fuzzy dice hanging from the rear view mirror. It occurred to me that LaRosa's boyfriend had probably decorated this truck to his taste.

"Have a nice day ma'am," he said, handing me back my piece of paper with a strange smile. They must have been used to seeing all kinds here. "Just pull under this overhang and follow the arrows to the parking structure."

I struggled to put the long heavy shifter into gear. This was no easy feat, since someone had creatively substituted an 8-ball for the gearshift knob. Looking down, I could see the pavement through the floorboard from which the shifter protruded. The transmission made a grinding noise as I tried to keep one of my dainty black heels on the clutch, the other on the accelerator. As I let up slowly, the creaky old truck lunged and jerked and finally lurched forward, passing under the overpass which read Maximum clearance 7'3".

To be honest, I don't know that I even gave that measurement much thought until I was halfway through the garage and I heard the awful scraping sound of tin against concrete. At first, I thought it was just some machinery. I continued on my merry way, following the yellow arrows. I began to suspect there might be a problem when I glanced in my side mirror and saw sparks flying and then got a whiff of the burning steel. At this point I stopped, pulled out the handbreak and jumped out of the cab to see that the camper had been shaved down an inch shorter than when I'd arrived. I looked around the parking structure suspiciously for Alan Fundt and his Candid Camera crew. But no, this was actually happening to me for real.

Once inside the building, a receptionist gave me directions to the fourth floor where the auditions were taking place. When I got there, I entered a large reception area filled with applicants of all ages and ethnic groups; none of whom were wearing anything more formal than skirts or Dockers. It was a Saturday, and the show was supposed to be fun and casual. I sat quiet, almost sullen, in my cocktail dress and gold earrings as groups of ten were called and ushered into another room.

Twenty minutes later it was my turn, and along with yet another group of hopefuls, I was shown into a small amphitheater where nearly two hundred people were seated, filling out forms on clipboards. In front of the semicircle of tiered bleachers was a stage, podium and microphone. When I had finished filling out the form, the game show host came out from behind a curtain, as bouncy and ebullient as any adult I've ever seen. It was as if he snorted a drinking glass of cocaine before his arrival. I have never seen a person happier and more energetic.

"Go-o-o-o-d afterno-o-o-n pee-e-eople!" he thundered out his exaggerated, manic greeting. I seemed to be the only one who didn't echo back his exact inflection.

"Go-o-o-od afterno-o-o-o-n, Chuck!" they yelled back.

Was I missing something? Had I arrived late and not gotten the instructions? All around me men and women were grinning and I saw more straight white teeth here than at an orthodontists' convention.

"Okay then. Let's get to work straight-away," he screamed. "You have been selected from among thousands of applicants to try out for Wheel O' Fun, the game show where everyone has fun, even if they don't win anything. There are just a few rules I must share with you before we begin," he continued. He then went on to read a litany of do's and dont's, which mostly revolved around the cardinal rule that we must all smile all the time. We would be chosen according to our energy, enthusiasm and whether we had a genuine laugh or not. There was no mention of minimum display of intelligence. "Remember," he sang out, still grinning madly, "our motto is 'the people at home are always winners,' and they like to live vicariously through our contestants."

Ordinarily, I'm just as fun-loving and energetic as the next person, but it seemed I'd gotten in way over my head. These were professionals; people who were permanently happy. There would be four "cuts," Chuck warned us with a huge grin. At each stage of the audition, fifty or so people would be eliminated until only ten remained out of the original two hundred. My chances looked as dim as my mood.

"Okay! We'll begin in a moment but first I must warn you that when, and if, you go on stage in front of millions of viewers across the country, the camera is going to "dumb you down," and fatten you up a bit! Fair warning!" he cackled. His bellowing laugh was then mimicked exactly by 199 others. "What I mean to say is, you need to be extra, extra animated with your gestures and your smiles, or the camera won't pick it up. And, unfortunately, you will all look about ten pounds heavier on camera. So don't sue me when it happens!" He just couldn't get over how clever he was.

"Okay, so that's it. Lets begin with round one. It's quite simple, really. When I point you out, just stand up, tell us your name and tell us a bit about yourself." *Oh yeah, real simple Chuck.*

I began to squirm in my cocktail dress. The room was getting warm. Everyone else seemed to be wiggling in anticipation of being called first. I tried to slide down lower on the bench. Then, as my luck would have it, I was sitting in the first row of contestant wanna-bees that he called on. I was sweating profusely when he worked his way to the potential contestant seated beside me. She was some little teacher's pet, I could tell, and she did some perky little song and dance for ol' Charles. I was next. "You, you there in the lovely black dress. Stand up and tell us about yourself." I could feel the camera going into full intense zoom. The room went silent and my hands and face became clammy and wet. "Come on, don't be shy! This is the Whee-e-e-el O' Fun." He threw his body into a gesture approximating a wheel.

I jumped up like I was shot out of a cannon. I bit my lip, "I'm 19 years old and I'm a governess." (I thought I'd use a more impressive sounding title for this group of scholars.) I blundered on, "I'm Suzanne and I don't really want to look fat and dumb." The audience screamed and hooted in laughter. I sat down quickly and waited for Chuckaroony to move on to another row. As soon as his attention was elsewhere I grabbed my purse and stumbled over thirteen sets of knees to the end of the bleachers and ran out the two large doors. I didn't stop running until I reached my "RV" and was safely inside it. Maybe I didn't have what it took to run down the aisle telegenically for this Bob Barker wannabe, but I could've used the money. So much for a future in TV.

After I caught my breath and had started the ignition in the lovely truck, I remembered that it was jammed up into the rafters. I was on fragile emotional ground here, having just endured a public humiliation—I didn't know if I could handle the mocking scream of the metal scraping the camper on the ceiling again. But what to do? In a moment of sheer brilliance, relatively speaking, I got out the driver's side and took a ball point pen from the dash to let just enough air out of the tires to lower the truck just over an inch.

Later, when Maria and Concetta asked about my new star status, I told them I didn't even make it past the first cut. They all laughed and said that maybe I was a candidate for *The Gong Show*.

Okay. I'm still a wimp. What did I learn today?
1. I need to take some public speaking classes
2. I need to think carefully about my wardrobe before I go out in public
3. I'm not as gregarious as I thought
4. Don't drive other people's cars
All of the above.
Note to self: Join Toast Masters.

#1 priority: Start looking for my own car.

Steven was out with clients or at meetings every weeknight, with rare exceptions. On those nights, Julia had issued a general invitation for me to eat with her and the kids. She said that on the rare nights when Steven was home for dinners she didn't want me there during their family time. I totally understood and was glad that they valued their infrequent week-night dinners together. Most nights, however, the normal routine was for me to sit down with Julia and the children in the family dining room and be served our meal. Maria or Concetta watched the baby in the kitchen and served us. There I was at the "big table" with my friends waiting on me. I never did feel comfortable with the whole scene. In between courses, Maria or Concetta would go back to the kitchen and wait to be summoned by the buzzer that was on top of the lazy susan in the middle of the table. The buzzer was Joshua's favorite toy and torture device.

Buzzzzzz! "I want ketchup!"

Buzzzzzz! "Take away this soup! I hate this soup!"

Buzzzzzz! "Amanda touched my fork. Idiot! Get me a new fork!"

Buzzzzzz! "That's all."

Sometimes he'd buzz it just for the buzz. At least this was what happened when the buzzer was in its place at the center of the table. There were many times when it seemed to be suspiciously missing.

Dinner was almost always an active time for me. I'd pop out of my chair to intercept Josh's hand on its way to the buzzer and get up to retrieve the ketchup myself, reminding him that he needed to be considerate of the people who were taking care of him. I wanted Julia to correct his behavior, but instead it felt like she wanted to correct mine. We always managed to make small talk, but I definitely felt on duty rather than at home. Sometimes Julia was friendly and almost at ease, but more often her guard was up, and so was mine. It was a priority for her to eat dinner with her children, but she didn't seem to feel comfortable handling it on her own. Although she was an accomplished gourmet chef in her own right, with expertise in orchestrating dinners for crowds of Hollywood stars, she seemed overwhelmed by the complexities of managing her own little clan at mealtime without a staff.

One or two nights a week, Steven would send someone from the office to pick Julia up so the two of them could attend one of his company-related functions together. The first night I observed this ritual, I assumed they must have had special plans because Julia was dressed to the nines in a stunning black sequined dress. She seemed excited as she stood primping her hair in the hall mirror, waiting for a driver to pick her up. I was talking with her, telling her how great her dress looked, when the front gate buzzer went off. Someone was at the intercom box. *It must be the limo driver,* I peaked out the curtain to see a weather-beaten, dented 1960s Volkswagen idling in the driveway.

The driver, who was very young, stuck his head out of the window, waved and honked the horn once. Seeing me at the window he yelled, "I'm here to pick up Mrs. Swartz. I can't shut the car off. Can you send her out?"

It was the first time I remembered feeling really sorry for Julia. She looked like an excited Cinderella, going to the ball, until she opened the door and saw her pumpkin sitting in the driveway. I watched the old bug as it chugged out of the driveway and I heard the car backfire. Later, I found out the driver had been hired to work in the mailroom three days earlier. Steven had a habit of sending whoever was handy in the office, in whatever car they happened to own, to pick her up. It seemed possible to me, that Steven didn't know that kid from the Hillside Strangler. And yet, I had heard that in LA, you are what you drive. I guess this didn't apply to Mrs. Steven Swartz.

When Julia was out with the Jeep during the day, I had to figure out an alternate way of fetching the kids from school. Maria came to my rescue, offering to lend me her car. I was very grateful, but the first time I took it, I was instantly aware of how out of place it was on the grounds of the private school. There I was, amid the Beemers, Mercedes, Jags and occasional limos, pulling up in Maria's rust-colored '72 Toyota. The bumper was hanging off and the paint job was chipped. To keep my place in the line of new cars making their way to the entrance of the school and the waiting children, I had to keep revving the engine to keep it running. I was definitely a spectacle, and I didn't know which would die first, the engine or me—from looks that I was catching.

I knew what they must have been thinking: Who the hell is that? And why does she keep revving that engine? What an eyesore. It shouldn't even be allowed on school grounds. Can't they do something about that, that…thing? I don't pay $50,000 a year for this! Someone ought to call the LAPD.

I was starting to figure out all kinds of things about my new home. One of them was why there was no answering machine or voice mail. I would have thought one so powerful as Steven would surely screen his calls—no telling who could get hold of his home phone number, though it was certainly unlisted. Later I realized that there was no need for such electronic devices because there was always someone home, usually at least four or five people. Many times Julia wasn't happy with the messages she received because everyone on the staff were native speakers of Spanish, except for me. It was difficult for them to write in English, and Julia was frustrated when she couldn't tell who had called. So they started coming to me after they had taken a message, and they asked me to spell the names correctly. I was happy to help them, mostly because gawking at the names of famous callers together helped us build camaraderie.

Once Concetta and Gloria came to me, all dimpled up with smiles and said they had a love message for me from Tomas Cruz. They wondered if they had the spelling right. They loved teasing me about my little infatuation with him.

As I got to know Maria and Concetta, I found out more about the recent history of the family. Maria had also been close to a previous nanny, Leticia, Amanda's special caretaker. Leticia had been with the family when Amanda was a baby. In between the two of us, there had been another young nanny who had only stayed two months. When I interviewed, Julia had told me that the last nanny didn't really understand what a nanny's job was. After awhile, the girl decided she wasn't cut out for the job. I just knew that I was different, that I *was* cut out for it. It never occurred to me to pay attention to this little warning sign. Maria confided that the young girl had been very snobbish with her and Concetta. She said that she had rarely talked to either of them. I wanted to make sure I wasn't like that. I was determined to be a part of their lives. Our conversations and the laughs we had together was a large part of what was sustaining me. It felt good to have other people live in Bizzaro World with me.

Maria said that when Leticia left there had been an unpleasant scene between her and Julia. After a few weeks, Leticia had called Maria asking to come back to visit Amanda. Julia had said she couldn't come into the house. Maria would periodically sneak Leticia over to see Amanda when she knew Steven and Julia would be gone for the day. She also had to plan the times when Joshua wasn't there, or he would tattle. Maria would never let her in the house. I think she was too scared to. So they would stand out on the sidewalk. I sympathized, but I told Maria that I thought asking Amanda to keep Leticia's visits a secret from her parents was too much pressure to put on a three-year-old.

The first time I saw their reunion from an upstairs window, I felt sad for both of them. When Maria told Amanda that Leticia was at the gate, she ran out the front door and all the way down the driveway. There, as if outside the prison walls, stood Leticia; a plump Hispanic woman, grasping the black iron bars and pressing her face into the space between. She was smiling, waiting for Amanda to push the button to open the gate and let her in. Little did I know that would be me someday, just another in a long line of departed souls.

Steven lived with a very strict diet. He worked out everyday and held a black belt in Aikido. Putting it mildly, he stayed in excellent shape. When he was home, he forbade using any salt, butter, additives or fatty foods in his meals. He strictly followed the Pritikin Diet. I was hanging out in the kitchen one night, while Maria prepared a meal for Steven and Julia. She was stirring a large pot of soup that Steven loved. As she stirred she smiled, hummed and poured salt into the pot.

"Maria! I thought he didn't eat any salt," I said, surprised. She didn't respond. She just kept humming and smiling as she shook the salt shaker.

"Little Soo-zita, Steph-on (what she called him when he wasn't around. It was Mr. Swartz to his face) would not eeet haf the dee-shez he asks me to make if I deed not put in a lee-tul flavor," she said as she laughed. "He luves all of my coookeng, I put everyong in that I need to make it muy bien. Then I just tell heem it tastes sooo good cuz I am such a good cook."

I pushed her on the shoulder and said, "Maria, I can't believe you put salt in his meals! He thinks he's on such a strict diet." She laughed again, and then I started, and neither of us could stop for ten minutes. I had to wipe the tears from my cheeks before I went into the dining room. Steven and Julia watched the children's diets too, especially monitoring them for fats. They were served only skim milk and they weren't allowed to eat butter, only margarine. Joshua had never even laid eyes on a Big Mac; and they had never eaten a piece of fried chicken, as far as I know. Grilled swordfish and salmon were typical Happy Meals for the children.

## The LAPD Almost Stopped Me From Getting to *90210*

Late one evening as I began to head downstairs to get Brandon's bottles, I heard Julia talking to Steven in the family room. When I heard my name, I leaned over the banister as far as I could. I put my hair behind my ear as if I was Jamie Sommers and it would help me hear, just like the Bionic Woman.

Steven said, "How is Suzy doing?"

"She's night and day difference from that last girl. She's great," Julia said. *Maybe I misread her.* I was thrilled at what I had overheard. Until now, I had taken the lack of communication between the two of us to mean that she just didn't like me. Maybe I had misinterpreted her. *Maybe she really hasn't been judging me all this time.* Then the kids started screaming and I couldn't hear the rest.

The next day, while I was with the kids in the family room, Julia came in and said that Steven had offered to pay for my nails to be done. She wanted to know if I would like to have my nails done like hers. If so, she would send me to her "girl" and pay for it. I'd never given a thought to how I was going to maintain acrylic nails. I was sure I would need to remove them, but it was so kind of her to offer. I thought maybe I could try keeping them up, and they *would* help me stop my lifelong habit of biting my nails.

"I'd love to. Thank you, Mrs. Swartz," I eagerly responded.

"We're not going to the beach house, so you can take my Jeep this weekend," she offered. I was stunned. The voice in my head changed its story. *Maybe Julia likes me after all. Things are definitely looking up.*

CUT TO:

EXTERIOR - ELEGANT SPA - DAY

Girl gets out of stretch limo onto red carpet. A stylishly dressed lady greets her in perfumed lobby.

                    GREETER
Good afternoon. You must be Ms. Hansen.  We've been
expecting you, the Swartz family wants to treat you to
an entire day of personal pampering.  Come right this
way and we can begin.  You can start in the dressing
lounge. Slip into the robe, it's on the warming shelf

beside the sofa. The heated slippers are underneath.
Help yourself to the herbal tea, and look over the list
of services. The Swartz' want to give you a full day
of luxury, so choose any five services. Our consultant, Mary Beth, can help answer any questions, and then
she'll get you started.

Greeter hands young lady a menu of choices, and shows
her to the dressing room.

Young lady looks around in awe at the beautiful décor,
the plump sofa, the chandelier and the Perrier sitting
on the glass coffee table. She slips into the plush,
white robe and opens the menu of services. Six hours
of luxury await her.

The following day I readied myself for my salon visit. Julia handed me
the keys to the Jeep Cherokee, along with a piece of paper with the
address of the salon. I hadn't traveled more than four blocks from the
house, when the short blips of a police siren went off. I turned to see red
lights swirling in the rearview mirror.

*Oh my God, what have I done?* I couldn't have been driving more than
twenty miles an hour down the residential streets of Brentwood, but with
my infamous record I couldn't afford another citation.

*Shoot! I haven't changed my Oregon license with the DMV.* I remembered there was a time limit, once you were a California resident, or you
would be fined.

My pulse quickened as I pictured myself in handcuffs, being stuffed
into the back of the police cruiser. The next picture that came to mind was
being let out of my cell to make my one phone call. Would I call my
mother or Julia? My heart began to do butterfly kicks in my chest as I pictured the Jeep being pulled onto a tow truck to be whisked away to some
lot in the bowels of Los Angeles. I was afraid that the officer would
research my record and discover my four moving violations and that inde-
cent exposure incident, although I wasn't formally charged for that. (Okay,
it was during Homecoming week and I was pulled over for speeding on

"Toga Day." When I got out of the car I accidentally stepped on the twin sheet I was wearing —I was thinner back then— and the tube top went with it, giving the officer an eyeful. He was having a better day than I was.)

Back in Brentwood, I rolled down my window. "Driver's license and registration, ma'am?" the officer said in an official manner.

"Uh, yes, I've got it here somewhere, Sir, let me look in the jockey box," I replied as I began to dig around.

"THE WHAT?" he said.

"Oh sorry, glove compartment" Mental note: ask my father if that's just a family term. "Jockey box" doesn't appear to be a word Californians understand. My first thought was to lie and tell him I'd left it at home. I could give him the Swartz's address as if I were a California resident and perhaps he'd just give me a ticket using my name and that address. I figured that if I gave him the Oregon license, he'd be able to pull up my citations and I'd soon be wearing a striped uniform.

My final decision came when he said, "Did you know that your plates are expired?"

"Uh, no officer, I didn't. This isn't my car. It belongs to my boss," I said, "My boss, Steven Swartz." I made sure I stressed the word Swartz clearly, hoping he might have heard of him.

"*The* Steven Swartz?" the officer asked surprised, as if there were many Steven Swartz' in town.

"Yes."

The officer never did ask for my license after that. He just said, "Okay, I'm giving you a verbal warning. Tell Mr. Swartz to get his plates renewed. Have a nice day." He tipped his hat and walked back to his car. My heart began to slow to normal again as I put the car in gear and pulled out into traffic. This was the first time in my entire life that I had been pulled over and NOT received a citation. *If this is how "name dropping" works, I'm definitely going to try it again the next time I see lights in my rearview mirror.*

On my way to the salon on Hillman Avenue, I passed through Brentwood, Santa Monica and then through Pacific Palisades, mostly in circles. When I finally did locate the address, I was in a very seedy section of some unknown city. Just as when I'd finally found the Nanny Institute in a less-than-upscale section of Portland, I was dismayed to see that I'd arrived at the right place. The address Julia had given me was an old and run-down apartment building with paint chipping off the walls. I couldn't imagine Julia going here to get her beautiful nails done, but there was no mistaking it. The addresses matched.

I climbed the two flights of stairs to apartment number 223 and knocked. The door opened with a burst of stale, hot air. The strong odor greeting my nostrils combined heavy perfume and nail polish remover, it was nearly overwhelming in the tiny confines of what looked like a one-bedroom apartment.

The woman who answered the door said, "You must be Suzy." My prayers that I was in the wrong place vaporized. "Come on, darlin'. Come on in. You're lettin' all the hot air in," she said, as I stepped cautiously inside.

I glanced at one of the windows, which was covered with cardboard and taped shut, and then I turned to her. The woman was immense, about five-foot-six and 250 pounds. She wore a black tank top from which her meaty arms protruded. Her buttocks and thighs were screaming to be released from their sausage-like encasements—a pair of shiny black Spandex pants that had obviously stretched far beyond their intended limits.

"Come here, sweetie. Sit down. Let's have a look at your nails," she said as she wheeled her tray of supplies between us.

## Mad Money

When she was all done, I had to admit the nails looked terrific, but my dream of a day of leisure at the salon didn't meet my expectations any better than my other new experiences in Hollywood. I tried to visualize Julia driving into this section of "Wherever" and sitting on this orange and green plaid couch amid the pungent odors of solvents, just to save a few bucks on her acrylic nails.

Never mind. Steven *had* offered to pay for my nails and I appreciated it, regardless of the environment. However, when I returned two weeks later for a fill, two of my nails had broken. The woman in black spandex promptly repaired them. Grateful that the cost would be put on Julia's tab, I thanked her and left without paying. The following visit, I broke several other nails again and was forced to return to the other side of the tracks; only this time, after the woman fixed them she said, "You owe me four bucks."

"Huh?" I said. "Julia said she was paying for it," I informed her as I reached for the doorknob.

"Sorry girl, Mrs. Swartz didn't pay me for last week. So you owe me two bucks from then and two bucks for today. She said she wasn't going to pay for broken nails, only for your fill. I guess Mrs. Swartz thinks if you break them, you pay for them."

I gave her the four dollars and a generous tip and gave up on having my nails done. It wasn't very practical, anyway. It was obvious that nails were not going to be part of my nanny costume.

I don't get it. The whole thing with the nails is weird. I wonder why Julia made sure I paid $2. Oh well, It's ridiculous to think I could keep acrylics, anyway. Julia seems like she's afraid she will be taken advantage of. I bet she and Steven didn't talk about it, because he was the one that offered to give me the nails as a little extra gift, and I know he wouldn't care about two bucks. I think he wanted to show me that he appreciated my work. I think Julia must be like Oprah, who still buys her false eyelashes at Walgreens. I know she wasn't as poor as Oprah was as a child, but I know she didn't grow up with the kind of money she's surrounded with now. It seems like money is Steven's domain, in the house. So maybe one area she feels like she can control is how much she gives the hired help. Maria says it has always been like this so not to take it personal. The whole thing, seems kinda sad to me.

A few weeks later, Julia and Steven called from the Mediterranean, where they had gone on a week-long private cruise with a group of friends. While at sea, they placed a ship-to-shore call to check on the children and the house. The phone rang at about two in the afternoon and I picked it up.

"Hello, the Swartz residence. This is Suzanne."

"Hello, this is the overseas operator. Mr. and Mrs. Swartz are calling."

"Okay."

"Go ahead, sir. The charges will be $3.52 a minute," the operator said.

Steven came on the line first and the connection was awful. "Suzy, we're calling you from somewhere in the Mediterranean. Is my art okay?" he asked. *Did he just say what I thought he said?*

"Yes, Mr. Swartz. Everything is fine. Brandon's taking his nap and Amanda and Joshua are outside," I told him as the connection broke up again.

"I couldn't hear you, Suzy, bad connection. Is everything okay?"

"Yes, sir, everything is fine."

"Can we talk to Joshua?" he asked.

"Yes, of course. He's outside. Hold on a minute." I put the phone down, ran outside and called to Joshua. It took two or three minutes to get him to the phone.

"Hello. Are you there, Mr. Swartz?"

"No, Suzanne. This is Julia. For God's sake, where is Joshua? This call is costing us a fortune."

She said a quick hello to Joshua and then he handed the phone back to me.

"Hello, Mrs. Swartz. Amanda..." buzzzzzzzzzz. The line was dead. She'd hung up.

It still doesn't make a lot of sense:
- $20,000.00 cruise– Don't give it a second thought
- $ 4.00 nail repair to make nanny feel valued. Hold on there! We can't provide these extravagances for the hired help
- $15.00 phone call to check on the kids - Way too spendy!

Go figure.

I never did understand money logic in the Swartz household, despite my excellent analytical skills in such matters. Julia made Concetta scrub stains out of a cheap T-shirt of Brandon's instead of buying the child new clothes. At other times, on oddball things, they would spend money like they minted it in the attic. I wanted to know how they decided what was important and what wasn't.

One time when Steven and Julia were on vacation, I walked into the laundry room where LaRosa was using an iron with a frayed cord. It was so old that I could see a flash of the copper wire through the cloth insulation, a definite health hazard, not to mention a fire just waiting to destroy the house. *Never mind the inhabitants— think of the risk to the art collection!*

I said, "For God's sake, LaRosa, we need a new iron. They must not know that this one is in such bad of shape"

Maria, on the other side of the kitchen, responded, "You know how Julia is bout mouneey."

"I don't care. I'm going to the hardware store where they have an account and charge a new one. This is ridiculous," I said with great authority.

When I was out, I bought a new iron with a coated electrical cord. Then I wrapped the frayed cord around the old one and put it in the garbage.

Two days later, when they'd returned, I overheard Julia talking to her friend, Jane, in the foyer. "They sure love to spend all my money."

I interrupted, "Mrs. Swartz, I was the one that bought the new iron." No answer. I continued, "I insisted that we need a new one." *So my friends don't get electrocuted.*

"We could have put a new cord on the old iron." Julia explained, "Do you have the receipt Suzy?" Fortunately, Maria had retrieved the old iron before the trash went out, knowing Julia far better than I did.

## Struck by the Stars

Maria may have been a great cook, but when it came to the Swartz' dinner parties, professional caterers ran the show. My first one was unforgettable. Up until that time, I had spoken to many industry giants on the phone. But the closest I'd come to meeting a celebrity was Steven's partner, Rick Dyer; who wasn't really a celebrity - though he did look a lot like Sylvester Stallone. My most exciting encounter so far had been a phone call from Tom Cruise, my teenage heartthrob. He called to talk to Steven, and Joshua picked up the phone to answer it. Coincidentally, Josh had been glued to the television, watching a tape of *Top Gun* for the hundredth time when he called. When I overheard who it was, I was so excited I ran to the extension in the kitchen and quietly picked up the receiver to listen. I stopped breathing.

"Hi, Tom," Joshua said excitedly. "I'm just watching you in *Top Gun* and my favorite part is when you go into the spin!" *I* was about to go into a spin!

"Hi, kiddo. What part is on now?" Cruise said cheerfully.

"Oh, the part where you say 'I have a speed for need,'" Joshua blurted. I had to suppress a laugh and cover the mouthpiece, but I continued hanging on his every word.

"Uh, oh, that part," Cruise stuttered.

He was so sweet. He remained on the phone with Joshua for five minutes, answering all his questions about the movie. Although he had a vested interest in being polite since he had been essentially "discovered" and was represented by Joshua's father, I think he really got a kick out of talking to his little fan. I could hear he was at a loud party, but he never rushed the conversation.

Finally, he asked if Steven was home and Joshua yelled out, "Daaaaadddddddyyy! The Maaaaverick is on the phone." It took everything I had to hang up and not stay on to listen to that wonderful voice, but my sense of propriety and self-preservation finally kicked in. I placed the receiver back on the hook very delicately.

## Guess Who's Coming to Dinner?

I had heard so much about Steven's love of entertaining that I could hardly wait for the upcoming dinner party. Maria and I looked at the guest list a few days before the event. As I read the names, I made some guesses about who they were.

**Michael and Jane Eisner** (I'd met them before and knew they were good friends and had something to do with Disney.)

**Irwin and Margo Winkler** (I made a note to call home to let my family know that Mr. Arthur Fonzarelly himself was coming to dinner. My sisters and I were big *Happy Days* fans, and I was sure this Irwin guy must really be Henry Winkler.)

**Steve Martin** and his wife, Victoria (Maria said she thought she was an actress, but I had never heard of her.)

**Sean and Micheline Connery** (Mrs. Connery had called that day asking for Julia - she refused to believe that Julia wasn't home. She kept telling me WHO she was, demanding to be put through, as if I was the social secretary that had been told to hold all calls. I must have told her five times that Mrs. Swartz was REALLY not in. Finally she just hung up on me in disgust.)

**Barry Diller** (I had never heard of him. Phyllis Diller's husband?)

**Diane Von Furstenberg** (I was pretty sure she was *the* clothing designer.)

**Aaron and Candy Spelling** (Now, I did know who he was. I loved *Charlie's Angeles*. I had all the action figures of the female crime fighters.)

Last, but certainly not least, **Barbara Walters.**

"Oh God, I hope Steven doesn't seat me next to Barbara Walters," Julia had said to me several days before the party. "He can seat her next to Jane. She's much more well-read then I am." I was shocked. Julia was both intelligent and beautiful, she was used to interacting with public figures. I'd never before seen her hidden insecurity.

In the dining room were two square marble tables placed a few feet apart. Each table sat eight people, and generally there would be anywhere from eight to sixteen people invited to the dinner parties. Steven was known for getting up and rearranging everyone and their food about halfway through each meal, regardless of whether they were through eating. He didn't want anyone spending all his or her time with just one person. He enjoyed mixing the personalities and conversations. I guess that was why Julia was nervous. She knew the chances were good that she would eventually sit next to the famous and well-read Ms. Walters. She didn't seem to have a choice where she sat at her own party. Apparently Steven decided that.

My role during the dinner parties, I figured out, was to sit in the family room with the children until the guests had been seated for dinner. Joshua would run back and forth from the family room to the dining room to talk to the guests during the cocktail hour. Throughout the arrival and pre-dinner time, waiters would come into the family room and bring us hors d'oeuvres. Intermittently the celebrities would parade through to see the children. I never knew whether I was supposed to dress up or wear my usual T-shirt and shorts. I thought I would have looked stupid sitting in the family room, the only adult in an evening gown, so usually I just stayed in my shorts. Just before the guests were seated for dinner I'd have the kids go in to say a final good night and take them all up to bed, just like Maria in *The Sound of Music*. I was always slightly embarrassed when it was my turn to carry Brandon into the dining room to bid them good night. In my working clothes, I felt like I was a mutt entering a stuffy dog show filled with purebreds.

The night of this first party, I had a good time practicing nonchalance as celebrities dropped by the family room from time to time. I was able to talk to Steve Martin briefly, until his wife interrupted him because he was eating cashews. She scolded him for eating something so full of fat. He asked her, like he was a child and she was the mother, "Oh, are these not healthy?" He kept such a straight face that I couldn't tell if he was putting her on, and I'm not sure she could either. She looked at him in disgust and turned around on her skinny heels and left the room. By the looks of her nearly transparent body, she took a passionate interest in the pursuit of caloric restriction.

It turned out that the Winkler guy wasn't ever on *Happy Days*. He was the guy that produced a whole lot of major hits like *Raging Bull*, *The Right*

*Stuff* and all the *Rocky* movies. Ever since then, I've seen his names on the credits of lots of major film hits. Barry Diller, the CEO of an entertainment company, wasn't Phyllis' husband. This was a good thing, since his date was the fashionable Ms. Von Furstenberg. Barbara Walters cancelled the day before the event. Julia was relieved, but I was very disappointed that I only got to talk to her on the phone. I had been a huge fan of *20/20* since I was a child, my mother blames that show for my over-zealous interest in other peoples' business.

Not long after my first dinner party, I was introduced to the Swartz' movie-screening tradition. They had a monthly ritual of showing pre-released movies to the family and a few close friends. They were always kind enough to invite me to view it with them. In one of the living rooms, that doubled as the screening room, we would watch the movies on a giant screen that pulled down from the ceiling. An ACT employee would run the huge projector from a small room in the back wall. It was like a miniature movie theater. One evening Steven invited Dustin and Lisa Hoffman to join us. The featured movie starred Matthew Broderick with an unknown actress named Helen Hunt, along with a bunch of chimpanzees. Almost immediately after the movie began to roll, Mr. Hoffman began to chatter and kibitz, either to himself or to his wife.

"The characters are crying before we are," he spit out. I gathered this was not good. "The monkey could teach him how to act." He rose up and jabbed toward the screen, like he wanted to start a fight with anyone who would disagree.

This went on and on. I felt the same way I do at a movie theater when seated close to the inconsiderate clod who has either seen it before and now wants to narrate it for the rest of us, or who's seeing it for the first time and offers a stream of constant criticism. That night, I had to remind myself, that *the* Dustin Hoffman was the critic. Perhaps, he'd just been in a bad mood to begin with, but he was definitely not enjoying the film. Finally, after commenting extensively on just about every scene, he stood up and said "Bad movie," and walked out of the room to get his coat. Steven and Julia exchanged shocked glances. Mr. Hoffman just muttered, "We have to get going," and hurried his wife out the door with a quick good-bye.

### The Fall Guy

My best friend, Kristi, called me from Eugene where she was in her freshman year at the University of Oregon. She asked whether she could come to visit me during her spring break. I was ecstatic at the possibility of having some company. I asked Julia if she could stay the night at the house, and she agreed. When she got there, Kristi was wowed by her first up-close and personal look inside a Hollywood home. She thumbed through a book by Danielle Steele, her favorite author at the time. She was pretty surprised that it had a long personal message to my employers. "This is just like *Lifestyles*!" she said.

I gave her a tour of the house, the art gallery and the grounds where the gardeners were pruning the shrubs. We waved to them and they smiled and waved back. I brought her into the four-car garage to show off the car collection too: the black Jaguar, the black Mercedes and my own personal favorite "the Porsche." I waved my arm over it like Vanna White on *Wheel of Fortune*. I was trying to be smooth, but instead I set off the car alarm. *WAAAAA! WAAAA! WAAAA! WOOOP! WOOOP! WOOOP! WOOOP! WAAAA!*

"Damn it! I can't believe I set off the alarm!" I wailed.

"Are the police gonna come?" she asked.

"I hope not! Ohhh! I can't believe I just did that!"

The gardeners came rushing up - Carlo, Jose and Miguel - pruning shears in hand. Then Maria and Concetta came out from the house.

"Su-zee, was that you again?" Concetta said.

"Yes! Steven and Julia are going to kill me."

The alarm was still ripping through the air—*WAAAA! WAAAA! WAAAA! WOOOP! WOOOP! WOOOP! WOOOP!*—It seemed to be getting louder, or maybe it was just my imagination, and we had to shout over the noise. *What was I thinking when I went near that car?*

"I feel like such a dork!" I yelled over the noise.

"You're not a dork," Maria said. "I've done it too. Dere are a lot of alarms 'round here. But don't worry, you'll get dee hang of it."

But I never did. During my time at the Swartz', it seemed like I was always setting off alarms. But that comes later.

"I know the routine," Concetta shouted. "Come on out of the garage. I'll call Steven's assistant and ask how to shut it off and reset it. Steven does not have to know you did it."

Everybody left the garage and we shut the door behind us, muffling the horrible wailing. We all walked back toward the house, stopping by the backdoor to discuss what to do.

"Don't worry, Suzy," Carlo said, "I'll tell them I accidentally sprayed it with the hose."

"Really? You'd do that for me?"

"It's no problem," he said. "It's okay. You won't get in trouble."

"But what about you, Carlo? Won't you get in trouble?"

"Noooo. They never bother me."

"They leave him alone," Concetta said.

"It's true," Maria said. Jose and Miguel stared at me and nodded. "To dem, Carlo can do nooo wrong. He's de best landscaper in de neighborhood." She put her arm around my shoulder. "Anyway, Soo-zita, we're like a family here. A familia within la familia, you know? We look out for each other."

After she called Sarah at the office and de-activated the alarm, I felt much better. I hoped and prayed she wouldn't tell Steven about my little mishap.

The third day of Kristi's visit, we went for a walk with the kids. Little Brandon was in his big-giant, fuddy-duddy English pram and Joshua and Amanda were walking alongside it. At one point, Joshua insisted on pushing the pram. I hesitated, but he was being so bratty and demanding that I finally gave in to avoid a scene.

"Only for a minute," I said. "This baby carriage is very big and heavy. It's not really meant to be pushed by little boys."

"I'm not a little boy!"

*Great, I just committed the cardinal sin of all sins for a nanny—always call a little boy a big boy, or don't say anything at all.* "I know you're not honey; I forgot—you're a big boy."

"I'm not a little boy!"

"Okay, Joshua, I said I'm sorry. Now here you go." I stepped out of the way and let him get in front of me. Then he started to push it a bit too fast. I picked up my pace to keep up. "Joshua, not so fast, be careful."

"I don't have to be careful. You can't tell me what to do."

"Yes I can, honey. And you do have to be careful."

"I know how to do it!" he yelled. The next thing I knew, he was popping a wheelie. It all happened in one frightening flash: the top-heavy pram started to tip over and the baby slipped forward, feet-first, heading straight for the pavement. My heart was in my throat. I rushed in and scooped Brandon up before he fell. Then the pram went crashing over sideways, its wheels spinning in the air. I was so scared that I didn't even reprimand Joshua. As we walked back to the house, my arms were shaking so much that Kristi offered to carry Brandon for me. I didn't dare put him back in that pretentious—and *dangerous*—English pram. When we reached the gate to the Swartz's house, my heart was kicking against my chest like in *Alien* before the creature popped out. In that moment I thought, My God, I can't control these kids. I can't take them anywhere and keep them safe because they won't listen to me.

Inside the house I told Julia what happened with Joshua and the pram. She was immediately angry and shouted "Go to your room, mister!"

"I won't go to my room!" Joshua yelled back. "Don't tell me what to do!"

"You don't tell *me* what to do! I've had enough of this disrespect from you." Julia chanted back.

"You don't know anything." Josh spit out.

"How can you say that to me? You're so incredibly condescending."

"No, Mommy, you're credibly sending!"

"Oh God, I can't believe you act like this. Forget it!" Julia stormed off and slammed the door. Joshua just stood there grinning, knowing he'd won the battle.

Day after day it was the same thing. Joshua would do something just begging to be disciplined, Julia would give him a time out, he'd refuse to go and then she wouldn't follow through. I don't think she knew what to do, so his behavior just got worse. How was I supposed to get anywhere with a child whose own mother didn't know how to claim her authority over him? She fought with Joshua the same way he fought with his sister. Amanda often witnessed these scenes, and she was climbing on board the bratty train, too. I could see that poor, sweet little Brandon would probably model his older brother's behavior once he got old enough to understand how things worked in the household.

What do I do when Julia doesn't support me when I try to discipline Joshua? He doesn't really pay attention to her, so why would he ever listen to me? I'd love to give her one of my parenting books, but I don't think she'd take it too well. I looked it up in my school textbook, but nothing in the index relates to the children treating the nanny with as much regard as they do an insect. Actually none of these parenting books I have, even address having a nanny in a home, let alone that there might be some ISSUES.

Note to self: Write to the editor of that Nanny Newsletter that I subscribed to and tell them that there's no section "Nanny Education" at Barnes and Noble

## Spago for Two

Kristi and I wanted to go out to dinner while she was visiting. I called Sarah at the office and asked her where we should go. She said she would make us a reservation at a trendy place where we were sure to have some star spottings. We were both excited since neither of us had ever been to Spago, we were dressed up as if we had been invited to the Academy Awards ceremony. She'd been wearing nothing but jeans and sweatshirts most of the time at college and I spent most of my days in shorts and t-shirts, so we were both thrilled to get all dressed up. I didn't think much of it until we got to the restaurant and almost everyone in there was dressed casually. And there we were, me in my "fits-all-occasions" black cocktail dress and Kristi in a similar costume, only in dark blue with a strand of pearls around her neck.

The night was a little disappointing for star sightings; lesser luminaries, such as Sally Struthers and Ricardo Montalban were the only ones on view that night. Sarah had listed the reservation under Hansen/Swartz so that they would give us special attention. The meal was excellent. Then they brought us a great dessert and made a point of telling us that Steven had paid for it. That was very kind, I thought, as I took out my checkbook and paid the rest of the bill. I had planned on thanking him the next day, but I didn't see him until the day after that, and then only briefly. When I thanked him for the desserts, he seemed a little confused.

"They were supposed to put the entire meal on my tab. So you paid for it with your own money?" he asked.

"Yes, of course."

"Hmm. I told them to pick up the whole thing. Here..." and with that he pulled out his checkbook, asked me how much it had been and wrote me a check. I thanked him profusely, recognizing that this was Steven's way of showing his appreciation for all the care and love I gave the children.

I can't believe that Steven got us into Spago and paid for our dinner. Not just anyone can get reservations. Sarah said if a "no name" calls there it can take over a month to get in. Wolfgang Puck himself made a point of asking if everything was all right with our meal. It's so weird. It's getting routine to see celebrities, and no one in the house here acknowledges how surreal it is. As I look back in my journal to the page where I listed all the stars who've come around or called, it seems a little silly. I've already gotten used to living in a place where answering the phone might mean talking to Cher or Chevy Chase or discussing diaper rash with Christina Ferarri. The other day I took a message from John Travolta and he seemed really nice, like an average kind of guy. Maybe it's like Oprah always says: you're still the same person you were before you became famous, it's just that millions of people know you.

## Face Off : The Sequel

My next big outing came a few weeks later when I asked Julia if I could use the Jeep on Saturday because I knew they weren't going to the beach house that weekend. She said yes. I was thrilled at all the things I would be able to do with the freedom. Since I had no friends to spend time with, I decided to cheer myself up a different way. I'd spotted a nice little salon when I was in Brentwood buying shoes for the kids. I'd been disappointed in the nail salon experience, but I hadn't given up on my spa fantasy. I'd decided to spend my day off at the Brentwood salon. All I could think of that morning was my noon appointment and how I would luxuriate in all the little attentions they would provide. The facial package included a neck and foot massage, which sounded heavenly. I drove there ready for some well-earned time in Eden.

The sign in the window read *Salon Fleur de Lis, Hair Styling, Facials and Pedicures*. I approached the girl at the desk and let her know I was there for my appointment. She immediately whisked me to a back room and told me to change into the white bathrobe that was hanging on the back of the door. I was to have a seat in a large Naugahyde chair after I had changed into the spa attire.

Within minutes a small woman with very dark eyes wearing a starched white lab coat began circling me. She was stroking her chin, poking at my face and saying "Uh huh. Uh huh," under her breath, as if I were an antique piece she was appraising. I didn't know what her ethnicity was, but her accent intrigued me. You don't get a lot of cultural diversity where I'm from, and it sounded exotic to my ears. She introduced herself as "Sa-meen-a."

"Hi young lady," she said with a heavy not-from-Oregon accent, "we-e-e must geeve you a pee-e-el."

I thought she meant "appeal," and I was so embarrassed. I couldn't believe I looked so bad that she had to comment on my need for improvement. *I knew I should have put on make-up before I went to the appointment.*

My facial expression probably showed what I was thinking because she shot back quickly, "No, no, my de-e-ear. A peel. You need an acid facial pe-e-e-l. The sun has caused your ske-e-e-en great damage. And you have had act-nee in your life." *No kidding, I am still a teenager.* "We-e-e must go beeyond a seemple facial. Something that penney-trates much deeper. You must be from the country" she added.

"Uh, yes. I guess I'm from the country." *This woman must think I'm in the blazing hot sun, out on the prairie each day, with no sunscreen. Just like Laura Ingalls. Now I know why Nellie Olsen always had such pale skin. She was from "the city" of Walnut Grove.* "You can actually tell where I lived from looking at my skin?" I said.

"Oh yes, most defineetly. Wait, you weel see. When I am done, your skeen will look and feel like silk, like a little bambeeno's behind. I suggest our most powerful peeel."

"How much will it be?" I asked. I'd only brought $140 with me, thinking that would more than cover the cost, a generous tip and lunch at the quaint little bistro next door to celebrate my new glowing complexion.

"Eeet is not cheap. How much do you have?"

"Uh, one hundred forty dollars."

"Perfecto. Eeet is eeactly one-hundred-forty doe-lahrs," she said as she grinned. *So much for my lunch.*

Simina commenced to move like she was possessed, draping me in a large plastic apron from my neck to my ankles. Next she worked up a healthy lather of cleansing cream over my face and then wiped that off with a scalding hot towel. I felt as if I'd been instantly sunburned. With my face still glowing, she slipped on a pair of twelve-gauge rubber gloves that ran past her elbows, the kind firemen wear. Then she draped a heavy fire-retardant apron over her neck. She opened a large jar and began to dip a small paintbrush into it. Next, taking great care not to spill the toxin onto herself, she spread the chemical jelly over my entire face. Only my eyelids and lips escaped the treatment. I was then told to sit motionless. Almost immediately I could feel a pleasant tingling sensation.

"Do not move, Miss Su-sahhna. Eeet weel take seven minutes to activate. I weel come back to check on you," she said, leaving me in the room.

The tingling was changing to a stinging sensation, and of course I began to worry. Agonizing over the unknown is part of my DNA. *Did she say it would take seven minutes to activate? If it's kicking in already, maybe a full seven minutes will gain me admission into the burn unit.* As the minutes ticked away ever so slowly, the stinging was intensifying and I thought my face might be disintegrating. I leaned up, squinting, trying to read the ingredient label on the jar of gel. I saw a long word and then "acid" afterwards followed by propylene glycol! *I'm in trouble! I may not know any foreign languages, but I did get an A in Auto Shop and I know that word. She put antifreeze on my face!* I tried to yell but remembered Simina's orders to remain motionless. Though my lips were pursed together and I was afraid my face would crack in two if I moved my mouth, I did manage a feeble mumbling sound, "Suhmeenhah, Suhmeenhah." No answer.

Suddenly an oven timer went off, startling me. The seven minutes were up, and at that precise moment Simina reappeared, checked her watch quickly and then began applying scalding hot towels once again to rinse off the nuclear residue. I was afraid to touch my skin.

"Eeet weel be a leetle tender for a day or two and then you shall see. You weel have dee skin of a baby. That weel be one-hundred-forty doe-lahrs, pleeze," she said, and with that I was left to my own devices. I had 43 cents left to my name.

Simina was right. When I got home I noticed my skin was tender, but not as bad as I expected given the burning sensation I'd experienced. What I didn't know was that the chemical was supposed to penetrate the first two layers of skin. She had given me what she said was a special lotion that I was to use once in the morning and once at bedtime to ease the discomfort. I think it was pure Novocaine because after I smoothed it on, my entire head went numb and I began slurring my speech, so I only used it at bedtime.

The next day Grandma Swartz was over. She remarked on the nice pink glow I had, asking if I'd enjoyed my facial. I told her yes, it had been quite an experience and left it at that. On the second day when I woke up and faced the morning mirror, I was stunned to see that my entire face was peeling, just as it does after being sunburned. I looked like I'd survived a fire. By that night I was shedding complete layers of skin, somewhat like a rattlesnake in August.

I couldn't keep my hands from peeling it away in large sheets. Underneath was yet another layer of hot red skin, just waiting to dry out and scale away like the previous layer. I began to panic. Julia told me I looked like I'd just escaped from a leper colony. That afternoon, in terror, I drove back to the salon and approached Simina.

"Oh my God, Miss Su-sahn. You have touched your face, haven't you? You're not soopposed to pick at it," she said, as if putting all the blame back on me. *How could I not peel it? It itched terribly and for the most part was falling away on its own anyway. I just wanted to keep the flakes off my clothes and the furniture.*

Skin Peel fiasco!
It's now the fourth day and my skin is still very blotchy, something like a Guernsey cowhide. I had no idea it would take so long for all these layers to slough off. It seems like the lady could have given me just a tad more info on what to expect. I know they say you have to be ready to suffer for beauty, but the ratio of torture to aesthetic enhancement is pretty steep here, not counting the humiliation factor. If I'm doing this to impress anyone, I don't think I've been successful.

Note to self: Get more information before allowing anyone to paint me with a chemical you can buy at a local auto supply store.

# Down and Out in Beverly Hills

## Doogie Howser Saves a Baby

I'd had enough weekend adventure for the time being, so I wasn't too sorry when Steven and Julia decided to go away the next weekend and Steven's parents came to stay and help out. Steven always had them come and stay with us when they were gone because he wanted them there in case of an emergency. On Saturday evening, Brandon began to get sick and by nine o'clock he had a temperature of 104.2 degrees. Grandma Swartz and I began to worry and decided we needed to call the pediatrician's office. The on-call doctor told me to bring him to the emergency room, and he would meet me there. We headed out. Grandpa Swartz drove Brandon and me to the hospital, while Grandma stayed at home with Joshua and Amanda. Brandon was burning up, but oddly enough he seemed to be feeling just fine, smiling and cooing at me. When we got to the ER, the doctor was just arriving and helping to find a seat for, what appeared to be a woman straight off the cover of the *Sports Illustrated* swimsuit edition. He looked about Doogie Howser's age, and I could hardly contain my irrational rage—*Focus, buddy! On the baby, not your Victoria's Secret model date; who I might add is probably just dating you because she thinks you are worth big bucks, because in all reality you're nerdy enough to be wearing a pocket protector, as far as I can tell!*

The doctor ushered us into a small examining room and took Brandon from me. He felt the glands in his neck, his forehead and then the top of his head. "Here," he said. "feel this." He put my hand on the top of Brandon's head over the fontanel, the soft spot that every baby has.

"Is this normal?" he asked.

*You're a doctor and you're asking me?* "No, no, of course not," I answered. I was screaming inside. Brandon's soft spot was bulging right out of his skull, yet Brandon just kept smiling. When the doctor said that he was very concerned, I started to get scared.

"He may have meningitis," he said. With that I really got shaky. Grandpa Swartz and I looked at each other in fear and disbelief. *What do we do? What do we do?*

Apparently, this young doctor was just starting in practice with the older pediatrician, Steven and Julia's regular doctor, who I had met previously.

"I've got to make a call," the doctor said. I felt reassured he was consulting with someone more experienced. He picked up the telephone and Grandpa Swartz and I listened intently.

"Yes, Brandon Swartz," he replied. "No, you don't have to come down here, I can handle it. Okay, if you insist, all right, goodbye."

When the older doctor arrived, I began to relax a little. Right away he said, "This baby isn't sick. Look at how happy he is." *Hey doc, looks like your young cohort is a little sharper than you,* my fearful self yelled in my ear.

The younger doctor disagreed with his mentor and I felt my loyalties switch quickly back to him. *How can he make an assessment on this child just by looking at him? How long has this old guy been around? When's the last time he had a refresher course?*

"I want to do a spinal tap," the young doctor blurted out.

"Are you kidding? You know whose child this is, don't you?" the older doctor responded.

"Yes, that's why I want to call them right now and get permission."

"They're on vacation," I said. "But I've got an emergency number."

That's when Grandpa Swartz stepped in. "I'll call Steven, everyone just stand by." After Grandpa talked to Steven, he handed the phone to the young doctor.

"Yes, Mr. Swartz," he said. "Yes, that's right. I want to do a spinal tap and I need your permission." Silence for a second. "Well, uh yes, Mr. Swartz, uh me personally, I've done a hundred of them." Steven must have sensed how young the doctor was. Then he handed the phone to me. At this point, Steven asked me for my opinion. *What did I know about meningitis?* So I just told Steven that it didn't look normal, that his soft spot was very swollen and I'd never seen it like that.

"We'll be there as soon as we can. We'll try to get a plane out tonight," Steven said.

With that, the young doctor took Brandon down the hall. He had along an assistant, who he explained, would be the one holding Brandon down while they put a needle into his back. "It's all in the holding down," the little Doogie Howser said. I could picture this tiny person stretched out under glaring lights while a young girl pressed down his arms and legs and the doctor plunged a needle into his spine. I wanted to be there to soothe him and hold him. I tried to follow along but the assistant turned me back. Grandpa Swartz and I sat in the waiting room fretting together. I felt so bad for Brandon that I was getting a little nauseous.

After we had been waiting about twenty minutes, the assistant came back out to the waiting room and advised me to call home to check on the other two children. She said, "Have them touch their chins to their chests. If it's painful or stiff, they may have the same thing."

Now I was starting to panic. By then it was nearly 11 pm. When I called, Maria picked up right away and when I told her what to do, she said, "I can't wake dem up. Eet's the meeddle of de night. Et will be terrible," meaning she knew that Amanda would scream for hours afterwards.

"Please Maria, just do it. This is serious," I told her. I called back in ten minutes. Over Amanda's wailing in the background, I could hear Maria saying they could move their heads just fine, with no pain.

After another ten minutes, a nurse came out carrying Brandon and my heart just did a tilta-whirl. He wasn't smiling anymore and I could see that he had been crying a lot. He was stretching his arms out to me from all the way across the room. He needed me. He wanted me. I started to cry.

I started to cross the room toward him and the nurse said, "No, no. We're not done yet. He was crying and I wanted to bring him out here to let him know you were still here. We have some more tests to do and the doctor wants to admit him." And with that, she walked back through the swinging doors with Brandon's cries echoing behind her. I tried to pull myself together as I sat in a heap, my face in my hands, and Grandpa Swartz's arm around me.

We waited again for what seemed hours until another nurse came and escorted us to the children's ICU ward. When we walked in, Brandon's foot was all bandaged up and he was lying in a horrible, cold, steel cage-like crib with an IV stuck in his little foot. The poor, sweet little guy! I asked if I could hold him and they said yes, as long as I was careful with the IV line.

By now it was way past midnight and I told Grandpa Swartz to go home and wait for Steven and Julia; I would stay the night. I couldn't stand the thought of my little baby Brandon being alone in that awful place, even if he fell asleep, which he didn't do for another two hours. I just held him on my lap with his chest on mine for the rest of the night, and he seemed content.

I woke up at five in the morning, stiff from scrunching up in a chair like a cat curled up on a small stool. I think I'd slept a couple of hours. Brandon was still sleeping on me. At around eight o'clock, Steven and Julia arrived. Julia came right up to me and kneeled down in front of my chair. Steven called for the doctor. Julia took Brandon from my arms. I felt so bad for her because Brandon immediately squirmed around and began crying and reaching for me. Julia looked into my eyes with an expression I'd never seen on her face and gently handed him to me. I wanted to cry all over again.

"Oh look, he wants Suzy," she said quietly to Steven. Then she said, "Why don't you go home, Suzy. It's been a long night and we can stay with him now."

I rested my cheek on Brandon's soft hair and cradled him against me until he stopped whimpering. When I looked up, Julia was still looking at us. Her eyes were soft and her voice was gentle. In that moment, a wave of genuine compassion and empathy filled the space between us. And it came from both directions.

Although I did not want to leave him, I knew I needed a break. I went home and slept most of the day. Julia had said that I could have Maria and Concetta watch the kids. I had a new appreciation for being in my own bed. When I called and checked in around 5 pm, Julia said they hadn't gotten the test results back yet and to just stay at home, because she had hired a private duty nurse to come in and take care of him. My heart sank when she said that he had been crying a lot because he wasn't used to the nurse. The next morning when I returned to the hospital they were getting ready to discharge Brandon. His temperature had gone back down to 99 degrees.

The test results showed that he did not have viral meningitis, it was only a bacterial infection.

When I got home there was a large bouquet of beautiful flowers sitting on the foyer table with a card that was addressed to me. I opened it immediately. It was from my friend, Mandie, from nanny school. I had called her out of desperation the day before and to talk with her about what had happened.

> *Dear Suzanne, I am thinking of both of you. I know how much the children mean to you. I hope Brandon is okay and I hope you're holding up.*
>
> *Love, Mandie*

For about the fifth time in two days I broke down in tears and sat at the foot of the stairs. At about that moment, Steven came in and saw me sitting and sobbing, holding the flowers in my hands.

"Who are the flowers from?" he said nonchalantly.

"From my friend, Mandie," I sniffed.

"What for?" he said, with a face devoid of emotion.

"Because, I've been having a hard time about Brandon." I mumbled. I was actually a little embarrassed that I was so upset, since he had taken it all in stride.

Steven looked at me blankly. *Hello! This was traumatic for me. I love your son. I can't believe you wouldn't know that this has been difficult and that I was very scared.* He didn't seem to understand. He paid me to take care of his kids, but not to fall in love with them. I did that on my own.

## I'm Going to Have My Daddy Fire You!

Steven was as protective of his children as he was demanding of his employees. Concern for their safety was one of the ways he showed his devotion as a father. The more powerful he became, the more preoccupied he was with that issue. One time, he even sent two plain clothes security guards to accompany Julia, his parents and the children to an amusement park that was in a less than upscale neighborhood. I was noticing that people of wealth and fame had to live with the real possibility of their families being harmed because of who they were or rather, because of what they had. Ironically the more you had, the more vulnerable you became.

Julia, too, loved her children deeply. She enjoyed doing things with the older children, and they were always hungry for her company. It seemed like taking Brandon along with the other two was too much for her, with the diaper bag, stroller, etc. Sometimes she and Grandma Swartz would take Joshua and Amanda to Disneyland and to other fun places. They shared special things, but not many of the ordinary things.

The children, like many other children with live-in nannies, had already experienced their fair share of caretakers before I arrived on the scene. I'm sure the children bonded with the first nanny and maybe even the second. By the time I joined the household, they had learned to protect themselves. It seemed obvious that they didn't want to lose another friend so they did their best not to make one. When I first arrived, I hadn't been prepared to have them treat me like they often did, as if I were an annoyance in their lives. I was used to caring for kids that were excited to see me when I walked through their door to spend the day with them. It hadn't taken me long to realize that it was naïve of me to think that these children would immediately bond with me. But I hadn't given up yet. I had seen how affectionate they could be when Kristi had visited. Since she wasn't their official caretaker, they were very open and loving toward her. It seemed easy to figure out what was going on. Josh knew that he didn't have to keep his protective devices up with her because she was just visiting.

Shortly after she left, I decided to use their fondness for her to get them involved in an after-school activity, something I usually had difficulty enticing them to do. I had the table in the family room all set up with construction paper, glue and glitter. Then while they made cards for Kristi, I wrote their words down in a letter to her. Despite a few skirmishes over the glitter, they had a great time. Josh loved to make rainbows and Amanda was enjoying using the glue sticks.

Kristi always wrote back. She sent the kids T-shirts with the U of O mascot, the Fighting Duck, on them (Yeah. I know, great mascot, but folks in Oregon are used to weird team names. Their in-state rival is the Beavers at OSU, a few miles up the road.) They loved making cards for her and dictating letters. So even though they weren't open to most nanny-generated arts and crafts activities, I could usually count on prying them away from the TV or VCR once in a while to have some good old-fashioned fun.

Aside from rare times like this, I had just about given up on getting close to Joshua. The two of us seemed to be at odds most of the time.

Amanda, when she wasn't having a tantrum, was starting to warm up to me. She once told me she wished I were her mommy. It was during dinner and Julia was sitting next to me. I'm sure it was as embarrassing to her as it was to me. I wasn't sure how to handle the innocent comment. The best thing I could come up with was, "Oh honey, I'm too young to be your mommy."

Julia said, "Amanda, it probably made Suzy feel good to have you say that." I almost fell off my chair because of Julia's comment. She usually seemed like I irritated her. And her difficulty setting limits for the kids had led me to believe that she was simply lacking in parenting knowledge. Just when I stopped expecting anything from her, she would respond to her children or me in such a wise and caring way that I got my hopes up all over again.

On the other hand, Joshua threatened on a weekly basis, to have me fired along with the rest of the staff. The first time I can remember him threatening me was when I stepped out the front door one morning as Julia was getting ready to take him to school and I found him peeing on a tree. Waiting until he'd finished his business, I approached him and reprimanded him for his behavior. *I thought* my admonishment was appropriate. After all, he was in full public view in the front yard that faced the street. He yelled back at me, while trying to wipe the missed aim of urine from his loafers, *"Mom said its okay!"*

"I doubt your mother would want to see you peeing in the front yard," I replied.

"Oh yeah, you don't know anything! My mom said I could and my mom is in charge of you," he shrieked emphatically.

He added in for good measure, "Annnnndddddddd.....I can have my daddy fire you, if I want to" *allrighty then.........*

Julia entered the conversation as she glided toward us. "Oh yes, Suzy. I told him it was okay. We're in a hurry and I didn't want him to go all the way back into the house."

Joshua silently stuck out his tongue at me and walked away. *Okay, I give up. I'll be sure and add this to my list of rules. Make this #42, article 12, section 6 of the house bylaws: It is okay for the children to relieve themselves in the front yard, if we're running late.*

After the peeing incident today, I am doubting whether I'll ever fit in. One day I feel as though I'm doing a great job and the next, something like this happens. Me working here is like trying to mix Metamucil in water—I never fully blend. Wish I had someone to talk to. I need some friends here! I try and get the mail everyday, hoping there's something for me. It's the high point of my long day. I love getting funny cards with news on the latest happenings at home. Cottage Grove updates:

- Football stadium condemned......... finally!
- Got our second fast food restaurant- Taco Time. In the Bi-Mart parking lot, of all things.
- There's rumor that Burger King is going to be built in the Vintage Inn Restaurant parking lot. What the heck is the deal with restaurants in parking lots? Do other towns do this? Is Cottage Grove real estate all that pricey?
- Amy's dad Bob won a new barbeque at Bi-Mart last Tuesday. No more lighter fluid and briquettes for him.

Note to self: You're living in the entertainment capital of the world, and the highlight of your week is to hear about your home-town friend's dad's new grill. Get a social life. Actually, a life of any kind would be an improvement.

## Friends in Low Places

A couple of nights later, Mandie called and announced that she wanted to come and work in Los Angeles. She had finally realized that most people in her home state of Montana didn't have nannies, so she would have to look elsewhere for a job. I was thrilled. Finally, a way out of this loneliness! I told Mrs. Swartz about her, giving a glowing account of her abilities and personality and asked her to think about recommending Mandie the next time someone she knew needed a nanny. Of course I didn't tell Julia about the "count to ten before you speak" rule of conduct her father had offered her.

Julia said that their good friends, the Goldbergs, happened to be looking for a nanny. Leo Goldberg was the head of a production company, a real bigwig. I told Mandie about the job and within two weeks she came to LA with her mother just as I had, to interview with them and a few other families the agency had found for her.

After she completed her interviews, Mandie called me for advice. She asked if I had seen the movie *The Untouchables* because she and her mom hadn't, and the man she had just interviewed with in the San Fernando Valley said he was in it. I told her that I had never heard of either the movie or him. I also clued her in on a basic principle that I had already learned from my life in Hollywood: a lot of people say they're actors when, in reality they're just trying to break into the business. So, I told her the guy was probably exaggerating about his role in the movie. For all we knew, he could have been a caterer on the set. This seemed plausible; especially since Mandie had reported that the family was remodeling their home and only had the use of one bathroom currently. That was the clincher for me. *What Hollywood star could get by with only one bathroom?*

I had learned another immutable movieland law: no one who's really important lives in the Valley. Mandie kept insisting that she really liked the guy, his wife and kids and she really wanted to take the position. In my infinite wisdom, I convinced her to take the job with the Goldbergs so we could live close together. I told her, "Just call the placement agency and tell them you decline the offer from this Costner guy, whoever he is."

Yes, Mandie and I are still friends. Years later we still laugh about that, but she stopped asking for my advice on her career choices a long time ago. I was glad she chose the Goldbergs, for totally selfish reasons. They lived in Bel Air, not far from Brentwood. We could see each other occasionally, and it was going to be great to finally have a friend to talk to, especially one who understood the challenges of the job. The best part was that Ellie, the youngest child she'd be caring for, was only a couple of months older than Brandon and the moms had commented on how great it would be if we got the babies together for play dates. *Yippeee! Adult conversation!*

From the very first day she moved in, we started sharing nanny tales almost nightly over the phone. There were times when we laughed so hard we had to hang up, catch our breath and call back. Right away Mandie sympathized with me because the Goldbergs had an eight-year-old who apparently had a mantra similar to Josh's "I hate you. You're an idiot." But she got to hear a more customized version that added on "You're fat and ugly."

I still remember the first time she called. She was in dire straits. She'd only been with the Goldbergs for three days. "Suzy, can I ask you something?" She sounded so hesitant.

"Sure. What's going on?"

"How do you eat at your house?"

"Huh?"

"I mean, where do you do it? Can you just do it when you want? Can you just take what you want?"

"Don't they let you eat? You sound like a starving refugee. When did you last eat?"

"Well, actually, it's really been three days. Nobody's said anything about it. They have a maid that also does the cooking, but I haven't really talked to her. So far they've just eaten out all the time. It's not like your house where you have Maria and Concetta to talk to and eat with. It's more formal here. My first hint was when she told me **not** to call her Margaret, that it was Mrs. Goldberg to me. I didn't exactly get the message that it would be okay to make myself at home in her kitchen after that."

I cut her off to give her a serious pep talk, which would become the template for most of our calls. "Stop right there! You haven't eaten in three days? March yourself into the kitchen, open the Sub-Zero and make yourself a big fat sandwich!"

"Nobody's shown me around the kitchen—I feel so uncomfortable going in there. What if I take something they're saving for something special?"

"Right. Better you just stay in your place, hiding in the servants' quarters. Maybe someone will take pity and throw you a crumb."

After I hung up, my brain started spinning: I gotta sign that girl up for some "take charge of your life" classes, but then I've always been much better at giving advice about what people should do with their lives, instead of minding my own. On second thought, maybe I'd better attend, too.

### Super Cuts

During one of our nightly conversations, Mandie said that she had a new look and couldn't wait to tell me the story of her over priced haircut.

Mrs. Goldberg had stopped Mandie in the hall one day. "You're thinking of getting your haircut, aren't you?"

"Um, no, not really. I just grew it out."

"You might want to consider going to my stylist at Salon Capelli. He can work miracles...on *anyone's* hair."

Mandie ignored her boss's suggestion. But later that day, Mrs. Goldberg stopped her again. "I had to pull a lot of strings, but I got you into Capelli for tomorrow at one."

After two conversations with Mrs. Goldberg about it, Mandie felt self-conscious about her hair and ended up keeping the appointment. Walking into the salon and seeing all the glamorous people there, she felt like a real Montana hick.

Mrs. Goldberg's hairdresser seemed very nice. Mandie asked him if he cut a lot of movie stars' hair. He said yes, he had a lot of famous clients, but he couldn't say who they were. For a hairdresser, he was pretty closed-lipped. She didn't ask anything after that. But while she got her hair styled, she was free to listen in on the hairdresser next to her talking to his client; a woman with dyed red hair and a ton of make-up.

"...The other day one of my clients, with hair so thin even I can barely do anything with it, runs in here with her hair all plastered to her head going, 'I need body! Give me body!' I go, 'Look, honey, I can't squeeze blood from a parsnip.' She goes, 'I don't care how you do it. You make me look like Kathleen Turner in *Romancing the Stone*. I want rain-forest hair!' So I whip out these," he picked up a bunch of hair extensions, "and start weaving them under and over, all around her frickin' head. And she keeps looking in the mirror and going, 'More, more, that's not enough.' I tell her less is more, but she won't listen. She just wants what she wants, which is what she doesn't have and never will, I don't care how famous she is and how much money she has. She leaves here two hours later looking like a cross between Don King and the Cowardly Lion. I'm thinking, *please* don't tell anyone I'm the one that did that to your head. I have a reputation to protect too, you know. I plan on going places in this business..."

One hour and much eavesdropping later, Mandie was out of there. She had to admit that her hair looked great, but she nearly started crying when she realized she had to shell out $80 for her new look. It killed her to think that in Montana she could get her hair cut for $12 at Sir Cuts-a-Lot.

She didn't know if the chatty hairdresser next to her ended up going far in the business, but her quiet hairdresser certainly did. When Air Force One held up runway traffic in LAX for two hours because President Clinton was getting his hair cut, Mrs. Goldberg's hairdresser was the one clipping the presidential mane.

Mandie and I often laughed about how our daily predicaments would probably sound a bit odd to other people outside of our gated homes. "Okay, here's one for you. Mrs. Swartz came into the kitchen and saw me loading the leftovers from the children's plates into one of those green plastic trash bags and she was aghast. I'm telling you, it actually took her a moment to catch her breath and I thought something was terribly wrong. I ask her if she is okay and she says, 'Suzy, never, never use those bags for the trashcan. They're heavy duty and only to be used for the *trash compactor*. They're too expensive to put in the garbage can.' Then she walks into the pantry and comes back out with a box of *thinner* bags and puts them into my hand."

I started giggling, and then Mandie started in "That's nothing. The other night I was cooking my dinner with the housekeeper and we got to talking, and before I knew it, the pan's burning. It really stunk up the place."

"Wait, stop," I interrupted. "Whoa, you're eating now?"

"Oh yeah, the housekeeper told me that Mrs. Goldberg asked her if she had ever seen me eat…so I got that straightened out. But the best part about being a spineless jellyfish is that I lost three pounds."

"Woooo hoooo, that's great. Living in a house where you feel like you're always just visiting *does* have its advantages. Okay, go on with your story, sorry I interrupted."

While I'm scrubbing to get the tar out of the bottom of the old stained pan, Mrs. Goldberg comes in and goes ballistic. 'My God, what have you done?' she shrieks at me. Then she runs over and grabs the pan out of my hand and says, 'You've ruined this pan.' Then she tells me I'm going to have to buy her a new pan.

"Why didn't you just clean the one you burned?" I asked.

"I was trying to, but she had declared it legally dead and that was that."

"So what happened?"

"Yesterday I had to go down to the May Company and buy a whole set of pans. It cost me nearly a week's paycheck."

"Why a whole set—I thought you only burned one of them?"

"I know, but she made me buy my own set to cook with. I can't use hers anymore. So now there are four pans in the pantry with Post-It notes on them that say 'Mandie's pots and pans.' It's like they have cooties. When I think about it, I shouldn't be surprised. I should have seen it right away."

"Seen what?" I asked.

"That she was tight. I didn't tell you what happened with the agency yet."

"No. What happened?"

"Well it was a mess and, of course, I ended up paying for it—or at least half."

"Paying for what? Did you break something at the agency?"

"No. But get this," Mandie said. "Since you recommended me, Mrs. Goldberg didn't use the agency she normally gets all her help from."

"Yeah, so…"

"Okay, so when I flew down and interviewed with them, there was no agency involved and since they were going to hire me on the spot, Mrs. Goldberg was thrilled with the fact that they wouldn't have to pay a fee to an agency. I didn't think much about it because I just wanted to go to work here closer to you."

"So what was the problem?"

"The other nanny who was here before me told the agency the job was opening up because she was leaving. After I interviewed, the agency called. So when I was hired, I guess they figured they were entitled to the fee. Mrs. Goldberg was so outraged that the agency had gotten her name. I ended up offering to pay half of the $1,200 placement fee because she was so upset about the mix-up."

"Oh my God, half, that's two weeks of pay for you. I can't believe she let you pay half of the fee so she could save a few bucks."

"At least she isn't making me pay it all at once. She's going to take $100 out of each paycheck until my half is paid."

"Unbelievable! Mandie, can you imagine what half a month's pay is to them? If you broke down Mr. Goldberg's earnings, he probably makes $1,200 an HOUR. Yet, she thinks nothing of letting you give up over two weeks of your income, for something you had no responsibility for. Mandie, you have got to get a backbone!" I almost started to laugh again but I could tell Mandie was taking it hard. So I offered my condolences.

"I gotta go," I said, having to abruptly end our conversation. "Brandon's crying." I told her I'd call her later in the week and ran to the baby.

It's my usual ten o'clock lockdown time, sleepwalk-proof lock is double checked. But I can't sleep, thinking about Mandie and the Goldberg's. Maybe I was a little hard on her tonight. I can tell she's really frazzled and worn out. Can't believe she agreed to get up with the baby seven nights a week, even on her days off. Margaret said she has a sleeping problem and if she wakes up in the middle of the night with the baby she can't get back to sleep.

Maybe I ought to quit criticizing Mandie...Helloooooooooo, Suzy, you're on call 24 hours a day too. Let's see, that works out to about 99 cents an hour. Man, we're both such wimps. At least I have two nights a week that Concetta covers for me. I'd better get to sleep. Brandon will be awake soon. With the cold he has, he's been up every two or so hours for the last few nights. I put the humidifier on in his room so maybe he won't be so congested after tonight.

## Where Was Jose Eber When I Needed Him?

With all my pratfalls, Mandie was beginning to call me Lucy. I quickly added, "Then you must be Ethel." Almost every day I had another story from my pathetic life to offer. One night I couldn't wait to get her on the phone so I could relate my latest episode. So I told her the whole story: about how Julia had been working out with her personal trainer, Jennifer, a gorgeous aspiring actress, and they had started talking about hair. Then Jennifer had mentioned her favorite salon in Westwood. I was sitting nearby with the baby, and out of nowhere, the personal trainer Jennifer offered me the name of the salon and the man who cut her hair. There are only two reasons a woman would suggest a hairdresser to another woman. One is if she were asked. The other would be if she thought the woman needed a little help with…….. I got the picture. I decided to try the unsolicited recommendation. Julia agreed that I could take time off for an appointment that next Friday. I didn't realize that things always take longer than they are supposed to in LA, and I didn't fully comprehend the idea that appointments are only made as starting points. In all the years that our family friend Diane cut my hair, she was never more than fifteen minutes late. So I set aside precisely an hour and a half, for which Julia gave her permission.

I had never been to a salon where so many different people attended to me. First, the receptionist confirmed my appointment. Then a greeter offered me a drink. Next I spent forty-five minutes reading *Glamour* and *Vogue* cover-to-cover. After that another person escorted me to the sink washing station, and then another attendant washed my hair. After that a girl put in my perm rods. I was told that after I was finished processing, then and only then would I see Franck, who would actually cut my hair. At least this was a little closer to my spa fantasy than my other two attempts, ghetto nails and scar face. By the time I met with the salon's owner Franck (pronounced just like the wedding coordinator in *Father of the Bride*), I was already starting to worry that I would be late getting back to the house.

I had my heart set on a perm, so I was trying out a new thing called an air-dry perm. An hour later I was still sitting in a chair with my hair in curlers the size of sewer pipes. I realized it was going to be over an hour before my perm would be "dried." I started to get very nervous about being late. I called the house with a report. Maria answered, sounding frazzled. She said she couldn't talk and was busy with dinner. She hung up abruptly after I apologized and told her I would be on my way. There was a knot gripping my stomach. Julia relied on my help at dinnertime. I somehow knew that she wouldn't take it well if I got home late.

I decided in a moment of sheer brilliance that I needed to leave and go home with the curlers intact. The prep girl said that leaving would be fine. I could take the rollers out myself in the morning and bring them back the following day—so much for getting my hair cut by Franck.

On the way out, I remembered that Maria had asked me to pick up yogurt for the kids' lunches on the way home. I stopped at a grocery store by the house so I could quickly run in. Since it wasn't all that uncommon in Cottage Grove for women to do their grocery shopping in curlers it never occurred to me to think about how I looked. I was worried about having to face Julia two hours late, so I hardly noticed that my hair was in giant curlers with four long pink drinking straws through each. There I was, running down the aisle of a crowded Ralph's grocery store looking like I had just stepped out of an alien aircraft with all my antennae on high alert. I noticed a few shoppers who had nothing better to do than stare and point me out to their companions. I thought, as I whirled through the aisles, *What's the matter with these people, anyway?* I suppose they'd never found themselves in a similar situation. They had obviously never had the desperate need to shop for yogurt and ignore their petty focus on *their* looks. *People are sooo shallow.* It wasn't until I got a look at my reflection in the glass cases of the frozen food section that I saw what they saw.

I wanted to just melt away like the Popsicles in Ralph's malfunctioning freezer case. I buried my head as best as I could in a copy of the *National*

*Enquirer* as I moved through the checkout line. I knew the reaction at home would be even more humiliating. Why were other people able to negotiate the ins and outs of self-maintenance with ease, when I always ended up feeling and looking like a baboons butt?

Maria and Concetta greeted me at home, doubling over with laughter at my appearance. Brandon took one look at me and started crying. Josh said, like a stern, wary dad, "Suzy, I want you to tell me what happened to your head." He was so earnest and concerned that it made me feel better, momentarily. I reassured him and gave him a big hug. I even started laughing along with the others. But then Julia came into the kitchen.

"I didn't see how you were going to be able to be back by four o'clock if your appointment was at two-thirty." *Then why didn't you tell me that before I left?* She glared at the curlers and spikes—my head looked like a land mine. And what did you have done to your hair?"

She sure wasn't seeing any humor in the situation. Maria and Concetta had to leave the room because they couldn't stop laughing and they could tell that they were not helping my situation with Julia. She was getting irritated with them now, too. I set the grocery sack on the counter and just let my heavy, oversized pink head hang.

*I tried to get back here as fast as I could. Why didn't you tell me how long these appointments take? Can't you just sit down and be served dinner minus the nanny, one night?*

I decided that the best policy was to keep my mouth shut, given the thoughts that were parading through my head. I had missed dinner, and when Julia left the kitchen Concetta got out a plate of food they had saved for me. She heated it in the microwave, while I went up and got Brandon ready for bed.

I started having overwhelming feelings of loneliness, and my brain found an old, old way of dealing with it: I started thinking about Troy, the guy I had left back at home for all the right reasons. After I tucked Brandon in, I opened my journal to get some rationality back. First I focused on the immediate situation with Julia. Then my mind did the rebound thing again.

Just when I was feeling like things were working out, grateful that she let me leave for my hair appointment, this happens. Either she's under a lot of pressure or she doesn't like me. I can't figure out which. I don't foresee me winning her favor, anytime soon.

I now see what Maria is talking about when she says Julia doesn't like her.

About the Troy thing, today I found an ad in the newspaper for a support group of "Women who love too much." Must be an offshoot of that book I loved. Maybe it would help me get over Troy. I swear that author must have been spying on me. I am guilty of every stupid thing she mentions. Including driving by his house a million times while his new girlfriend is visiting him to see if I could see through the curtains.

Daily life with the Swartz was unpredictable. Just when I'd decide that it was totally crazy, there would be days when everything would seem pretty normal.

Jennifer the trainer had been in several TV commercials, including a spot for Secret antiperspirant. When I saw it on television one night, I was delighted for her, yelling out to everyone, "Look, it's Jennifer!" I got far more excited than the others in the house about such things. I was really pulling for Jennifer's career because I liked her. She was a bright woman, but I think she missed the boat on a great opportunity when she turned down Steven's offer to help her get some auditions. She said she preferred to "make it on her own." Considering what he had done for his martial arts instructor, who went on to be a big-time action hero, I was worried that she'd missed her ticket to stardom.

Steven was practicing aikido one day when the phone rang. I answered and I recognized Dustin Hoffman's voice. I said, "I'm sorry, he'll have to call you back. He's taking his Karate lesson." When I relayed the message to Steven, it was clear that he was disappointed in me. He explained to me that no one knew about his aikido until a story had run, just recently, in the *New York Times* about his martial arts expertise. He was clearly not happy about it. It was then that I began to get just how much he valued his privacy. He did not want his picture in the papers. He didn't want stories told about him.

Steven was very kind when he was trying to explain this to his naïve little houseguest. While he was talking he actually put his arm around me. Once more I had the sense that he did appreciate my work. I wondered why I didn't ever feel like I could relax around him, he was always nice to me. But I knew I wasn't the only employee that felt that way. Once Maria had confided in me that after all the years she'd worked there, she still never felt relaxed in the home.

I'm beginning to be more observant of little things that I haven't noticed before. I've got to work on learning what things are secret and what things I can say. I'm just taking mental notes so I won't blow it.

No wonder so many things in this household and in LA seem out of whack to me. In C.G., everybody pretty much knows everybody else's business, and the level of wealth is significantly different. During the gold miners' charity breakfast every year at the old mine, the Kiwanis Club was lucky to profit $500 on the whole event. Here, an average fundraiser runs at about $1,000 per plate.

I'm seeing how different it is to grow up here amidst the rich and famous compared to where I came from. Doubt that Amanda's first "movie date" will be on Tightwad Tuesday like mine was. When LA teenagers want to watch a movie, they have custom-fitted projectors, reclining seats, big screens and professionally equipped speakers in their home. They might even have a guy from the studio set up the film and run it for them. This seems pretty standard for the neighborhood, but to my mind, it detracts from the romance that I've always associated with going out to see a movie. It even seems a little un-American. Oh well.

This started me thinking about what the children's lives would be like as they grew up. They'd probably live their entire lives with people being paid to take care of all their needs. They'd never be required to do anything, and as a consequence, they would never learn how to do much on their own. Then again, maybe this wouldn't be a problem.

I pictured Brandon, Amanda and Joshua all grown up trying to figure out how to work a broom and dustpan: wondering where you'd find such tools. I could see each of them getting their own set of wheels: a Porsche for Amanda, a Ferrari for Joshua and a Hummer for Brandon. They would all drive the seven blocks from the house to the local Ben and Jerry's for an ice cream cone.

It would certainly be different from my high school experiences, which included helping my friend, Christine, push her old Volkswagen down an inclined street to get it started. Amy and I would push it from behind and Christine would steer. I would be wheezing and gasping, holding onto the bumper of the '68 bug. She would yell out when we were going fast enough and then Amy and I would both pull on the door handles and swing ourselves up into the passenger seat, landing on top of each other. Christine would simultaneously pop the clutch and off we would go. She could never afford to get that starter fixed. Sometimes friends are a good substitute for money; I'm not so sure the reverse is true.

What would the Swartz kids do as teenagers if they ever had car trouble? It was a stretch to imagine them doing anything more strenuous than dialing up their personal assistants on their cell phones. One night as Maria and I were eating dinner, I brought up the subject. "What are these kids going to do when they grow up? They've never been asked to even put their own clothes in the laundry basket and they'll never empty a dishwasher in their entire childhoods."

"Soo-zita, eet dos'unt matter. They weel have so much money, they won't have to."

I couldn't help thinking about it for the next few days. How do children like this end up? How do they go to college and take care of themselves, prepare meals, iron a shirt, know how to separate lights and darks for the laundry? For heaven's sake, Amanda wasn't aware there were people in the world who didn't have cars with automatic windows. The first time I took her to the store with me in Concetta's car, she gave me a glazed look as she glanced back and forth between the roll-up window handle and me. She looked quizzically at the alien appendage. "Where's the window button?"

"Some cars don't have automatic windows, Amanda. Sometimes you've got to roll them up *yourself*," I said, putting the emphasis on the last word. "This is how you do it." I demonstrated the act with the driver's side door. She gave me a look as if I had just given her a detailed description of the theory of relativity.

CUT TO:

INTERIOR — COLLEGE DINING HALL — NOON

Expensively dressed young man looks around enormous cafeteria, perplexed as to how the restaurant works. Follows other students - Picks up a tray and starts through the line.

> YOUNG MAN
> What is this?

> LUNCH LADY
> That is Salisbury steak.

Young man still looks perplexed.

> YOUNG MAN
> Salsa berry what? I'll just have some of that cream of cauliflower soup.

> LUNCH LADY
> (laughing)
> That's not soup, those are mashed potatoes, the instant kind. Would you like some?

Young man leaves the tray and goes back to his dorm room. He finds all his clothes in a heap on the floor where he left them.

> YOUNG MAN
> Um, Matthew, that's your name right? Matthew?

> ROOMMATE
> Yeah bud, Guess we're gonna be bunk mates for this semester. What's wrong? You look baffled - you still looking for the girl's dorms?

> YOUNG MAN
> What time of day do they come to pick up the laundry and dry cleaning? I left this out this morning.

> ROOMMATE
> (laughing)
> Yeah, right on. Where are those maids when you need them?

ROOMMATE

This isn't a 5 star hotel Dude, the laundry room is two floors down in the basement. You need to borrow some of my quarters?

YOUNG MAN
(looking very confused)

I have to go call my dad. With the amount of money he's donated to this college, when he finds out about the lack of service, some heads are going to roll. You wait and see.

He storms out of room, then returns a minute later.

YOUNG MAN

Uh, Matt, I can't get service on my cell. They got this old freaky looking thing that someone said was called a "paid phone." Do you know how to get it working for me? I think you need to put coins in before you can get a dial tone. My dad is gonna hear about this little situation, too.

## Disneyland in Aspen

On the occasional weekends that Mandie and I were both off duty, we usually shopped. My wardrobe still consisted mostly of shorts, jeans, T-shirts and sweatshirts; clothes that could withstand barf, dirt, paint and snot. It wasn't what most women would call a professional wardrobe, unless you were in my profession. One particular shopping excursion, I wasn't really intending to express my sartorial self. But, I fell prey to a very convincing sales woman who brought half of her coworkers over to the three-sided mirror to rally support for the release of my credit card.

"Oh my dear, that is you," one of the strangers said.

"Do you travel? That would be great for traveling."

"Gorgeous, absolutely stunning, it makes you look so thin," said another.

That was all it took. "I'll take it. Wrap it up," I said. The sales lady lovingly folded the white cotton one-piece jumpsuit into a neat square and placed it in a bag. Mandie had eyed me warily during the fitting, but had not offered an opinion, which I thought was unusual. I was sailing so high on the compliments, I hadn't paid attention.

In hindsight, I think she was probably getting even with me for the Costner snafu. Why else would a friend let a friend walk out of a store with such a hideous outfit? Looking back, the entire store was made up of these "new" clothes that resembled that dress you've seen on the infomercial that can be worn 56 different unflattering ways.

I bought it, envisioning that I would wear it on an upcoming trip. After all, the sales ladies kept saying it was perfect for traveling.

I was looking forward to my first time in Aspen. When I had interviewed, Steven had asked if I skied and whether I could drive in the snow. I thought I might be helping the kids out on the bunny slopes. But as we started packing, nobody said anything about bringing ski clothes to me; I stuck to my new policy of trying to figure out what was going on, instead of asking questions. So I just packed my regular clothes and threw in a couple of Oregon sweaters for the chill, figuring I could rent skis if I needed to. I was excited about having a new traveling outfit for the plane anyway. When Saturday came and we were about to depart, I took one hasty look in the mirror in my room. Since it wasn't full length, I could only see my new get-up from the waist up. When I went downstairs, Joshua and Amanda were standing in the foyer with their suitcases.

"You look like an astronaut," Joshua blurted out.

Amanda said, "What is that?" pointing to the magenta sash tied around my waist.

"An accent," I explained, feebly.

Steven looked me over from head to toe, and gave me an expression I can't describe, somewhere between disappointment and embarrassment. I decided to go upstairs to change. When I got there, I pulled over the chair so I could stand on it to see myself "full-length" in the mirror. The kids were right; I looked like either a snowman in a children's school play or a member of NASA. When I turned around I could see that the little red hearts of my underwear were clearly visible through the seat of the suit. No wonder Steven looked at me as if to say the fashion train had long ago left this poor girl standing at the station.

I changed into my standard nanny uniform, substituting jeans for shorts with my T-shirt, and started loading luggage into the limo for our six-day vacation in Aspen with their good friends, the Eisners. It would be my first time in the Disney corporate jet. By this time, I had seen Mr. Eisner on *The Wonderful World of Disney*, so I had figured out that he was the CEO of the company. When we got on the plane, I thought it was hysterical that everything on board had either Mickey Mouse or Goofy printed on it, from the napkins to mugs and glasses. This is the absolute truth: on the rolls of toilet paper, each square had a big Mickey smiling back at you.

The entourage consisted of Steven and Julia, Michael and Jane, the Eisner's male nanny, Paul - who was a few years older than me, the Eisner's three sons, ages 9, 12, and 18 and my three little charges. We were going to meet Mr. Eisner's mother there and the oldest son's girl-friend was flying in from somewhere on the East Coast to join us.

The trip started out with Steven lecturing Joshua in the limo about how disappointed he was with his behavior. Josh had been quarreling with Amanda. Steven told Josh how good he had it to fly on a private jet. In the course of the speech he said that he, Steven, had never even flown on any plane when he was six years old. I guess that was Steven's version of the old "When I was a boy I had to walk eight miles..." Like the original versions, I think it failed to impress the son, although Joshua was always visibly impacted by his dad's disapproval.

Though the Disney plane was certainly comfortable and was able to accommodate the twelve of us, I wasn't feeling well, not at all well. My stomach was doing loops.

After we landed, despite my nausea, I helped to load the more than twenty pieces of luggage back into the limo and then unload it at the Eisner's house. I was beginning to get clammy and the queasiness was starting to roll over me like a tsunami. However, I chalked it all up to the flight and told myself it would all go away shortly if I could just make it to a chair to sit down for a few minutes. By the time everyone was inside the house, I knew there was something much worse going on. This was not going away. I realized that in addition to starting a menstrual melt-down of nuclear proportions, I must have picked up some sort of flu.

I went into the bedroom that Brandon and I were assigned to lie down, but it was only a minute before I heard my name being called. When I emerged, Mr. Eisner and his mother were standing in the hall and they both did a double take when they saw me. My face was sheet white and I was sweating profusely.

"My goodness, Suzy, you look awful. Are you okay?" Mrs. Eisner asked.

"You should lie down," her son said. I started to answer them when I saw Julia standing in the hallway with a confused expression on her face that said, "*what are you talking about? I didn't notice anything wrong with her.*"

Mr. and Mrs. Eisner walked past me into another room and I quickly went into the bathroom where I locked the door. Within seconds I was lying on the frozen tile floor in the fetal position feeling very sorry for myself, thinking, Julia doesn't have time for me to be sick. Her denial autopilot is kicking in. I could just hear her in my mind: "We didn't come all the way to Aspen to have to adjust our fun to the physical limitations of the help."

I wasn't crying wolf like my family always accused me of doing. I couldn't remember ever being as sick, with the exception of the time I had the flu when I was thirteen. I had asked my mother then, if it was possible that anyone could still contract the Bubonic Plague. As I said before, coming up with implausible medical conditions was kind of a hobby of mine as a child. But this was the real thing. Writhing on the floor, I could hear Steven in the hall loudly asking, "Where's Suzy? Where's Suzy? We've got to get going." I was in so much pain that I couldn't muster the strength to answer. I knew Brandon was safe in his crib. If they'd just leave, I could go lie down in bed and I might recover. Looking back now, I can't believe I wasn't able to answer him. I just kept the mantra in my head, Leave, leave, leave. Let me recover in peace.

"Where's Suzy?" I could still hear him shouting on the other side of the door, with the kids answering in unison, "I don't know, Dad. Let's go!"

Somewhere else in the house, I could hear Julia complaining about the less-than-pristine conditions of the Eisner's house. The place was a sprawling, indifferently-decorated, semi-rustic vacation home. It was a relaxed place, the kind that seemed to make the Swartz nervous.

After a few more moments, I heard the front door open and close. The house became empty and silent. When I did manage to grab the doorknob and pull myself to my feet, I walked out to find that everyone had left – except for Brandon, who was lying alone in his crib, quietly playing with his feet. They had all gone without knowing where I was, and they hadn't taken the baby with them. I don't know what must have gone through their minds. I kept thinking that they were irritated with me for being sick and missing in action. I had the shocking realization, right then and there, that they really didn't notice me enough to see that I might have my own needs. I felt very, very alone as I picked up Brandon and rocked him in my arms.

By the next night, whatever disease I had contracted had passed through me like a bad winter storm. The cramps were my constant companion for the next two days, but I could cope with that. I'd had experience with being incapacitated one or two days out of the month. Once I emerged from my stupor, I discovered that people were scattered all around the enormous house. The Eisner's oldest son was in the kitchen with his girlfriend. She was an heiress to some famous fortune and was more self-absorbed and aloof than anyone I'd ever met. I don't think she uttered more than a few words during the entire trip that didn't have some reference to her family's wealth.

I eventually felt sorry for her. I did have to give her credit for coming up with inventive ways to squeeze in references to her financial stature, regardless of the topic: the snowfall outside, her night's sleep, the way she salted her potatoes, the time of day. Hers was a most unusual talent, honed to an impressive degree. All right, I admit it: I couldn't stand her.

The following evening in Aspen, Brandon was in his port-a-crib in my room and the entourage had gone to dinner at Goldie Hawn's house. As luck would have it, they had decided to leave Brandon and me at the house since they would be out late. The Eisner's nanny stayed home too. He seemed like a nice enough guy; however, being that it is unusual for a man to want to take care of children, it made me a little curious about him. When I applied my mom's rule about wearing the other guy's shoes I knew I needed to be more open-minded. So I started a conversation with him.

Paul sat on the couch and I sat on the hearth. He was a small guy, and he was definitely the quiet type, so I tried to make small talk.

"What do you think of Steven and Julia?" I asked him out of thin air.

"Oh, I suppose they're all right, nice enough." I waited. He had finished.

"Uh, can I get your opinion on something," I said.

"What's that?" He looked curious. Now he was warming up.

"Now get ready for this. Julia suggested that I could date the oldest Eisner." I forced out a half giggle. He busted up laughing. "Now wait a minute, Paul," I blurted in defense.

"No, no. I'm sorry. I wasn't laughing at you. It's just that we nannies are at the lowest level in the pecking order. In fact, I don't know if we're actually in the order. There is no way in the world that an Eisner would date a nanny. Just wouldn't happen," he said. "They don't mix with the hired help." Then he stood up as he left the room, laughing to himself.

Obviously, I had more to learn about the social ladder of the wealthy. But maybe Julia did too, I think she had actually been sincere in her suggestion —she had mentioned it to me twice. Maybe it was a compliment to me. It seemed like she had thought that he and I were close in age, not necessarily thinking about the other dimension. I thought Julia always had an air of slight awkwardness about social status. I always wondered how comfortable she really was with her wealth. I'm sure she never believed, growing up, that she would be married to a man worth millions and millions. Maybe she thought it was just a fluke, something that even someone like me could blunder into.

The conversation with Paul put voice to some feelings that had already been brewing. Being treated like I was invisible much of the time was beginning to wear on me. I was getting more and more attached to the children, yet it seemed that the way our relationship was structured made things confusing for them and me. The subtle communication, the one that Joshua was already picking up, was that I cared for them because I was paid to. It didn't matter that my love and affection for them was authentic. They would soon learn that, by the measure of exchange, the care I gave wasn't worth a lot. I was beginning to feel that this was a decidedly low-status way to earn a living.

Brandon was asleep in his port-a-crib in my room, so I retired early to write in my journal. I had a lot to think about.

Paul was right. I'm just the help. I'm just like the hired hand on Dad's favorite show, Bonanza. I don't get to eat at the dining room table with the Cartwright family; I'm out on the cattle ranch sleeping in the bunkhouse. Even if I am ten times more attractive then Miss Prissy, it doesn't matter. I'm simply not in the same league. I'm not even playing the same sport to be able to join the league. My problem is that I don't like hearing the truth. Paul was just trying to tell me what my "place" was. Just facts, as they say. He seems to have accepted his role in the Eisner's family. Something weird he shared was that Mrs. Eisner seemed to have the standard practice of asking every guy she interviewed if they're gay. The nanny before him had warned him about this, and had suggested he "not take it personally."

I've decided to apply that logic to my situation with the Swartz. I just have to keep reminding myself that my employers aren't my friends. If they were, they would've at least asked about how I was feeling yesterday when I was so sick with the flu.

The truth is that they're the wealthy landowners and I'm the peasant farm girl. We have a working relationship. And the fact that I accidentally saw one of them naked one morning doesn't change the professional distance of our relationship.

Why am I complaining? I'm working in the job of my choosing and I'm being paid better than most nannies: $300 a week Buck up, Suzanne! And scrounge around for some Advil in the medicine cabinet.

The next day, we all traipsed out to the slopes and took the gondola ride to the top. Steven and Julia rode in one car with Joshua and Amanda, and Brandon and I rode up on a second chair. Only Steven was going to ski but we all went to the top anyway. When we got there, there was a man taking family pictures of everyone in their colorful and expensive ski gear. Julia approached him and discussed the price of a group photo. When she returned, she asked if I would wait over on the side while they had their picture taken. She said they just wanted the family in the picture.

"Yes, of course." *I do realize that you wouldn't want one of the nannies in your family photo album.*

Then they started taking off their ski jackets and caps and piling them on me to hold. Julia glanced back as she walked toward the photographer and said, "Suzy, I'm glad you're here. You make a good coat rack."

Well, today I felt like the Griswold's Aunt Edna, strapped to the top of the family truckster on the way to Wally World, in the movie Vacation. I have got to get a better attitude!

Note to self: Try that visualization/affirmation thing where I see positive changes in my life - OK here I go.
Tomorrow I will feel like Christie Brinkley driving the Ferrari along side Chevy Chase....
Tomorrow I will feel like Christie Brinkley driving the Ferrari...........
Tomorrow I will feel like Christie Brinkley ..............

The flight home was uneventful; the only sounds were coming from the kids playing and the heiress chattering on about her debutante ball experience. I found my thoughts idling on an image of her silver spoon becoming lodged in her over privileged throat. Ever the good nanny, though, I censored my little fantasy—I knew I would definitely be breaking the nanny code of conduct if the children witnessed the act of violence I was imagining.

Mandie had just arrived home after a trip to New York with the Goldbergs, and she called when I got home to tell me all about *her* private jet experience. She said this guy named David Geffen and his friend, Carrie Fisher, were with them on the plane. She recognized Fisher from *Star Wars* but didn't have a clue who the guy was; though she thought he was some sort of record producer. When he spent time chatting with her about the kids and turned out to be quite nice, we both surmised that he couldn't possibly have been anyone very important. Big Wigs don't waste their time visiting with nannies. Leave it to the country girls from Oregon and Montana to be wrong again. We didn't recognize the name of Geffen, the biggest music mogul of our time.

Mandie's trips were always more eventful than mine. She usually flew on corporate jets with interesting people, and she got to know them a little bit. The passenger list on the trip to New York included Goldie Hawn and Kurt Russell. She described them as great, normal folks. While they were flying, Kurt made sandwiches for the kids and Goldie led sing-alongs for everyone. I tried to imagine Steven asking everyone on the plane, "Did you want mayonnaise (without hydrogenated oils, of course) on your sandwich?" and then Julia breaking into a round of "Ninety-Nine Bottles of Imported Beer on the Wall."

# Nanny Comraderie

Mandie and I loved to swap stories of any kind during our nightly phone chats.

"Wait. Before you start, I have a question," she said.

"Shoot. What is it?"

"You had to pay to put in your own separate phone line in your bedroom, right?"

"Yeah, it's separate from the four lines on their phone," I reminded her.

"Well, when I moved in, Mrs. Goldberg said I didn't need to install my own phone, that I could just use hers. So now at the end of every month she goes through and highlights all the calls that are mine so I can pay her back. The problem is, she makes these little comments when we settle up, like, 'You talked to someone for an hour and a half.'"

"Why don't you tell her, 'Yes, I did. I *like* to have contact with the outside world'?"

"She goes through your bill and highlights all your calls? 5 minutes to Missoula, 43 cents.... oops there is another one. Bozeman, Montana......Oh here is a real whopper $6.28 to Helena, glad I caught that one."

Mandie interrupted me, "I am not kidding."

"She thinks she's that poor?"

"And get a load of this. They just had this small stained glass window installed in one of the downstairs bathrooms and it cost $15,000."

I couldn't hold myself back. "All righty then, I'm glad your reimbursements to them on your phone bill are keeping them out of the welfare line. Have you guys had your government cheese delivered to you this week?"

I needed these nightly conversations with Mandie more and more. I could talk to her about anything, and at that time I needed to talk. My relationship with the children still wasn't melding as quickly as I'd hoped. I'd come to love all three of them, and although Amanda was still sometimes warm to me, only one of them regularly wanted and needed me—Brandon. I knew Julia wasn't crazy about his preference for me over her, but she seemed to accept it as just a fact of their lives. When I'd only been working in her house for three days she had commented how she hated it "when the baby wants to go to the nanny instead of me." I didn't know how to respond, so I stayed silent, but now I had a new thought about it. She thinks that this is just one of the prices she has to pay for the convenience of having help, I decided.

It was different with the two older children. They always preferred their mother to me, particularly on school days when they hadn't seen her all day. When they came home, they immediately wanted to know where she was. Usually I had no idea what she did all day or where she went, though she often remarked on how busy she was. She didn't seem to shop much on Rodeo Drive or "do lunch" with the girls, like I'd expected. She didn't actually seem to be the proverbial high-maintenance socialite. She once told me she had never even had a facial. And after she witnessed my "facial from hell" results, she said she didn't think she wanted to ever visit an aesthetician.

Joshua still wasn't taking kindly to me. Oddly, it was his sister who had been so close to Leticia, not him, but I think the succession of nannies had taken its toll on him, emotionally. No doubt there was a Leticia somewhere in his past. Added to this, he was old enough to begin emulating his father to a degree, a role he was practicing more and more.

When Steven wasn't home, Joshua seemed to think he could control everyone in the house. I could see his behavior turn off all of the staff, and I imagined that he felt none of them cared about him. It was hard to deal with his outwardly difficult and hostile behavior, even though I understood that he was just a six-year-old boy determined not to let anyone new into his life. Underneath the layers, he was a loving child who had the ability to care. I could see that demonstrated with his love and devotion to his grandmother "Nana."

When I talked with him about her, Joshua corrected me regularly, telling me that I was not saying her name correctly. "It is 'Non-uh,' not 'Nann-uh,'" he would tell me, rolling his eyes, sometimes asking why I "couldn't get it right." When this happened, I was more interested than irritated. I was glad he felt such unreserved love for someone in his life. I wanted to help him learn to trust me, but I didn't know how to make that happen. While the rest of the staff was fed up with his behavior, I tried to show him everyday that I cared about him.

More than once when he was going off on one of his tirades, calling everyone on the staff "morons," I remember Maria saying to him (I don't know how to spell it in Spanish but it was pronounced) "Coma say chingas!" When Julia asked Concetta what that meant, Concetta told her, "Go in peace, little one." I can't repeat here what the real translation is. Julia was never the wiser and Maria used it often, always with a peaceful smile on her face. Maria had to put up with a lot of verbal abuse from a six-year-old. This was her private little act of revenge.

Amanda wasn't always a model of childhood sweetness and joy either. Sometimes, we got along famously, and we had fun dressing up and doing silly dances to Raffi tunes. We played "telephone" and "baby" and "guess what I think." She was an adorable moppet. But often, right in the midst of our fun, some tiny thing would set her off. She wanted the kind of crackers she'd had at school, or she wanted to watch a video instead of going out or she couldn't find a toy. Or for reasons only she could know she would scream and wail and throw things, both hers and mine, long past the point of exhaustion.

Once, Amanda spun out of control because Julia was leaving. She flew out of the house after her mother, kicking and screaming. She was three; she knew what she wanted and it was not going her way. There was no end to her frustration and fury. She screamed, she kicked she cried huge gulping sobs. I started to carry her to her room and she wriggled out of my hold. She almost fell down the stairs. I think it scared her that she wasn't able to control her angry little body, and neither could I. So we just stopped there on the steps and she sobbed more quietly. I finally sat down below her and looked up at her sad, wet face. I said, "Amanda, I am so sorry you're upset and having such a hard time." I told her I loved her.

She said, "I love you too," for the very first time, and plopped her heaving body onto my lap. We hugged and sat together until we felt better. Sometimes it's hard to figure out what we're so mad about. We just know that we are.

The butter incident with Josh when I first arrived hadn't helped to promote a trusting relationship. We had our good times and our bad, but I always felt like Josh was just trying to prove the theory he'd already developed: when you start to care about people, they leave. The air of suspicion he carried with him was very unusual, and discouraging, coming from a six-year-old. I wished he would let down his guard and see that I was on his side. Our best times seemed to happen just after I brought him home from kindergarten, when I could get him to talk about his day at school. He would tell me about his classmates. We quickly worked out an understanding that I would not tolerate hearing them described as stupid, mean or ugly. Instead, we agreed to call them "characters," with much lifting of the eyebrows, as in, "Suzy, Chantel was a *real character* today. She broke the wheel in the hamster's cage." Or, "Tayla dropped my project. *What a character!*" The way he'd ham it up was really funny and he loved being in on a joke.

It seemed to me like life was difficult for Joshua because he was an extremely bright child and a tightly-wound perfectionist, very much like his father. We'd sit down together and go over his homework, which he undertook with great concentration. He would become extremely frustrated when he made a little mistake on one of his handout pages, rubbing holes through the paper with his eraser. When we worked together on something like this I felt we were gaining ground; at least he let me help him with something he cared about.

I was remembering an incident that happened my second day on the job. I always thought that it might have set the tone for his lack of trust in me. I wondered if he would ever forgive me for my lack of knowledge of bathroom safety paraphernalia. He reminded me of the mishap, almost every time I filled his bathtub. What had happened was, when I went to take the toys out of the tub and turn on the tap, I noticed the spout was covered with something that looked like a giant prophylactic, over the faucet. *Now, why in the world would someone want to protect their bath spout?* I had no immediate answer, so I pulled it off. *How else was I going to run the water?*

As with most other things in the Swartz's house, there was a reason, but it just wasn't evident to me. After the water was warm and the tub half-filled, I told Joshua his bath was ready and he got in while I helped Amanda get undressed in the connecting bedroom. Within seconds, there was a wailing that nearly rivaled Amanda's temper tantrums. I turned immediately to see Joshua sitting in the tub, holding his head and screaming, "You idiot! You're so stupid! I hate you." I definitely did not hear, "Suzy, you're such a character!" He was on his mantra. Then I realized that the cover I had removed had been placed there to protect the children's heads, not the spout itself. While horsing around in the water, Joshua had knocked his noggin. Fortunately, this incident didn't require stitches, but I had one more strike against me on his 'Suzy as enemy' scorecard.

I spent so much time around the house that my world had narrowed and these little scenes gained importance. It had become apparent early on that I was never to leave the house on a weeknight. My workdays were endless because I was always on duty. I couldn't leave on Friday nights because I had the night shift with the baby. And I certainly couldn't stay out on the weekend and come back as early as I needed to Monday morning. That would set off the outside alarm when I opened the gate and the interior alarm and wake the family. So my time to myself consisted of Saturday morning until Sunday night: a 36-hour work-release period. I was starting to kick myself for never mentioning a contract, and for never discussing how many hours I would work or what my responsibilities would be when I accompanied the Swartz' on their vacations.

I knew I had to get out of pity-party mode, so Mandie and I decided to take matters into our own hands with our littlest charges and sign all of us up for a Gymboree class in Santa Monica. We figured it would give us something else to do together besides taking our babies to the park. Gymboree is basically an activity that allows parents of babies of a similar age to play, sing songs and socialize with their babies and other adults.

By the time we had been attending for several weeks it came to the attention of all the other moms, that Mandie and I weren't moms at all, just nannies. They were all blown away.

At first I took it as a rebuff, but then one of the moms explained, "No. No. I can't believe they aren't your children. You're so good with them and they obviously enjoy you." Then I noticed for the first time how each baby looked like us. Brandon had rosy round cheeks and dimples like mine, and his hair was coming in about the same color as mine. Ellie,

"Mandie's baby," had straight black corn-silk hair and a round face, just like her nanny.

## Falling for Braveheart

"Suzy, you're not going to believe this one." My nanny buddy launched the nightly conversation. "I've just got to tell you my big news. I finally met Mel Gibson in person." *Like duh, what other way would you meet him?* "And I was such a klutz I can't believe it."

"What happened?"

"Remember I told you last week the Goldbergs were planning their own anniversary party?"

"Yeah."

"Well, I peeked at the invitation list that was on Mrs. Goldberg's desk. Talk about a *Who's Who*. I mean everybody was on it, from Dolly Parton to Quincy Jones, and there in the middle was Mel Gibson." Mel was to Mandie what Tom Cruise was to me.

"Oh boy, I thought, I'm finally going to meet him. So I volunteered to let people in. You know, to be the greeter at the door so I'd make sure I'd get to shake his hand or something."

"So did ya?"

"I'm getting there. So, I'm standing there, saying hello to Shirley McClaine, Kelly LeBroc, Don Johnson—I could hardly catch my breath. I was wearing that blue dress you like. Finally, after I've let about forty people in, there he is. My God, he's good looking, better than in the movies."

"So, whatja do, try to hug him or something?"

"No, no. I started to say, 'Hello, Mr. Gibson,' but nothing would come out but air. Suddenly I was breathing like a thoroughbred that had just crossed the finish line. I started to turn away, not wanting him to see me like that, and I fell head over bumpkin across a chair and landed on my back with my feet in the air, minus one shoe. I almost died."

"Did he help you up?"

"Not exactly, he tried, but I saw Mrs. Goldberg out of the corner of my eye looking very irritated with me, so I just scrambled up by myself. I wonder what he thought—or do you think he gets that all the time?"

I never did a somersault for Mel Gibson, but some of our nanny tales were remarkably alike. For instance, Mandie and I noticed a similar tendency within our respective families to blame the "help" whenever anything was amiss. It is frustrating to lose something, that feeling is universal. Fortunately, if you are blessed with household help, you have a ready-made lineup of suspects. One Saturday when Mandie and I were out, we decided to actually make a chart comparing the weekly missing item stories. It was amazing to see the similarities, boiled down into that form:

| Crime Scene | Mandie's Story | Suzy's Story |
|---|---|---|
| The Missing Item | Baby Outfit | Toddler Car Seat |
| The Accused | Construction Workers | Gardener's Assistants |
| The Tirade | "Leave it to them to steal baby's clothing!" | "These people are always taking things from me!" |
| Our Search Committee | Graciella, the Housekeeper | Gloria and LaRosa, the Housekeepers |
| Our Comments during Our Frantic Search | "Are you sure you didn't leave it in the car?" | "Are you sure you didn't leave it in the car?" |
| Time We Spent Searching for "Priceless" Items | One and One Half Hours | One Hour and Fifteen Minutes |
| Where Found | In Diaper Bag in the Car | In Maria's Car, Left after Transporting Amanda |

When we looked at the chart, we broke into a fit of giggles, the kind that release the built-up tension of weeks. We were still laughing as we left the coffee shop, the list in hand. We had done our therapy for the week and we were ready to go back to our assigned posts with perspective.

## When Tammy Met Sally

One day I overheard Julia talking to someone on the phone. I heard my name mentioned, so I listened more closely. I couldn't believe what I heard, given the recent tension in the house. "Oh yes, you'll definitely need a nanny. Mine, is a lifesaver. I don't know what we'd do without her. She's like my right arm." *My right arm* about fell off as I listened to her praise, from the next room.

"She does more than just take care of the kids. In fact, just the other day she saw I needed to make lunch reservations at the Ivy and she took it upon herself to call for me since she knew I was busy."

I almost fell through the doorway. It was the kindest thing Julia had ever said about me. Later that night, Julia told me she'd spoken to Sally Field on the phone that day. She asked if I knew of another nanny I could recommend to her. She said that Sally's baby wasn't due for a few more months.

I immediately thought of Tammy Munroe, who was a year ahead of me in high school. I knew she would be perfect. In truth, Tammy was perfect at everything. I had always looked up to her. The entire town loved her because she was beautiful and incredibly *nice* at the same time, not an easy feat.

I called Sally, who was pregnant and at home on bed rest. I addressed her as Mrs. Field, just in case she had formality issues like Mrs. Goldberg did, and told her how great my friend would be for the job. She seemed like a genuinely kind person, and I thought the match would be ideal. She was really easy to talk to and I felt very good about giving Tammy an excellent reference. When I got off the line, I called Tammy and told her about the job. I'd been bugging her to be a nanny ever since she started working at the local frozen yogurt shop with my sister. I told her that she could hurry up and get through nanny school before Sally had the baby, and then she should interview right away to secure the job. She said she'd fly down as soon as she could get time off. We set up a tentative interview.

Tammy came down and stayed with me for two days before her meeting with Sally. I gave her directions to Sally's house. She was really nervous as she set off. I waited for her with my fingers crossed. I just knew this was going to be a good fit. When she got back an hour and a half later, I insisted that she share every detail. She said that when she got there she was so nervous that she was sick to her stomach. She wanted to turn back, but she knew she'd have to face me later, so she decided to forge ahead nausea and all. She was too chicken to chicken out. She buzzed the gate and Sally's husband came out. She explained he was so g-g-gorgeous, she became light headed. After seeing him she felt better at the prospect of living in Sally Field's household, if only for the scenery.

When Tammy met Sally, she found her not at all intimidating. She felt very at ease in the house. Both Sally and her husband, Alan, asked her some questions about her experiences in life. She had the impression that they thought she wasn't very street-smart. Where did they ever get that idea?

Alan had said, "With our lifestyle, we're going to need someone that's going to be comfortable with us. How do you feel about that?"

She replied, "I feel okay about you. I'm comfortable enough. How do you feel? Are you comfortable with me?"

She said that Alan had burst out laughing. Here was a nineteen-year-old girl from Mayberry USA asking him if HE was comfortable around HER. He said that he was sure she'd fit in just fine.

Tammy and I spent most of the weekend holed up in my room because I didn't want to go downstairs when Steven and Julia were home. We were starving. Tammy couldn't believe that I didn't feel that I could bother them or that I lived in such an unpleasant situation. She said that she hoped it wouldn't be like that for her if she got the job with Sally.

After having Tammy here I realized how accustomed I've become to feeling uncomfortable most of the time. I'm kicking myself for not following the advice I got at nanny school about the contract. I used to consider myself fairly bright, but I gotta admit I was a nit wit not to be more assertive when I interviewed here.

I'm always quick to criticize Mandie for not standing up for herself. But it's so much easier to berate Mandie for being a doormat than to stop being walked on myself.

Goal #1: Ask if I can go out next Friday night at 8pm and meet Mandie for dinner.

## Nannies Anonymous

Not long after reading a monthly *Nanny Newsletter*, I decided that Mandie and I needed to go to a nanny support group meeting. Yes, there are such things. Mandie was worried. "Is it going to be like an AA meeting? Hello, I'm Mandie and I'm a miserable nanny."

I'd found one in Beverly Hills, the city with the highest per capita rate of households with nannies, I was sure. The ad in the newsletter read:

*Nanny Support Groups*
*Learning to cope with the isolation and stress of the job.*
*Support groups offer friendship, mentoring and a sense of identity.*
*Gain the career credibility and the social opportunities that nannies*
*deserve.*

I couldn't agree more. My hope was that this might end up being similar to the times at the Nanny Institute when we'd shared our challenges with our practicum families. Not exactly a social opportunity, but I thought it might be helpful.

When we got there, Mandie's fears and my lowest expectations were confirmed. There we were with girls even more pathetic than us, working for $150 a week; doing all the housework, cooking and child-care. Now that I was with an audience of my peers, I felt enough power to assert myself. Mandie and I began blabbing on about the families we worked for. I pressed the girls in the group to stand up for themselves and continued on my tirade when the group leader stood up and abruptly interrupted me. She said that Mandie and I had highly unusual and unlikely jobs, not the type of situations the other girls had to manage. It wasn't normal for anyone to be making as much money as we were, and certainly not to be working for such employers. This group was for the "average" nanny, not for the likes of us. So much for the support group.

This was the tenth time I'd considered calling home for advice from Carolyn and Linda, but I realized it would be too embarrassing, given the fact that I'd never even entered into a verbal agreement about my working hours and responsibilities, the very thing that they must have drilled into us a hundred times in school.

That night I was too depressed to write in my journal. I hadn't finished with my *Nanny Newsletter*, so after I locked myself in, I turned to the last page of the issue, which dealt with Nanny/ Family relationships. The article was apparently intended for parents to read.

This edition featured a questionnaire for parents. It was supposed to be an outline that a parent might use during a formal job evaluation, at six months and at one year of employment. I didn't foresee that ever happening in my current position, so I decided to take the inventory myself. The first category was "job performance" and the employers were supposed to give each question a value of 1 to 5.

So I decided to rate my own performance:

#1 **Does nanny limit personal errands during work hours?**
*Nanny doesn't own a bicycle, so it hasn't been a big issue.*

#2 **Does nanny offer options for handling child's behaviors when appropriate?**
*Maybe I could casually mention that Penelope Leach does not recommend to parents to reason with a three-year-old as though she's thirty. But what do I know? I'm only 19 and my entire net worth is less than $700.*

#3 **Does nanny take the initiative in planning activities for the children?**

*Yes, but then I sit alone at the table with the art projects.*

**#4 Does nanny support parent's discipline style?**

*Have not been given the "Swartz Discipline Guide" yet. But I will be very amenable to following it once I get it*

**#5 Does nanny support parent's TV restrictions?**

*Note to self: Try to figure out if there are any types of restrictions.*

The next section was my evaluation of the family regarding such things as respecting nanny's time off, supporting nanny in discipline issues and paying overtime as stated in the contract.

I thought it best not to read this evaluation model any further. I was beginning to have some very unconstructive thoughts. I had been gradually becoming more and more dissatisfied at my job, and the idea that I had 578 more days to go, was enough to make me feel like having MYSELF committed.

I rolled over to turn on my thirteen-inch black and white TV, in time to watch Robin Leach, on *Lifestyles of the Rich and Famous*, profile yet another one of our recent dinner guests.

Mandie seemed to have gotten more out of the nanny support group than I, so she returned a few more times on her own. During her second visit she met a girl she liked. After the meeting, the girl seemed a little troubled and asked Mandie if she would join her at the local IHOP for coffee. Mandie obliged, sensing the girl wanted someone to listen to her problems.

Once they were sitting in the booth, Mandie asked the girl what was troubling her. She responded by going on a five-minute jag about celebrities on TV talk shows.

"Mandie, I just hate it when I see all those holier-than-thou over-privileged stars lie in front of millions of people."

"What do you mean lie; lie about what?"

"About everything; their children, their lifestyles, their causes." Then the girl broke down sobbing into her paper napkin and Mandie realized that perhaps this poor unstable soul was mistaking Mandie for some sort of professional nanny counselor.

"What exactly are you talking about, Sheila? Are you talking about someone in particular or all celebrities in general?"

"I don't know about all of them but I do know about one for sure."

Mandie was on the edge of her seat now.

"Who? Which one? What did he or she do?"

"Mandie, I swear to you, I had to leave the house because the guy had a huge cocaine problem.

"Since I was doing some of the housework, as well as playing nanny, I would occasionally help clean the bathrooms. More often than not, there was a pile of white powder sitting on a hand mirror on the bathroom counter in the morning. When I realized, or at least guessed what it was, I used a hand vac to suck it up."

Mandie's not an entire prude; she worked to suppress a snicker at the thought of hundreds of dollars worth of drugs being vacuumed up with a Dirt Devil.

"Oh my God—did he know you did it?"

"No, and I don't care if he did know, it serves him right. At least he never said anything, probably because he had so much of it all the time. What's one small pile?"

"So who was it?"

And Sheila told her.

"No way!"

"Yes. He was my last employer."

"That squeaky clean guy? At least that's his image in the PI show."

"The very one."

"No-oo-o!"

"Yes."

"But Mandie, it wasn't just the cocaine snorting at home that got to me. It was watching him on a talk show. There he was, telling the understanding host about all the evils of drugs and how he was afraid it was going to influence his kids, living in LA, the drug capital of the U.S. Next he said he now had to move to Wyoming to keep his kids from falling prey to its evil spell, blah, blah, blah. What a crock of shit!" Sheila cried as she wiped her runny nose with a wad of napkin. "And to top it all, they won't let me see the children since I quit, they said it wouldn't be good for the kids."

After Mandie related this story over the phone, I started watching the talk shows when I could. I began to realize that I had met or knew the nannies for most of the celebrities I saw interviewed. And the mothers' descriptions of their own homemaking and childrearing prowess were vastly different from what their nannies would describe. If any of their employees ever came forward with the truth about what they **really** do behind closed doors, they'd probably need to be placed in a Nanny Witness Protection Program.

### Stress for Success

One day it occurred to me what the real reason was; why I was having a hard time adjusting to life at the Swartz'. It wasn't the long hours, or Julia's quirks. The problem was that they seemed to take everything so seriously. No one ever really laughed about every day happenings. The Swartz household basically was a stressful place, with the exception of the laughter that the office and household staff and I shared over some of the crazy things that went on around there.

One especially revealing incident that happened on the day of their wedding anniversary was an example of why our thinking was so different. That day, as was the case nearly every day, I had received many different deliveries and had numerous workers, ACT employees, and others traipsing through the house. The Swartz residence was always a buzz of activity, even when they weren't home. Late that afternoon, a delivery man showed up at the front door with a large box, about three feet wide. I signed for it, noting it was from Micheal and Jane Eisner. Aha, I thought. It must be an anniversary gift. When I started to place it on the bench in the hallway I noticed that one side was covered with a blue cellophane window. Though it was large, the box wasn't heavy so I picked it up, held it closer to the window for light and looked through the cellophane. I was startled. Grinning back at me was Mickey Mouse. Sitting next to him was Minnie. At first, I thought it was a gag gift, but the more I thought about it, how cute. And, to be honest, what else would you get two people who have everything—another crystal vase? And further, maybe it wasn't an anniversary gift at all. I put the box back down and went upstairs because I could hear Brandon waking up.

Later, Steven and Julia coincidentally came home at the same time that evening and upon arriving in the foyer Julia lit up with a big smile and said to Steven, "Honey, look. That must be our anniversary present from the Eisners." She was like a bubbly little girl who knew she was about to get a new pony. "What do you suppose it is? It's so large," she said.

"I have no idea, Julia. Why don't you open it and see." Steven said.

With that Julia tore into the box, opened the lid, reached down inside and pulled out a stuffed Mickey Mouse.

Silence. Julia looks at Steven. One eyebrow goes up slightly. He shrugs.

"I don't get it," she finally said, as she reached in again and pulled out his bride.

"Do you get it?" she asked incredulously to Steven.

"Do you get it?" she turned and asked me.

"Is this a joke?" she said to Steven, shaking Mickey by one of his ears.

Steven didn't have an answer. Neither did I, so I reached into the box and pulled out an envelope.

"Here, Mrs. Swartz. It's a card," I said, handing it to her.

> *Dear Julia and Steven,*
> *Wishing you a lovely anniversary.*
>> *With Love and Friendship,*
>> *Jane and Michael*

"That's it? Do you believe it? The Eisners have more money than God—certainly far more than we do. And what do they get us for our anniversary? Two stuffed rodents."

Another long silence.

"I'll bet they didn't even pay for them!"

That was when I left the room thinking, I doubt that Michael Eisner had to *buy* a Mickey and Minnie doll. I saw it differently. Maybe, Jane saw it as a symbol of unity that couldn't be broken, very appropriate for an anniversary, yet she could only see the monetary value.

Now, I am not saying that I grew up on the set of *Leave It to Beaver*, but my family was pretty easy-going and we found humor in a lot of things. My parents were very involved in my activities at school, and our home was the one where all the kids hung out. There were no house-keepers, cooks, nannies or chauffeurs. We did old-fashioned things like bake homemade chocolate chip cookies with my mom. We also had the family ritual of singing (and I use that term extremely loosely) Credence Clearwater Revival's "Proud Mary" as though we were the Osmonds in concert. Talk about humorous. I had a hard time imagining Steven and Julia rocking out with their kids. No wonder I felt ill-at-ease so much of the time with this family.

Julia showed her flair for organizing and managing large events at one big major event each year: at the premiere for a big studio release. These were huge, star-studded affairs and Julia worked with legions of caterers, publicists, decorators and studio executives to pull them off. I couldn't tell whether she enjoyed it, or whether she did it because Steven wanted his wife to do it. He would decide which movie he thought would be really big that year and Julia would focus her talents on that one.

Julia took obvious pride in her husband's ability to pick the hits. She explained to me about his uncanny ability to 'just know' which one to choose. I realized that she believed that he contributed more to the evening than she had in the months of work that she had invested. Steven seemed to appreciate her work, but I had never seen him show his recognition of what she had put into the event. He wasn't one to gush with personal affection.

Honest. I was NOT snooping. One day shortly after the premiere, I saw a card on top of a stack of mail on the dining room table. It was even open. The envelope next to it was marked "Personal." I admit to excessive curiosity, at times, but I would never open something with that marking. I did, however, read it. It was sent from the A.C.T. offices, addressed to Mrs. Steven Swartz.

> *Dear Julia,*
>
> *We don't get the chance to talk or see each other much. I just wanted to take this opportunity to express my gratitude for the professional and thorough job you did on the premier. It went extremely well. Your efforts in such matters are always appreciated.*
>
> > *Love,*
> > *Steven*

I almost got a little teary eyed, thinking how nice that must have been for Julia, to have him give her such a big complement. I also made a mental note to find a husband that does not work as many hours as my boss does.

## Comforting a Baby: A Beginners Course

One night, Amanda, Joshua and I became violently ill with food poisoning. Steven and Julia were out for the evening. I spent hours running to help first one kid and then the other, and then going to throw up myself. When Steven and Julia got home around eleven, we were all still up. We had awakened Brandon with all the commotion.

Julia offered to put Brandon to bed and to get up with him if he woke up, which he often did. I was so afraid of being seen as less than the perfect employee that I told her I was fine and that I would get up with him the rest of the night. She seemed truly sympathetic to the fact that I'd been heaving my guts out, and she said that if I needed her I could come get her out of bed. "I sleep on the side of the bed next to the door."

On some level I was afraid she wouldn't "do it right" and it would be confusing to Brandon to be out of his routine. I guess my sense of over-responsibility made me want to persevere even though my stomach was sore from the last hour's activities. It seemed like it would take more energy than I had, to explain to her how to heat his bottles in the night so I thanked her, excused myself and went into my own bathroom where I proceeded to dry heave for the next ten minutes.

Interestingly enough, several months later, when Julia and I were getting the kids ready for bed she said that she'd like to put Brandon to bed. I was really happy that she asked. I walked down the hall to finish getting the two older ones ready for bed.

"How do you do it?" she quietly inquired.

"How do I do what?" I replied.

"How do you put him to bed, what do you do?" she asked. I felt so sad for her. She hadn't even experienced what most moms learn to do in their sleep, literally.

"Don't worry. He's really easy, I'll heat the bottle in the warmer for you," I suggested, "then give it to him in the rocking chair." "After that, you place him in the crib face down** because he likes to sleep on his tummy,** and then you pull his favorite blanket up over him," I explained as I got the crib all ready for her. *Oh shit, does she know how to put the side rail down? I'd better put it down now so she isn't embarrassed; I'll just come back in after she leaves to put it back up.*

"Sometimes I sing him a short lullaby, before I turn out the lights." I continued.

Julia said, "Can I rock him a little after he has his bottle?"

"Yes, of course, you can rock him, he loves cuddling time."

Julia doesn't seem confident about meeting the needs of her own baby. The fact is that she could do a fine job. She just has no confidence in herself since she's given all responsibility...and joy of her baby to others. In some ways, this choice of lifestyles has left her powerless. It's sad. They have more than

---

** For all you safety monitors out there, (yes Danette, I'm talking to you) this was BEFORE they said babies needed to sleep on their backs.

enough money to live a comfortable life and spend plenty of time with their children, and yet they don't. I don't understand it.

CUT TO:

EXTERIOR — OUTSIDE OF LARGE HOME — MORNING

Very cold day, snow falling. Several inches of snow covers everything. Street is quiet, no cars are seen driving.

INTERIOR — KITCHEN OF BEAUTIFUL HOME

Frantic mother looking in the refrigerator, looking in the cupboard, looking at baby in highchair.

> MOTHER
> (yelling)

Have you got a hold of the agency yet? Hurry up, what's taking so long? What are you doing?

Husband in next room calling on telephone.

> FATHER

We need some help immediately; we'll take anyone who knows how to deal with children.

Long Pause
I know there's a blizzard, that's why I'm calling you. Our nanny can't get to the house, the roads are too bad. I need someone immediately. Neither my wife nor I know what to do. Find someone who has a 4-wheel drive and is not afraid to drive in these conditions. I'm telling you I need someone now! Well then, put me through to someone who can help me. . .Okay, I'll expect a call back in less than five minutes.

Father slams receiver down and goes into kitchen to try to help Mother. Father finds some canned soup in the cupboard.

FATHER
Here, give him some of this.

MOTHER
He can't eat that; I think he only takes a bottle.
Find some formula!

FATHER
How old is he? He's sitting up in the high chair;
doesn't that mean he's old enough to eat real food?

MOTHER
I don't know. I've only seen the Nanny give him a
bottle. I don't think she feeds him anything else yet.

Baby is wailing in the background.

FATHER
I saw her mashing a banana with a fork yesterday morning. Do you think he eats fruit? Can't you at least
call the Nanny at home and ask her these questions?

MOTHER
I already tried, she doesn't answer. She's probably just
using this storm as an excuse to have the day off.

FATHER
For God sakes, can't you find some of that formula
stuff?

MOTHER
Here's some. Do I mix it with water or milk? Does it
need to be heated?

I had been working for the Swartz' for about six months when Steven
walked into Brandon's room and stood by my side while I cared for the
baby. This was part of his daily routine: he came in the nursery nearly every
morning to kiss his youngest son and tell him goodbye. This morning he

stood there quietly for a moment. He reached toward Brandon to hold him. Brandon nuzzled into me.

Steven responded reflectively, "Do you think he knows I'm his father?"

"Well…" I paused. "Yes… I think he does know."

"I'm not sure he does," he replied, kissing Brandon.

I watched him walk down the hallway like he usually did, as fast as possible, the lower half of his body moving while the upper half remained motionless and in control. I could only imagine all the thoughts running through his head; the lists of the "important" things that he needed to accomplish that day. I felt sad standing there holding Brandon. It occurred to me that Steven barely knew his own children. He revered them as *the most important thing in his life*, and I had no doubt about that. He would do anything for them. And yet he barely laid eyes on them for more than a few minutes during a work week. And since he wasn't a part of their everyday lives, he hadn't really learned how to play with them. I mean, Steven Swartz was not the type of dad to take his kids fishing or to the batting cages. It made me so sad that he had no idea what he was missing. There were people who were hired for this kind of activity. All except the fishing; that was something that his kids probably would never experience in their entire lives.

### The King and His Court

Shortly after Steven asked whether I thought Brandon knew that he was his dad, I got the idea that I should take Brandon to Steven's office for short visits with his father. My motivation was, admittedly, partially selfish. So far I'd dismissed what I heard in nanny school, that it was important to build a social support system; now I was realizing the wisdom in that advice. I was beginning to feel like Gordon on *Sesame Street*. All I ever talked to were children and puppets. I craved some interaction with adults in the outside world. By going to the office I'd have a chance to have a little adult communication.

What a sense of freedom to just get in the car and go somewhere interesting outside of our neighborhood! I had developed a relationship with Sarah, Steven's assistant, when I vented to her on the phone… say, a few times a week. Now we would get to talk face to face. Sarah knew, perhaps more than anyone, what it was like to live with Steven because he spent most of his life in the work domain, not at home. I don't think Julia or Steven ever realized how much Sarah and I talked, or that I relied on her a great deal, especially when I got discouraged about the long hours.

Sarah was a good listener, and she once supported my feelings of frustration by saying that she and the other people who worked at the office couldn't imagine living in their house. One day she told me that she was getting a better idea of what my role was. She said that many times when Julia had called her at the office she'd refer to me as "the nanny." Sarah said she had always tried to call her on it by saying, "You mean Suzy?" Sarah said that it hadn't changed anything, and Julia continued to not call me by my name.

"She acts like I don't know who you are, or like you're not a real person."

"At least Julia admits to having a nanny," I replied. "I've met lots of girls in LA whose employers won't even admit that they have a nanny."

By going to the office, I was beginning to understand Steven much better, especially when I saw him in his real element and when I heard Sarah's stories. I already knew how important Steven's time was to him. For heaven's sakes, he had his hair cut every few weeks right in his office so he didn't have to waste time going to a salon. One day, while I was sitting in Sarah's office with Brandon, one of the guys from the mailroom, which is to say a gofer, came in and reported to Sarah that he was going on a "recon." She replied, "Gotcha."

"What's a recon?" I wondered.

Sarah leaned in toward me across her desk and lowered her voice, obviously not wanting anyone to hear. "It's shorthand for reconnoiter, like in the war movies. You know, they send out a scout to recon the area to make sure there are no enemy soldiers around."

"So what's that guy doing, checking for other agents who might be hiding downstairs waiting to snag one of ACT's clients?"

"No. He's going out to scout the best route for Steven's next appointment."

"So he can avoid any land mines that might be in his path?" I laughed.

"Yeah. You know Steven can't stand to waste time or to be late; he'd rather die. So whenever he's going on an appointment across town or within about a twenty-mile radius, he sends a gofer to check the traffic and figure out which of the various routes are fastest. Then he phones back and tells Steven to take such and such a street to whatever other street. You know, he comes up with a game plan. Sometimes I even draw up a map for Steven to take with him."

Sarah explained to me why Steven was considered so powerful in Hollywood. It had taken him a relatively short time to acquire all the "big names" in the industry. He had a multimillion-dollar client list and he was a master deal-maker. From managing his employees with his iron will, to negotiating deals with big studios, his power was like an octopus with tentacles touching everything. Virtually every employee who interacted with him had experienced his self-assured charm and they were aware of his reputation for ruthlessness when it came to the people that tried to get in his way. He drove himself fiercely, and he drove his staff just as hard. He demanded nothing less than perfection from his employees, and the staff was driven to meet his expectations. Despite the stress, the ACT staff was amazingly loyal. They were on a championship team, and Steven was calling all the shots. They were the powerhouse in town, and they were intimidating.

But there was a down side to the company's culture. Sarah told me about the time her childhood friend's father had died unexpectedly. Just after she heard the news on a Thursday afternoon, she went in and asked Steven if she could have some time off to attend the funeral on the upcoming Monday. "I told him I would probably be back in the office by noon. I knew he wouldn't be pleased by the request. After all, Monday is traditionally our busiest day."

I was as usual, naively shocked (sometimes in Cottage Grove they would close businesses for the afternoon so the owners could attend a memorial service) "You're kidding! This was for a funeral."

She continued to recount the conversation to me. He had said, "Sarah, I can't believe you'd leave me on a Monday." He delivered this with a look of grave disappointment. That was how their conversation and the subject of her being gone for several hours on a Monday, had ended.

"If you're surprised by that," she said, responding to my dismay, "wait until you hear about Karen's request for time off. She's one of the most important people in this building. She does the payroll for the entire company every two weeks. Three months ago, she was due to give birth. She came to me and asked for my advice on how she should approach him about her upcoming maternity leave. She wanted to know how she could continue to do payroll from her home. I joked, 'Leave time? You'll be lucky to get out of the office on the afternoon you deliver.' Only problem was, that prophecy turned out to be true."

"You're kidding! What happened?" I was bouncing Brandon on my lap while I listened to this recounting of his father's family-friendly policies.

"Steven is very big on not wanting anyone to know how much money anyone else in the agency makes. It's a secret that's guarded as closely as the envelopes from Price-Waterhouse on Oscar night. Karen is probably the only person besides the CFO who does know, and I'm sure Steven had her sign a forty-page non-disclosure agreement in blood.

"At any rate, as it turns out she was going to go into the hospital to be induced on a Saturday night, and with any luck, she hoped to deliver on Sunday, which is what Steven was planning. I told him that Karen was certainly not going to feel up to coming into the office on Monday. I said that she'd probably be out for at least three weeks, maybe more."

"So what did he do?"

"He had me send a computer, printer and all the accounting ledgers to her house. He said she could do the payroll from there. She was happy with the arrangement because she could spend more time at home with her new baby.

"He was probably too afraid to have anyone else do it," she commented. "If he could have handled it himself and taken Karen out of the equation, he probably would have."

CUT TO:

HOSPITAL — BUSY MATERNITY UNIT — LATE AFTERNOON

                    FIRST NURSE
Can you believe what's going on in room 322?
                    SECOND NURSE
I've never seen anything like it in my thirty years as
a nurse. Did you see the machine in there? Three
delivery guys had to bring it in.

                    FIRST NURSE
Yeah, and what was with the duct tape?

Couple in their fifties are seated holding hands outside room 322. The nurse exiting the room is stopped
abruptly by the woman.

WOMAN

Nurse, how much longer is it going to be? We've been waiting here for eight hours. I'm getting worried about my daughter.

MAN
(Interrupts woman)
Where's the doctor? When's he going to be here?

NURSE

Takes a long breath and wipes the sweat from her brow.

Your daughter insisted on having some sort of computer delivered to her room so that she could finish processing the payroll for her employer. She was dilated to ten centimeters an hour ago. Then her husband came in with a roll of duct tape and wrapped it around her knees. He said not to remove the tape until she's done with her accounting entries. The strange part is she asked him to do this! I'm going to call for a psychiatric consult. Maybe the two of you could go in there and talk some sense into her.

Man and woman stand up. Nurse looks perplexed. Man puts his arm around his wife, not replying to the nurse.

MAN

Come on, Donna, let's go to the cafeteria and get some dinner. I'm really hungry.

WOMAN

Yes, Melvin, that sounds like a good idea. Looks as if it's going to be awhile. Now, why didn't that nurse have the common courtesy to inform us hours ago that Karen was working on the payroll? We could've slept in this morning. Evidently this nurse doesn't understand who our daughter's boss is.

## Parenting Advice

One night after Brandon and Amanda had been visited by an attack of sibling rivalry at the dinner table and were safely out of the room, Steven and Julia started discussing their kids' behavior while I helped Concetta clear the dishes. Julia began the discussion, and then Steven expressed his thoughts. Then he asked me why I thought Joshua was so often unruly and prone to outbursts. I added my two-cents worth. Apparently, my thoughts had given rise to something he hadn't considered before. Julia started to say something in response. He stopped, put down his wine and told her very coldly to shut up. That was the first time I'd witnessed this kind of thing. I was embarrassed for Julia and for him. He continued, "Suzy, would you go on? I wanted to hear what you had to say." My first thought about the future consequences was: *Oh great. This is really gonna help my relationship with Julia.*

Whoa. Can't believe that Steven was so rude to Julia tonight. On the other hand, it was nice to be treated like somebody with a valuable opinion, for once. But was it ever awkward!

Did we ever have a lecture in nanny school about what to do when the parents don't seem to like each other all that much.

Special note: Call NNI and encourage them to start teaching Family Dynamics 301-302, whatever it takes.

# Fame, Food and Freedom

When I hired on with the Swartz, I had made it clear that I needed to go home in June for a three-day weekend to attend my Uncle Clare's birthday party. I had been looking forward to getting back to the land of sanity for some time. I needed a vacation from my day-to-day responsibility with the Swartz', but I also needed a break from the whole scene. So it was with relief that I headed back for a long weekend away from the land of the stars. A chance to get away from all the craziness for a few days!

In truth I had no luck at being home alone for even a few minutes, once I got there. From the moment I stepped into my parent's car at the airport until the time I left three days later, my so-called vacation was spent relating stories and answering the never-ending question: "What are they like?" That's all anyone wanted to know, along with the occasional inquiry about me: "How does it feel to be a nanny for the stars?"

Technically, I had to explain, I'm not a nanny for the stars. Steven and Julia weren't actors, and anyone outside of Hollywood who didn't subscribe to *The Hollywood Reporter* didn't know his name. So, I always explained, my employer was the guy who was important to the people *we* think are important. Since my letters and phone calls home had included my experiences with the likes of Barbra Streisand, I guess I shouldn't have been surprised by their curiosity. Even my best friends couldn't believe that I had actually visited on the phone with John

Travolta. Star power seemed magnified by distance, and here in my hometown, stars were glorified by peoples' imaginations.

By the third day of my visit, I was growing weary of answering questions. It seemed like it might be easier to go back to work in Tinsel Town than to tell one more story. But one of the guidance counselors at my high school had asked me to come in and speak to the students on Career Day while I was home. I felt I owed her. Besides, I've never been one to pass up an audience or a chance to talk.

Mrs. Pittman's typing room was packed with girls wanting to hear all about the 'Hollywood Nanny' or rather, the people she'd met. Their big question was the same: *What are they like?* I wanted to explain to them the reality of my life, but I didn't want to admit publicly that I might have made a big mistake or reveal how demeaning my job really was. I knew in their eyes that it was exciting to have rubbed elbows with the legends, so that was what I talked about. Once I got started, I couldn't stop.

I told them how quirky the family was regarding money, how it was difficult to get them to buy new clothes for the baby, while vacations on private jets was as common as changing socks. I recounted how little things that are everyday occurrences in average households, like losing a Barbie doll's shoe, were cause for uproar and accusations. I told them stories about dinner guests, screenings, parties and famous faces. I was beginning to feel a bit like a star myself, laying claim to my proverbial fifteen minutes of fame. This went much better than my previous attempt at stardom, when I lied to my fourth grade class and told them that I was Jan Brady's sister in *real life.*

After I was done answering the questions, a reporter from the local paper was waiting to interview me. They ran a story about my experiences and there was even a picture of me in *The Cottage Grove Sentinel.* Of course, I hated the picture. It looked like I was looking off into a far away galaxy contemplating the meaning of nannyhood. Fame is funny. The position that equated with servitude, neglect and even contempt in Hollywood had made me a hometown star. On the way back I had enough time and perspective to start thinking about one of the more persistent questions that had been plaguing me since I took the job.

*Why don't people with a great deal of money realize that their wealth is providing them with so many choices in life?* I see their abundance of resources allowing them to be able to spend MORE time with their family, not less. I grew up, with many of my friend's parents, constantly being limited by a work schedule that provided income for the necessities of life. They would have given anything, to never miss a little league game or be able to volunteer each week in their child's classroom. *I don't get it!*

When I got back to LA, I discovered that I had been in trouble without even being there. Apparently the day I left, Gymboree's schedule had changed to the spring schedule, and Brandon's class had been moved up an hour. During the time period that our class had met, the older children, or "walkers" were now meeting. Grandma Swartz had shown up early and found herself surrounded by older children, and she was livid. Concetta and Maria said she and Julia couldn't stop talking about me while I was away. I thought maybe it embarrassed her to be in the wrong place at the wrong time. I was at least as frustrated with them as they were with me. *How hard could it have been to play with him on the floor at the gym? What in the world would this family ever do if they ever had a real problem?*

## Planes Trains and My Own Automobile

Finally I was about to get more independence from the Swartz'. I had saved enough money for a down payment on a car of my own and I'd been researching the purchase for a while. I had decided on a brand new Celica. When I mentioned my plan to Steven, he surprised me by offering to help. He had his CFO at ACT call a dealership in Marina Del Rey for me to negotiate a contract. When I went to pick it up, the salesman complained to me that he wasn't making any money because some big shot had bullied him into selling the car at cost. I felt sorry for him, but I was also thrilled to be able to afford my first new car. Now I owned my own set of wheels—I was a real Los Angelino. Life was going to be a whole lot more fun now. And Steven had helped me out, and I was very grateful to him.

I hadn't heard from Mandie since I'd been back, and so I called to tell her that we now had transportation. Mandie's inconsistent transportation until now had been limited to the '79 Ford Escort station wagon that the Goldberg's let her drive once in a while, on her days off. We were both still boggled by the fact that these people let their employees drive their children around in automobiles that weren't exactly the highest-rated in safety crash tests.

Mandie got excited when I started talking about how cool we'd be tooling around LA in my new car. Then she said that she'd been saving a car story of her own for me. The weekend before, Mr. Goldberg had ended up with three cars at the beach house, so he had asked her if she would bring the Porsche home.

"I felt like asking him if he was feeling all right. I didn't want to tell him that it's been a couple of years since I'd even driven a stick shift. But I figured it out after a couple of false starts, lunges and squealing tires. There I was sailing down Pacific Coast Highway!"

"You had the convertible? Way cool!"

"Well yeah except I couldn't figure out how to work the roof thingy. It was hot as Hades and I wanted to put the top down and let my hair blow in the wind. But I was worried that he'd be able to tell that I had opened the roof. I pulled into a gas station and tried to figure out where the button was for the top. I poked around at things for a few minutes, but I was kind of scared that I'd screw something up. I figured I'd just settle for rolling the windows down, but I couldn't find them *or* the air conditioning buttons. And I was scared to just start pushing random buttons, not knowing what havoc I might cause. I was dripping wet by the time I got back. I'd been sitting in a mobile sauna for an hour." She paused. "And then I worried I might be screwing up the leather upholstery with my sweat."

I laughed. "Was it fast?"

She snorted. "Like hay flying through a baler." *You can take the girl out of the country...but you can't take...*

I laughed again. This girl was obviously still pumped up.

"I got it up to seventy, but then I got scared and slowed back down to the speed limit. But that's not the whole story. As usual there was a fiasco at the end."

"Oh my God, you didn't crash it, did you?"

"No, thank God. When I got to the house, I realized that Mr. Goldberg didn't have a house key on the Porsche ring."

"Oh, no! Whatdja do then?"

"The Goldbergs weren't going to be home until Sunday and I wasn't about to call back to the beach house to say I had no house key. Mrs. Goldberg would have had a fit and fallen in it because of MY irresponsibility. Then I remembered that Graciella, the housekeeper, had a complete set of keys. So I decided to go to her house and get them. Unfortunately, Graciella lives in a pretty seedy part of town, which I wasn't thrilled about exploring," she added.

"Sounds like the place I went to when I got my nails done," I commented.

"Yeah, only worse, this place was Gang Central as far as I could tell. Everywhere I looked there were bars on the windows and very scary-looking people around. I mean it was spooky."

"Like one of those ghettos you see on TV?" I asked.

"Worse, at least for me, it's like nothing in Montana. At any rate, I'm there, at Graciella's, but of course I don't want to get out of the car. There is no way I'm going to leave Mr. Goldberg's car parked on Pico, particularly since I didn't know how to use the keyless lock."

"Good decision. So whadja you do?"

"I sat below Graciella's window, lying on the horn. She probably thought it was just one more car alarm going off in the neighborhood. But finally she did poke her head out of the window and I yell to her that I need the Goldberg's key."

"What did she say?"

"She doesn't speak very good English and my Spanish still consists entirely of food dishes, so it took a while to sort it out. We finally settled on going down the street to a place that makes duplicate keys and duplicate drivers' licenses probably, too. When she points out the place, I know I'm in trouble because I can't parallel park, so I slow down to a crawl and Graciella kind of rolls out of the car. I tell her I'll circle the block until she's made the key, which is what I did. I drove around twelve times before she showed up on the curb again. I'm positive that the police officer on the corner thought I was a drug dealer looking for a sale."

Mandie sighed, and I could almost hear the smile in her voice. "God, what an afternoon, but what a car!"

## Wolfgang Puck is Steaming

One Saturday shortly after I got my car, Mr. Swartz asked me to do him a favor. He wanted me to go down to Spago and pick up some lox that they had special-ordered. I never had anything to do on the weekend anyway, so I didn't mind going. Spago isn't exactly a carryout place. In fact, I don't think they prepared orders to go for anyone. Wolfgang was doing him a special favor. I felt like when I was sixteen and first got my drivers license; I kept asking mom if she needed anything at the store, so I could test out my driving skills.

I took Amanda with me, and we got a parking spot near the front of the restaurant where there were two huge glass entry doors. Amanda and

I walked up and pushed on the door, but it was locked. *That's odd; it's the middle of the afternoon. Why would they be closed?*

The sun reflected off the doors so brightly that it was difficult to see inside. I cupped my hands around the sides of my head and pushed my nose on the glass trying to get a peek.

"Are they closed, Suzy?" Amanda asked.

"I don't know. I don't think so. There are people running around in there. I can see Wolfgang. Maybe they're doing a private party or something," I answered.

I pounded on the door to get their attention. Nothing. Perhaps they hadn't heard me. I pounded much harder the second time and then pushed my face back up to the glass. Inside there were several chefs dressed in their white outfits, glaring at me with their fingers up to their lips as if to shush me. *Don't shush me. What in the hell's going on?*

Now I was starting to get irritated. I decided that more drastic measures were needed. So I took off my loafer and used the heel to pound on the door repeatedly. Then I peered back in. This time men were gesturing with sweeping motions of their hands and arms as if to say, "Go away, little girl, we're closed." *Damn it, why aren't they opening the door for me?*

*Don't they know I'm Steven Swartz's nanny?*

*Bang, bang, bang* I pounded again and now Amanda had joined in. We were making one big ruckus. That's when I saw Wolfgang approaching full steam ahead. I could clearly see he was not happy. His lips were pursed tightly together, eyebrows pulled down toward his nose, hands on hips...

"Just what in the hell do you think you're doing?" he yelled at me through the still-locked doors.

I smiled weakly. "Mr. Puck, I'm picking up some lox for Steven Swartz," I said.

I don't think he heard a word I said. "Get the hell out of here. We are filming a television commercial. You're costing me money! Go away," he yelled as he shooed me with his hands and stormed back to the kitchen.

One of the members of the crew who felt sorry for me ran over to the door and asked what I needed. I told him I was supposed to pick up salmon and he told me to try around back where all the staff was taking a break. Amanda and I walked back behind the dumpsters and found the employees outside, sitting at tables. They kindly gave us our salmon, and we were on our way.

I embarrassed myself at Spago today, which is not a big deal. I'm getting used to being embarrassed. But what's far worse is I acted just like the kind of person I'm starting to despise: a coattail-riding, "don't you know who you're dealing with" Hollywood bore.

## Movin' and Shakin' up Hollywood

The sound began as some far-off locomotive that seemed to gain speed and intensity as it rumbled closer and closer, louder and louder. *Jeezuzzz, what in the world is that?* I took the bottle from Brandon's mouth, beginning to feel apprehensive. Then suddenly the entire house seemed as if it had been lifted by a tidal wave that was rolling underneath the foundation. I panicked and sat bolt upright, then I jogged downstairs with Brandon on my hip.

"Maria, Maria," I screamed. "What in the hell is going on?"

I couldn't find her or Concetta. Then, as I stood in the doorway of the kitchen and looked out into the family room the walls seemed to converge and twist as if they were made of tag board that some giant was playing with in his enormous hands. I heard Julia yell, "It's an earthquake, everyone under the desk!"

I could feel myself hyperventilating. I'd never felt so scared before. I crawled under the desk first, with Brandon in my arms, and then Amanda and Joshua huddled in after me. Julia was crouched on the outside, not really covered by anything. My first thought while all the commotion was happening was that I should be on the outside, since I was the hired help, and the family should be under the built-in heavy desk. I felt very guilty that I was in a safer spot than Julia.

Five seconds after the earthquake ended I heard the front door open. It had to be Steven coming up from the workout room. I could hear his footsteps and the door shut. I could hear him yell to us from the foyer.

"Did you guys feel that?" he yelled from the hallway.

"Yes of course!" Julia yelled back. The inflection in her voice implied, *Duh, obviously we did.*

We started piling out from under the desk. Steven still hadn't come into the room. I was surprised until I realized that the earthquake really wasn't big enough to injure us. I knew Steven thought there was the possibility that it might have damaged some of his smaller sculptures. So he was checking on the artwork before looking in on his family.

I'd never been in an earthquake before. Thunderstorms, yes. Lots of them. But this was a totally different experience. At the time, it felt like a train with a hundred freight cars had rumbled through the house, when in fact the whole thing lasted less than a minute. I wanted to run outside, not knowing if it was going to come back or not. I had read there were aftershocks, sometimes for weeks. I didn't know whether to sit, lie down or stand and brace myself against something. No one else really seemed that shaken up. I found Maria and she seemed unfazed and asked where we had gathered during the commotion. I told her I was scared to death and she said, "Oh Soo-zita. Ease no beeg ting. We geet dem all dee time."

## Picasso at Risk

Maria, Concetta and I had dinner together one night in the kitchen, as we liked to, sitting at the end of the enormous marble-topped center island. After we ate and I put the children to bed, I went into the family room for a rare moment of quiet and reading. I was determined to learn at least a little about this art that was all around me. Before now, my forays into visual art had consisted of attending the Country Fair each year outside of Eugene to see what crazy outfits the hippies had on, if indeed they were wearing anything at all. So I was trying to understand at least a little more about Steven's art collection.

Steven had told me when I was interviewing that he had one of the most extensive private art collections in California, and I didn't doubt for a moment I was living in an art museum: the living room and formal dining areas were all like galleries, enormous shrines to the art. There were lots of abstract paintings, which I studied; twisting my head at different angles, hoping to find something in them: a dog, a vase, a tree, anything recognizable.

I had seen several of Picasso's paintings in one of the art books Steven kept on the table in the living room. I made myself comfortable in a large chair and began to thumb through the book when the page fell open to what looked like the very same painting that was hanging in the living room. I couldn't believe it. This silly looking picture could cost millions of dollars!

The next morning, the construction foreman came in to ask if he could use the phone. There seemed to be an endless supply of these workers, doing exactly what, I never did figure out. Carl was a few years older than me and we'd become friendly. He was one of the few people there that I ever had the chance to get to know. He was working his way through college doing construction work.

After he hung up in the other room, he came back in. "Steven's art collection is really something," he said staring at the wall. He said, "Wow. That's a Picasso," pointing to the wall. "Is it a copy?"

"Certainly not," I chimed in confidently, having just boned up on the subject the night before. "No, that's the real deal," I continued, as I motioned for him to come closer. "Look, can you see that streak of paint?" I asked as I touched the canvas. Then everything broke loose. A shrill alarm sounded, like the kind you hear in the middle of the night from a car, only a hundred times louder. It was so loud Maria came running out of her room howling, waving her arms in the air, franticly, "Miss Soo-zita, it is thee Pee-casso alarm, oh my." She was running back and forth, and I still had my hands over my ears. I couldn't think.

"Miss Soo-zita, you must call Meeester Swartz."

*He'll kill me.*

I ran as far away from the sound as I could to make the call. I could barely hear the phone ringing on the other end of the line.

Silence.

*Oh my God,* I thought, *they'll never answer. They've probably got a hundred calls backed up, as usual.*

One of the ACT receptionists finally answered. "A-C-T."

She was having trouble hearing me above the still shrieking horn. She finally understood my scream: "I need Sarah in Steven's office!"

Sarah never got too riled up about anything. She calmly told me that Mr. Swartz wasn't in the office and that I should just hang up and wait for the security company to call. Apparently she'd been through this before and was familiar with the routine. She told me not to worry. It would stop after fifteen minutes and we could have the alarm company reset it. Sarah assured me she could take care of it.

As soon as I put the receiver down, the phone rang.

"Hello. The Swartz residence," I said in a loud voice.

"What's the code word?" the man said.

"Maria, come in here. What's the code word?"

"I have no ideeeuh, Miss Soo-zita, I only know thee code for thee house alarm, I don't know about thee Pee-caso"

By now the awful noise had been going for more than ten minutes and my ears were beginning to ring. Julia had told me the code word for the house alarm, in case I needed it, but Maria said this was an entirely different alarm.

"We'll notify the police ma'am," the man said.

"No, No, No!" I said. "Mr. Swartz' secretary is calling you right now to take care of this. Please, please don't send the police."

Maria and I both went out into the front yard, Brandon in tow. The alarm had really scared him, and true to form, I was already making up scenarios in which his hearing was being damaged for life. I realized as we stood by the front gate, nearly forty yards from the door, that the entire neighborhood could hear the damned thing.

I tried to avoid Steven that night and the next day at all costs, fearing for my life, but oddly enough, he never said a thing about the incident. And here I had thought his art would be the one thing that could get a rise out of him. Maybe he was distracted by his work, or maybe it was really no big deal. I could never predict.

I'm not getting any closer to figuring these guys out. I thought Steven would be really steamed about me setting off the alarm today, but so far nothing. Some things that seem petty to me can be cause for great distress in the house and the issues that seem huge to me don't seem to even hit the radar. Then again, maybe Sarah didn't tell him.

## Moving Violations, Part 2

It was announced that we were getting a new vehicle, a replacement for the Jeep Wagoneer. On the day of the new SUV's arrival, One of Steven's assistants, Jason, called me from the freeway on the way to the house in the new vehicle.

"You're not going to believe this, Suzy. It's a friggin' tank. Whoa! Watch out. I think I might have sideswiped a semi with the mirrors. This thing is as wide as a motor home, I swear. They don't expect you to drive this monster, do they?"

"Uh yeah, they do. I have told Julia I am kind of worried about it. How about you stickin' up for me and saying it's probably too much of a vehicle for the poor little nanny to drive?" I teased.

"This thing is too much for me to drive. Ok I'll do what I can for you. I'll be there in about fifteen. Open the gates so I can get this 18 wheeler on through!" he laughed.

Even though it was a good idea for me to have a safer car to drive with the kids, I had been dreading the arrival of the behemoth. Brentwood's streets were narrow and there were always cars parked on either side, with the ever-present fleet of construction workers. It was a winding maze. Julia took me out immediately for a test drive, "to help me feel more comfortable driving it." She kept saying how eeaasssyyyyy.... it was to drive.

I didn't doubt this, it was a flipping' automatic after all. Driving it wasn't the problem, for heaven's sakes, I had been driving since my Uncle Tubby took me out to the hayfields when I was six and let me drive the flatbed while he threw in the bales of hay. I drove my dad's '74 Ford pickup all the time, in high school. The old beater was so hard to get into second gear that I used to challenge my guy friends that they couldn't do it. They didn't believe that I, *a mere girl*, could drive a manual transmission better than them. I always won the bet and we'd end up laughing hysterically as they ground the gears, over and over. Finally I'd have to scoot over into the driver's seat and get it into second gear for the poor boys.

So the issue was not the mechanics of it. It was the SIZE of the thing, especially relative to the narrowness of the streets in the neighborhood. When we went out for my auto lesson in the new shiny Suburban, I felt like I was riding with my grandpa, who actually was a high school driver's Ed teacher for more than a hundred years. With Julia in the passenger's seat as we left on our driving excursion, I couldn't help imagining that she wished she had a brake on her side of the car; like they did when my mother was in school and was learning to drive.

Julia told me, "If you're so nervous about driving this, you should have both hands on the wheel."

*Allrighty then—10 and 2... 10 and 2. We're gonna get through this lesson.*

A few weeks after the monstrosity arrived, I was driving home and right in front of OJ's house I heard this loud, scraping sound.

Amanda seemed alarmed. "Suzy what was that noise?"

"Oh probably a dump truck unloading some gravel honey, don't worry about it," I looked in my mirror just in time to see an old work truck rocking back and forth. *Oh my God—did I just sideswipe that pick-up? I had to of; why else would it be moving.*

I began to perspire as I imagined the huge scrape down the side of the brand new vehicle. I pulled into the driveway, parked and jumped out as fast as I could. When I checked it out, all I saw was minimal damage to the mirror. I guessed that I had grazed the truck with the mirror.

I immediately ran inside and begged Maria and Concetta for help. They found me a rag to buff up the chrome on the mirror. It hardly showed, and I don't think anyone ever noticed it. I never even thought of being arrested for a hit-and-run, leaving the scene of an accident, or whatever it was called, until years later when I was telling someone the story. At the time I was so caught up in how I was going to tell Steven that I had just damaged his new vehicle, that a citation for fleeing the scene of an accident didn't even enter my mind.

Yours truly came too close for comfort today (literally). God. I'm afraid Steven's going to find out. He notices everything. Just yesterday Julia told me that he never makes mistakes, and that's why he has no tolerance for incompetence. It is not looking good for me.

I wonder if I'll ever have more than one week running without some kind of calamity.

Calamity Nanny. That wouldn't sound too good on a resume.

Note to self: Call Mandie and hear her latest story, and hope she did something worse, so that I feel better about my situation.

# Fireworks
# and Pacifiers

July seemed like the party month, if they were not going to one, they were having one. Unfortunately, the first party of the month turned out to be a bit of an unexpected fiasco. They had invited a group of people over for a big dinner party. For Julia, this afternoon was nothing short of cataclysmic. There was no particular occasion to celebrate, but I could see by Julia's behavior that this was still important. The guest list was packed with attendees at the last Academy Awards Ceremony, of course.

The guest list included:

>Sally Field and Alan Greisman
>Barry and Dianna Levinson
>Luanne and Frank Wells
>Marvin and Barbara Davis
>Christina Ferrari and Tony Thomopolus
>Aaron and Candy Spelling

The guests were scheduled to begin arriving around five. It was about one o'clock when Julia came home and asked me, "Where are the caterers?" She quickly asked the same of Maria and of course neither of us had a clue, besides it seemed a little early to me—guests wouldn't be showing up for at least another four hours. When two o'clock rolled around, she was shifting into full panic mode and at that point I did begin to think something was wrong.

Julia was running in circles, "Oh my God, where are the damned caterers?" she kept saying. Then she picked up the phone and called Steven at the office and chattered at him. And of course he had no answer either, but was just about to leave the office. He told her he'd be home shortly.

"This is a nightmare!" she kept saying as she dialed the caterers—

They had indeed had the wrong day written down. I won't bore you with the tirade Julia went on to the owner of the catering company. But she ended the call with "You can bet Steven will never ever let me use you as a caterer ever again."

"Suzy, we've got to do something. This is the biggest nightmare of my life. This can't be happening. Everyone is going to be here in less than two hours! Steven is going to kill me."

As Julia ran from room to room, Amanda kept yelling, "Mommy's having a nightmare. Mommy's having a nightmare."

I would have loved to save the day, but I knew my hamburger casserole from nanny school was not an option, so there wasn't much I could do. I called Sarah at the office since I knew she would have heard from Steven about the fiasco, to see if she had any ideas. She said that Steven had called Spago to see if there was any way they could help out. Sarah said she would call me right back.

"Oh God Suzy. No one is going to want to – much less be able to – come up here on an hours notice and feed this many people. This is a nightmare, my worst possible nightmare come true. Do you know I've actually had this dream several times?" she asked into the air. "We are going to be taking a lot of people out for dinner with no reservations" she said to me.

The phone rang, I quickly answered, and it was Sarah. She was so excited. Lo and behold, Wolfgang said he would send his people right out. I couldn't believe it. He was actually going to do it. Within the hour guests started arriving. Aaron Spelling and his wife were first. She was a true "Barbie Doll" kiss the air type. She was always saying, "Darling" as she greeted people and then pretended to start to kiss them, but would never really get any closer than about six inches from their cheeks. All you could hear was a smacking sound wafting by their ears. At any rate, shortly after the first guests arrived, Puck's people showed up in a large Mercedes followed by a huge enclosed truck. Five people jumped out of the Mercedes and two men leaped out of the truck, jammed a ramp in the back end and began to unload carts and trays and containers filled with food. God knows where they got it all on such short notice. They certainly didn't have time to cook anything. Never the less, there it was, a full compliment of hors d'oeuvres, salmon, grilled vegetables, you name it, all sizzling hot and ready to go. Maria and Julia had managed to keep the guests happy with Champagne and wine and I don't think anyone ever realized the "nightmare" Julia had gone through just two hours before— saved by the Puck.

CUT TO:

INTERIOR — RESTAURANT — NIGHT

Camera pans dining room. Harrison Ford is seated alone in one booth. Camera goes left to the next booth where a party of four is seated including David Geffen and a male companion. At the final booth sits Steven Spielberg and Kate Capshaw. Camera comes in close on Steven who has a menu in hand.

     WAITER
Mr. Spielberg. What would you like this evening?

     SPIELBERG
I'm starved. I'll have the Clam Linguini with white wine sauce please.

     WAITER
Oh, I'm sorry. We're all out of Clams. Is there something else you would like instead?

     SPIELBERG
I had my heart set on the Clam Linguini. Okay, then let me have the Veal Piccata with angel hair pasta.

     WAITER
Uh, I'm sorry Sir. Actually, we're all out of angel hair pasta as well.

     SPIELBERG
What? How can you be out of pasta? That isn't possible.

WAITER
Well, to be honest Mr. Speilberg, we don't have much
of anything right now. Some guy in Brentwood had an
emergency catering job and they took everything
Wolfgang had. We do have some Spumoni left however, if
you'd like some dessert?

The next event on their social calendar was the first time I was asked to go with them to a dinner party in the evening. Normally they didn't take the children to evening functions. I overheard them telling Joshua that we were going to Superman's house. Of course I was visualizing Christopher Reeve, who I think is a doll, and I was excited to go. It turned out this Superman wasn't Mr. Reeve. The party was at the home of Richard Donner, who directed the film, and his wife Lauren Shuler-Donner. Too bad.

I was invited because I was chauffeuring the children: Steven and Julia drove in the Jaguar, and I followed behind in Julia's Mercedes. They wanted the older kids to come for a short visit to the house and then be taken back home when dinner was served. Once again I faced the wardrobe dilemma: what the hell was I supposed to wear, the ole cocktail dress and heels? Not too practical while chasing my little charges around the house. I settled for my usual pauper-wear, my nanny costume of jeans and a shirt.

At about seven, we arrived at an enormous estate, surrounded by twenty-foot-tall black iron gates with extremely sharp points on the tips of each spear-like pole. The home must have been at least 25,000 square feet. It looked like a three-story castle. All the way there, I had clipped along behind the speeding Jaguar, like Samuel Jackson and John Travolta tailing Harvey Keitel in *Pulp Fiction.*

I had no idea how to find the house on my own. What if I lost them? As I followed along, my stress had increased with each mile. As we approached the valets' tent, which was set up under an immense porte-cochere, a couple of things caught my eye: the valets' ersatz Buckingham Palace uniforms—we're talking red velvet, gold braid and epaulets—with the two gargantuan guard dogs just inside the gate. These people were taking the castle thing a mite too seriously.

They were the scariest looking dogs I'd ever seen, and they were unrestrained. It seemed to me that thick chains and padlocks would be in order. Admittedly, I am not a dog-person, as evidenced by my run-in with the Rat Dog. Somehow every dog I come in contact with seems to know it. I can't count the number of times pet owners have told me "ole Tuffy would never hurt a flea" and then the thing turns seriously mean and snarly with me.

However, not even little Amanda seemed perturbed by the vicious guard-beasts. These dogs were so dangerous they each had their own "handler." All of the guests in front of me passed without eliciting even a doggie blink. Maybe these canines are actually made out of concrete, I wished, as I got closer and closer. Maybe they're just elaborate special effects. I was adjacent to them when they began to snap like fasting crocodiles—at me, of course, only at me. I thought my life was over in that moment. I sprang three feet into the air and crossed the front door threshold like an Olympic long jumper.

Thought I was a goner tonight when those two huge monsters decided they wanted to make me into a midnight snack. I was totally terrified, and I had to wait until one of the caterers would come out with me to take the kids to the car. I about peed my pants running the gauntlet back to the safety of the vehicle.

When I told animal-lover Mandie about it, she said that they must have sensed my fear. I told her I thought they were trained to sniff out my less than millionaire status.

### Independence Day

The Fourth of July was a huge event for the elite community of Malibu. Every year, one of Steven and Julia's good friends, put on a real shindig. It included a spectacular fireworks display, even bigger than the one they put on every year at our local Riverside Auto Racing Speedway, if you can believe that. Of course, this would be my first experience at the annual event. The location of the big event was about seven doors down from the Swartz's Malibu place. I knew Mandie was coming with the Goldbergs, so I was looking forward to seeing her.

Down on the beach where the grass meets the sand, there were several very large, unhappy-looking men in suits standing guard. Perhaps fifty foldout lounge chairs were all lined up neatly facing the ocean. Tons of people were gathered at an enormous buffet of amazing food. I told Julia that Joshua and Amanda wanted to go down with the other kids to the sand. I asked her if she could hold Brandon while I took the older ones to the beach area. She said yes, and she took Brandon from me, who was cooing very cutely and being fussed over by all of the guests.

There was music playing, and I played tag with the kids and a whole group of other children. I was having fun for the first time in quite a while. Then I decided to take the kids up to the buffet. At that point, I'd been on the beach for less than 30 minutes. On the way up to the food, I passed Mandie coming down.

"Where have you been? I couldn't find you," I told her.

"Oops. Big trouble," she chopped out. "Mrs. S is looking for you and she has mean in one eye and angry in the other."

"Now what did I do?" I say. "Oh, God. Would you stay here with the kids and get them something to eat? I'll go see what she's so upset about."

Julia was in a lather. "Where have you been? I've been looking all over for you. We were frantic," she snapped.

"What's the matter? Is Brandon okay?" I said the first thing that came to mind.

"I couldn't find his pacifier. Where did you put it?" she bleated. "He was getting all fussy."

"It was in his pocket when we got here. That's where I always put it," I said.

"Well, we couldn't find it. Steven and I searched all over the damned place and then I had to send him all the way back to the house! Steven's going to leave Brandon with Maria. You need to go back up there and help her take care of him right away," she directed me.

*I can see that this really put you out. I am so sorry this "crisis" has been so upsetting to you. I wasn't sitting in a lounge chair sipping margaritas. I was entertaining your two children. I feel so badly for contributing to your "hired help" woes— why don't you just rename me Slacker Nanny?*

And what did I say?

"Oh, I'm so sorry; I'll walk back to the house."

*Wimp!*

I wanted Julia, for just one minute, to see how things looked from my point of view. I don't think she ever realized that I grew up attending parties at our local Elks club! As you can imagine, this was *not* an establishment where it was routine to observe:

—Cheryl Tiegs, wolfing down two hot dogs like she hadn't eaten in a couple of days. By the looks of her, maybe it might have been weeks since her last meal.

—Kenny Rogers walking around and *not* singing. I'd never considered that he'd be a normally functioning person who didn't sing unless the occasion called for it. I was sitting next to him, just waiting for him to break into "I met up with a Gambler...." Apparently his preferred mode of communication *is* just plain talking.

—A slightly blitzed Goldie Hawn who tripped over me; apologized very sweetly and included me in her conversation with Ali McGraw about how a baby is such a little miracle.

—Sydney Pollack, the guy from Tootsie. I still had a disturbing image stuck in my brain of seeing him a little earlier in the day at the beach house, dressed in nothing but a purple Speedo. I was having a hard time getting *that* picture out of my mind.

—Ed McMahon was talking to me and mentioned *nothing* about the Publisher's Clearing House Sweepstakes and me becoming a millionaire. I was just coming to grips with the fact that my one and only chance for the prize patrol to stop by my house had just faded away.

—Not to mention Sylvester Stallone, walking around with prominent bags under his eyes, demonstrating unarguable proof of the expertise of make-up and lighting artists on movie sets.

—Also, the curious spectacle of the afore mentioned Sly Stallone surrounded by security guards, who appear to have heat exhaustion because they are in full suits in this weather. What possible peril does he fear in this social arena with fellow celebrities? Evidently he does not want to take any chances with some pesky autograph seekers. Plus the guy's short. *What's up with that?*

After the pacifier scene, I was banished back to the house. Mandie stayed with all the rest to watch the show. When I finally got to the house Maria was standing on the deck and Brandon was asleep. She and I watched as the shower of lights lit up the sky.

## Hit Me with Your Best Shot

The next week when we went to the Malibu house, I had better luck. The best part about going to the beach house was that I was able to sleep in a separate guest house. It was so nice to be away from everyone, in my own space. Either Maria or Concetta would always come with us. Wonderful friends that they were, they always offered to get up with Brandon so I could sleep through the night.

The room was big and open, with hardwood floors and a lot of art. Even if I didn't get to go there until very late in the evening, just the thought of having my own space AWAY from the group made the trip better. I'd usually set my alarm so I'd get up early in the morning to return to the house for the rest of the day.

After we had arrived, unpacked and settled in I took the children out on the deck, which overlooked a pristine beach. All the homes on Celebrity Row, as I called it, were tightly packed together. The balcony of the house next door was only about ten feet away. I noticed a young woman standing there, staring at the ocean. Then a sweet little toddler came out and said, "Mommy." The woman looked familiar, but I couldn't figure out who she reminded me of. Amanda said something to the little girl, and then the mom and I struck up a conversation that continued as we all gathered up towels and walked down to the ocean.

While the children played at the edge of the water, we sat and talked about raising children. She was toothpick-thin, with very narrow hips. In fact, she had the slightest build I had ever seen on an adult woman. She looked to be about 5 feet tall. About halfway through our conversation I finally figured out who she reminded me of, in fact who she probably was. That was right about the time that Julia began yelling for me to bring the children back to the house. I was disappointed that our conversation had been cut so short because I really enjoyed talking to her. She was one of the few people I met in LA that seemed what I called genuine.

That night I called four of my girlfriends back home and told them I had just spent the morning on the beach with Ms. "Hell is for Children" herself, Pat Benetar. And to this day, I still don't get what that title means; it seems like a disturbing song title. It's hard to believe that sweet mother sang that song.

## A Hug From Bill Murray

I was alone at the beach house with the kids the next afternoon and the phone rang.

"Swartz residence..."

"Hello is Steven there?" a man said. His voice sounded familiar.

"I'm sorry; he's not home at the moment. May I take a message?"

"Huh. Who's this?" he said.

"Oh, it's just the nanny."

"*Just the nanny?*"

"Yeah."

"I see. Well, this is Just The Roto-Rooter guy. We have the same first name, Just The. I never met another Just The before."

"O-*kaaay.*"

"Hey, Just The, where are you from?"

"I'm from Oregon."

"Ore*GONE.* I know a guy from there. Maybe you know him too."

"Um—"

"His name's Ken."

*Okay, there are three million people in Oregon. How on earth am I supposed to know the same guy? Oh the hell with it, I'll play along.*

"Uh, what is his last name?"

"Ken Kesey"

Now, what are the chances of this, Ken Kesey is the uncle of my health teacher's wife, and I had been to their house several times in high school.

"Actually," I said. "I do know him."

"You do? Wow!"

"Sure, I know him." I didn't explain my loose connection to the man. I also didn't let on that by this time I had figured out that it was Bill Murray on the other line. "He lives on that farm in Pleasant Hill."

"That's right. I've been there," he said. "That's amazing. What a small world."

"It sure is," I said.

"Hey, do me a favor. Tell Steven and Julia that some guy named Bill is coming over later today."

I hung up the phone and felt slightly guilty. My connection to Ken Kesey, the infamous Merry Prankster and celebrated author of *One Flew Over the Cuckoo's Nest*, was a little tenuous. I loved my high school health teacher and his wife, Sheryl, but I had never actually laid eyes on her uncle in my life.

Maria came in from shopping and I told her that Bill Murray called and what a strange conversation we had.

"Oh yeah," she said. "Bill, he's a beeg jokest'r, dat one. Veeery nice guy doe."

When Julia came home, I gave her the phone message.

"God, I hope he's not bringing that kid of his. Last time that little monster was over he hauled off and bit Joshua."

*Yes Julia, that has been know to happen with young children.*

"I couldn't believe it," Julia said. "He bit him right on the face."

"Can you imagine the nerve of that kid? He hasn't been over since, and I don't plan on inviting him. And why the hell they named him Homer I'll never know."

Bill showed up an hour later, without little Homer. I heard him in the foyer. "Where's the nanny? I gotta meet the nanny." Then he came busting into the living room. "Hey! You must be Just The. Come over here, Miss OreGON!"

He picked me up off the ground and gave me a bear hug. I have to admit that his warmth and good cheer were a welcome change. "And there's Maria!" he said, seeing her in the doorway. "Come here, you! I missed you." He picked up Maria too, and she started laughing.

Later, after he left, I said to Julia, "Wouldn't it be funny to live with a guy like that? His wife must have a pain in her side all the time from laughing."

Julia just stared at me for a long time and said, "Yeah, she has a real pain in her side all right"

I called Sheryl that night. She wasn't home, but I left a message on her machine explaining the whole thing. "So, to make a long story short, I had to use *YOU* as a name-dropping resource. Hope you don't mind." I knew she would understand, growing up in Cottage Grove you don't have a lot of names you can drop when it comes to connecting with people in high places.

## Escape From Planet Hollywood

I had been planning my trip home for months, and couldn't wait until Friday when I was due to fly out. Of course, I Ok'd it with Julia that I would need to get off about 2:30 on Friday afternoon in order to make it to the airport on time. The week at the beach seemed to drag on forever. It was about noon on Friday when Julia left Malibu with Amanda for a mother/daughter fashion show. The Swartz family would remain at the Malibu house until late Sunday afternoon and I had a flight at six that night. At one that afternoon, Maria said "Soo-zita, just go. Brandon ees napping en Meester Joshua is watchin movee. I take care of dem for a few hours. Deer's no sense in you staying."

I thanked her profusely. She knew how excited I was about going home. Though this gave me plenty of time to get to LAX, I nevertheless managed to get my fifth speeding ticket in three years on the Pacific Coast Highway while I was driving to Brentwood. I tried the little name-dropping technique with the officer this time, and it didn't really work. He retorted with a sarcastic "Well, I guess the Most Powerful Man in Hollywood won't be too happy about your ticket, now will he?" He gave me my citation and I was off. I was determined to not let that policeman affect my excitement about getting to go home.

When I arrived at the house to gather my things before the trip, Concetta came running out to meet me. She said that Julia was holding on the phone and she was steaming mad, madder than Concetta could ever remember. *What in the world had I done now?*

"Suzy, she just went off on me. I've never heard her so upset."

I tried to catch my breath, gulped and picked up the receiver, holding it a healthy distance from my ear.

"Yes. Mrs. Swartz, its Suzanne."

"I know who it is. What do you think you're doing?"

"Huh?" I didn't have a clue what she was talking about.

"Maria is not your boss, I am. And I'm very unhappy with you. What did you do, just run out the door after my car left the driveway? I was already letting you go early."

"And by the way, I am not happy about uh.....uh....the fact that some-times you don't pick up the kids' toys," she continued. *Where did that come from?*

For once I was speechless. Immediately after our call ended, I called my friend Sarah at Steven's office. I was engulfed in tears when she answered.

Sarah tried to comfort me by saying that Julia must have been under some heavy-duty stress in order to be that angry. "Surely it couldn't be you," she offered. "They always tell me how happy they are with you," she tried to console me. I told Sarah about the comment about the toys, and she laughed.

I can only guess that sweet Sarah must have called Julia after we hung up, because ten minutes later Julia was calling back to the house to apolo-gize for losing her temper. Her voice sounded sincere, but the main thing I remember was that she said that she was looking forward to my return. That struck me as a surprise, given the weather pattern of coolness alternating with thunderstorms when I was around her. My head began with a more hopeful mantra than the recent ones: *Maybe she does like me…*

I was holding onto any shred of affection I could find. If she was willing to throw me a crumb I was willing to accept it. Maybe this would be the start of a new relationship for us. I could hear Joshua in the background saying that he wanted to talk to me. I was still sobbing hard. Having just heard his mother's tirade a few minutes earlier, I was sure he was going to join in on the fun. Julia put him on the phone.

"Suzy? Will you still bring me back pictures of you water-skiing like you said?" Sometimes when I've been crying, any little thing can set me off again. I lost it.

Today was the first time Josh has ever opened his heart to me. And he did it even after he heard his mother berating me on the phone. It may seem trivial, but for Joshua to take any interest in me, to extend himself even that much, is a monumental break-through. I really have hope now that things can be better. I think this may be the turn-around point.

I had a great Oregon summer vacation at home, back in my world. It seemed like another planet than Hollywood. I went out with friends and spent a lot of time water-skiing out on the lake with the boat. I remembered to shoot a picture like Josh asked. When I gave it to him, he seemed excited, and I noticed later that he had put it on his mirror.

The trip back to my Hollywood home would have been uneventful except for the take-off. My alarm didn't go off in the morning and I went screeching out to the airport, praying that I'd catch my flight. I was petrified that I would be several planes late and Julia would just go ballistic, especially since I hadn't left on the best of terms. The flight was scheduled for 9am, and I got to the ticket counter to check my bags at 8:42. The agent said I might still be able to make it if I ran. So I sprinted off, my enormous purse swinging behind me and bouncing off my rear end. The Eugene airport is very small and there are no jet ways. You just cross the tarmac to where the plane sits, a distance of about fifty yards. They were just closing the door to the cyclone fence gate as I got there. After pleading with her as if for my life, the Delta girl let me through, and I tore off across the asphalt. Apparently she'd called the crew and told them to hold the door open to the plane. As I was running, I saw it open again and two attendants waved for me to hurry up before the stairway was to be pulled away from the plane.

I could see all the little faces filling each window on this side of the plane, watching the entertainment. About half way between the terminal and the stairway, I tripped and the entire contents of my bag spewed out across the tarmac—four tampons, coin purse, make-up bag, keys, wallet, a banana, two magazines, four loose sticks of Doublemint gum, my ticket, my bag claim checks, a paperback book, my address book, a pair of socks, a miniature flashlight, a small can of Mace, ear plugs, my reading glasses, a bottle of nail polish, about four dollars in change, several loose slips of paper with notes for journal entries, pictures of my family and the kids, three one dollar bills, a box of raisins, two earrings and a backup tooth brush (you can never be too prepared).

I lay there sprawled out on the hot black surface, surrounded by what looked like the contents of my apartment, with approximately 130 people staring out the windows. I imagined them groaning in unison. Luckily, one of the flight attendants, laughing almost uncontrollably, descended the stairs to help me stuff the thrift shop back into my bag.

Guess what seat I had? Right. The very last one in the back next to the commode. I felt like I was walking the Green Mile as I passed all the passengers who were either laughing out loud, snickering or tsk-tsking me.

It was a bumpy approach, but I was back on board to Nannyville.

# Lifestyles of the Rich and Famous

While I was home, my sister Cindy had confided in me about how bored she was with her life in Eugene and with her job there. I persuaded her to apply for a position in the accounting department at ACT. For whatever reason, it was customary for applicants to send in a photo along with their resume to ACT. Thank goodness Cindy is attractive, so sending a photo wasn't a real issue for her. People always did say we looked alike. *Why did they care what she looked like, she wasn't interviewing for a movie position – she was interviewing for a job in the finance department. Apparently, they don't want anyone unattractive or fat even at the office.* She must have been cute enough though because she got an interview and was offered the job. She was very good at what she did, and I was proud to recommend her, I knew there would be no problem with Steven having my sister work for his company because of her outstanding work ethic. Once he was aware of the quality of her work, he would be **thanking** me.

Cindy and I have always been great friends, and we were both excited to have her move close to me. She aspired to do great things with her career, and I aspired to get an occasional Saturday night off and stay at her apartment. She put me in charge of finding a place for her. My priority was proximity to the Swartz', of course. The best I could do was a two-bedroom box that cost $1,100 a month. Today you couldn't pay the utilities for that. Poor Cindy couldn't even muster that much, so she ended up bringing two of her friends with her to share a two-bedroom 500-square-foot flat not far from the Swartz house. One of the girls had to take up residency in the walk-in closet. I am not kidding.

At first, Cindy's job in the Capital of Glitter was a bit of a letdown. She worked in a room with eight women and no windows processing clients' compensation. Though ACT's clients weren't employees, their checks came through the office first, where ACT deducted their commissions immediately. Then the balance was sent on to the clients. Cindy later told me that she had once received a call from an actor's manager demanding that ACT pay interest on the money that he was supposed to have received the month before, which still had not arrived at his mansion. At first it seemed petty that someone with his wealth would be worried about some insignificant amount of interest, until she told me the check was two months late and it was supposed to be for $4 million! Of course she wouldn't ever tell me who it was; she has this confidentiality thing hard wired into her brain, and it has always been impossible for me to get information out of her.

## There are No Children in the Brat Pack

During Cindy's first week on the job she was asked to handle the phones for the CFO, while his secretary went to lunch. She was told to interrupt him if anyone "important" called. Of course, since it was only her third day, her first thought was, "How am I going to know who's important and who isn't? What am I supposed to say? Excuse me, but before I can put you through, I'll need to know how much your last film grossed." No, that wouldn't work. She had no idea what amount made a movie a blockbuster.

The truth is that my sister doesn't usually know any actors and actresses that are currently hot in the media, let alone the names of behind-the-scenes people whose names are common knowledge in the movie-going public. She probably doesn't even know who Roger Ebert is, to this day.

The first call she received was a memorable one.

"Hello, Dan Gibbon's office. How may I help you?"

"Is Dan in?" came the stressed-out reply.

"I'm sorry; he's not available right now. May I take a message?"

"Yes, it's extremely important. Tell him to call........." She didn't know what to do. She didn't recognize the name and hadn't heard it clearly.

"I'm sorry. I didn't get that. Could you give me your name again?" she asked.

"It's Steeefan.........." Garbled transmission.

This time the gentleman was obviously becoming angry and he spit his name out at her.

"I'm terribly sorry. Perhaps we have a bad connection. I don't understand. Could you pronounce your last name just one more time slowly?"

"S, DOUBLE U, A, ARE, TEE, ZEE." He spelled it loudly and dramatically. "SWARTZ!!!! He yelled into the phone.

She gulped. "Thank you. I'll put you right through."

Less than a week after she began her new job at ACT, the boredom of life in Oregon had already been replaced with plenty of excitement. The government had just required a new form in accounting, an I-9, which served as proof of U.S. citizenship. She was assigned to gather the necessary documentation on all of ACT's clients. Since ACT's clients included some of the most notable and reclusive actors and directors in Hollywood, I told Cindy that this was a job better suited for an *Entertainment Tonight* reporter.

These folks maintained their privacy at any cost, so what might have been a relatively mundane new procedure at any other office, quickly became a hot issue among the celebrity clientele. The I-9 required verification of your birth date, which probably upset more than one actor, trying to pass for younger than they were. Cindy needed to make copies of several documents: a passport, driver's license and social security card, and the law required that she "physically" see original documents. Trying to get a social security number, birth date or driver's license from the likes of these stars should have been a task assigned to Interpol.

The adventure began when she went to the local clients' homes with her portable copier on wheels. This gave her the look of a traveler perpetually headed to the airport with her baggage in tow. Then came the complication of the out of town clients. Driver's licenses and passports aren't exactly the kind of documents you want to be mailing here and there. Cindy kept hearing some of the same comments over and over: "Oh, the government didn't care if I was an American citizen during the past ten years when I paid millions of dollars in taxes, but now suddenly it's imperative," or, "Who's going to see these documents; why do you need it?" *Translation: who's going to know how old I really am, or how I lied about my weight on my driver's license?*

One of her first assignments was to go to Demi Moore's apartment to get her I-9 information. Cindy told me that when she returned to the office all her co-workers were talking about Demi and the "brat pack." She informed them that they must be thinking of someone else because this Demi lady didn't look like she had any kids. I explained to my non-*People* magazine-reading-sister that they were referring to a group of actors that included: Emilio Estevez, Charlie Sheen, Rob Lowe and Ally Sheedy. I tried to remind her about the big hit *St. Elmo's Fire*.

"I don't think I've seen it" was her response, "Do you think I saw it at the drive-in?"

"Cindy, in the future, just pretend like you know what they are talking about and then run and call me if you need any more celebrity trivia."

"Suzanne, quit acting like I don't know anything. I will have you know, that this girl in the office just invited me to go with her to a wedding for that girl that used to play "Lucy" on *Dallas*, and I knew exactly who she was talking about. Now what is her name in real life?"

"Cindy that show hasn't been on the air in years, of course you are up to date on it,"

We laughed.

It's so refreshing to have Cindy's perspective here in Glitterland. None of the status stuff matters to her, and I'm sure it'll give me a perspective. Now we can laugh at craziness together. I also am excited to have a place to get away to sometimes without having to deal with the alarms when I return.

## Double Parked at the Beverly Hills Hotel

One of Cindy's next assignments was to get the information on Chevy Chase and a director he was meeting with. She was told to go to the Beverly Hills Hotel that afternoon where they would be in a suite together. When she pulled up, she was mortified that she would have to use valet parking. She drove an old clunker, and suddenly there she was, surrounded by every expensive and exotic car imaginable. She said she felt a little like the girl in class who was wearing faded jeans from the Goodwill, while the cool kids had on name brand clothing.

The meeting with Chevy Chase was tough enough, but she did manage to get the information she needed. However, as she left the meeting and was about to retrieve her car, rummaging around in her purse for the tip, she found to her dismay that she was virtually broke. Outside the hotel's massive glass doors were two valets dressed like palace guards. In queue were a Rolls, a Bentley, a Mercedes and a Lamborghini, each driven to the entrance by a valet who would then dutifully stand by the open doors, awaiting guests. And a big fat tip.

Cindy stood frozen, not knowing how to handle her predicament, when a young valet in the purple uniform approached her and asked for her receipt. She winced and handed it over. A succession of cars came and went for nearly ten minutes. Evidently her car had not been given top priority.

Cindy discovered that Chevy was standing behind her, waiting for his car as well. Now she was becoming nauseated. What would he think about The Agency of Creative Talent, if their trusted accounting person was seen climbing into a 1975 Datsun with two bald tires and a "non stock" baby blue paint job? Worse yet, what would Cindy's boss think? She could only hope that somehow her car would be hidden on the other side of one of the limos when it came time to get in.

The way Cindy tells it, the valet was quite tall and so his arrival in the tiny rattletrap, in front of more than fifteen waiting businessmen and dignitaries was even more ridiculous than it might have been. His legs were so long he had tangled one of them between the steering wheel and gearshift knob. As if the appearance of the sky blue Datsun had not been embarrassing enough, the sound of the horn blaring under the valet's twisted knees certainly was. There might as well have been a contingent of Marine Honor Guards firing a twenty-gun salute along with a loudspeaker announcement "Will the very poor person with a very old foreign car please come to the valet station immediately and take this pile of trash off the premises before more of our important guests are further offended?"

By the time she reached the car she'd found a single dollar bill in her purse. She carefully folded it in fourths so that the numeral one wouldn't show, not so much to hide the denomination, but to make it look like there was more than one bill folded.

The valet opened her door and stood formally by as she climbed in. She then engaged the clutch, put the car in first gear, put her other foot on the accelerator and tossed the tiny green square of paper at the valet. She careened down the driveway, knowing that by the time she cleared the hedge protecting the hotel from street view, he would just be unfolding his largess and she would be safely out of sight, never to be seen again. That was Cindy's crash course in Hollywood Class Consciousness 101. She shared with me the lessons she had learned:

- It's not who you are, it's what you drive.
- Appearances really are everything.
- Fake it while you can, then bolt.

After Chase, Cindy continued to work her way through the "C's." She came upon a name that seemed out of order, Mapother: a name she didn't recognize, certainly not a big star, perhaps a director? When she asked Mr. Mapother's agent why his client was in the "C's", she was quickly ushered upstairs by two male employees.

"Here, make a copy of this passport and be quick about it," he said. "Now listen to me," the agent said, "This Mapother guy is really Tom Cruise. That's why he's in with the "Cs". You're not to tell anyone else about this—ever. Do you understand?" "Yes. Yes, I understand," she replied, feeling as if she had been kidnapped momentarily by the secret service. She had just entered the secretive Society of the Keepers of the Name, and her lips were sealed. She wouldn't betray it to a soul, not even her own sister. I had to look up his real name to write this book.

I am a wimp. It is currently 9:15 pm on a Friday night. I want to leave and go stay the night at Cindy's. But I am afraid to ask. Here is what Ms.'Doesn't have a backbone' has done the last three Fridays.

7:50 get Brandon ready for bed, pajamas, rocking etc.

8:00 take him down for kisses and hugs from the family and then lay him down for the night (he is always so sweet, and usually goes right to sleep)

8:05 get bottles on ice etc. and put in upstairs bathroom

8:08 confirm with Concetta that she will sleep in Amanda's room and get up in the night with him

8:14 pack my bag to stay Friday and Saturday night over at Cindy's

8:24 walk downstairs to the foyer and listen to see what the family is doing at the dinner table

8:32 pace back and forth, attempting to get up the nerve to ask to leave

8:40 go in the kitchen to get moral support from Maria and Concetta, that YES, I should be able to leave, since the kids are eating with Julia and Steven and they want to spend time together with the family

8:46 Tell myself that I should be able to leave, it is Friday night, Saturday is my day off, I have put everything in order, Brandon is in bed, and I should be able to be off duty now.

8:51 get a knot in my stomach thinking what Julia will say

8:58 decide to wait until it is 9pm, since that sounds sooo much later than 8:59 so I can say "It's 9 o'clock, can I go to my sister's now"

9:02 march into the dinning room and announce, with as much confidence as I can muster (with my bag over my shoulder) I am going to stay at my sister's now

9:02 and 30 seconds Steven says Great, see you later, Julia says huh what? where are you going? Is Brandon in bed, did you tell Concetta you were leaving? When are you coming back?

9:03 hug kids, say good-bye, Steven says "Thanks Suzy," Julia continues to look confused by the events that have just transpired

9:04 get in my car and scream "Yes, I am off work"

OR

as is the case tonight at 9 pm I chicken out, come up to my room and decide to wait and leave first thing in the morning, as soon as Steven shuts the alarm off in the morning. While silently steaming that I SHOULD be able to leave the house on Friday nights. How bout that contract Miss Suzy????

PS........Stop by the bookstore tomorrow and pick up some self help book with a title, such as "You and your boss, working together for a mutually satisfying relationship"

My stomach can't take the stress, I think I might get an ulcer, it's too stressful pacing back and forth upstairs, contemplating in my head all the reasons I should get to leave but not wanting to go down and ask/tell them I'm leaving.

## Great Moments in Wretched Excess

Throughout history men as well as women have been guilty of excessive behavior...

A.D. 60—Roman emperor Nero decorates one of his palaces with a 120-foot tall statue of himself and installs ivory-inlaid ceilings that are equipped with pipes to sprinkle perfume on dinner guests. *Steven never installed perfume sprinkling, though he did have a fire sprinkling system in the house to protect the artwork.*

1782—Parisian jeweler Charles Bohmer creates the gaudiest piece of jewelry ever; a necklace that contained 647 diamonds in the vain hope that Marie Antoinette might buy it. The price tag? In today's dollars, $100,000,000! *Of course he'd never seen Grandma Swartz' pearl, sequined and jewelry encrusted sweaters.*

1880—George Vanderbilt, grandson of the railroad baron Cornelius Vanderbilt, builds the largest house in America for himself, his wife and his daughter. It is 172,000 square feet with 34 bedrooms and 43 baths.

1990— Aaron Spelling's new 37 million-dollar home measures 56,550 square feet with 123 rooms. It includes a bowling alley, full-sized ice rink, doll museum, four bars, a rose garden on top of the garage, a French-style "wine and cheese room" and two rooms just for wrapping gifts.

2002- Tyco Chairman indicted for fraud. It was reported that he paid $6,000 for a shower curtain!

Mandie's moment of excess was a long vacation with the Goldbergs to France during the Cannes Film Festival. While they were there, Mandie accompanied Mrs. Goldberg on several shopping excursions. We're not just talking typical shopping trips here. These were expeditions of monumental proportions. Of course there were two vastly different credit limits on the two women's plastic. Mandie's was $500 and Lord only knows what Mrs. Goldberg's was, if she had any.

On the first outing, Mandie fell in love with a $400 purse. She lusted after this purse like she was Dolly Parton in a wig shop. The problem of course, was that she didn't have Dolly Parton's budget, so she knew it was out of the question, or was it? She approached Mrs. Goldberg, desperately trying to find some rationale for buying it. What better ally than Margaret the Super Shopper? Mrs. Goldberg agreed that it was beautiful, but even she felt it was far too much for Mandie to pay for a purse. Not the least discouraged, Mandie found a pay phone and called Montana. Since they were in France, the call likely cost her nearly as much as the purse. She hoped that her mom would provide the necessary support to step over the line.

"Of course, dear, you must buy it. When will you ever be in France again?" her dear mother responded. Buoyed with this very sensible thought, Mandie went back to the store and maxed out her Visa card. That night she slept with the purse on the pillow next to hers.

The next day was another shopping adventure. Now it was Mrs. Goldberg's turn. She spied a Jackie-O style small clutch purse about the size of two cigarette packages. God knows what would fit inside it, beyond a pack of cigarettes and a lighter, and Mrs. Goldberg didn't smoke. She fell in love with the purse and decided without hesitation to buy it. While forking over her platinum, she remarked, "I'm on vacation. I should be able to do this." The cost of the purse? $6,000 U.S. dollars! Later that afternoon, she paid $343 for a key chain.

Before she left, Mandie had said to me that she would write me letters from Paris and Rome, but all I got the first week were two wish-you-were-here type post cards. Finally, probably owing to slow overseas mail delivery, the day before she returned, I got a letter from her.

*Suzy,*

*You'd think that being all the way over here in France would be nice, but oh my God, it only makes me homesick for Montana. I mean it probably is a really beautiful place and all, but Margaret—excuse me, "Mrs. Goldberg"—is making my life hell. I thought I was going to see at least a few famous sights. But so far the only big adventure I have been on turned into a disaster. The whole family and I went on this really big boat, some super-yacht or something, and I was so sick I thought I was going to lose my noodles over the side. The water was so rough that I could barely even walk along the deck without weaving all over the place and stumbling into things, like a sailor who's three sheets to the wind. People must have thought I was drunk. But maybe they didn't notice, because it seemed like a lot of other people were seasick too. Or maybe they were drunk!*

*Anyway, I'm out on the deck feeling like I'm late for my shift driving the porcelain bus and this big swell comes up and suddenly I go crashing into this guy standing by the railing. Luckily, I didn't barf on him. He helps me steady myself, and then he kind of squints at me and asks me if I'm all right. I*

felt like a total loser! But that was nothing. I start to say, "Thank you very much," but before I can get the words out, I whip around and start dry heaving off the side of the deck. Then I'm like OH MY GOD, because he says, "Ma'am, can I get you anything?" and he looks at me again, all squinty and stuff, and I realize its Clint frickin' Eastwood!!!

"Do you need anything?" he says, and I'm thinking, all I need now is a hole in the earth to disappear into. I've never been so embarrassed in all my life. With the possible exception of my falling down incident with Mel.

Love you, miss you,
Mandie

After she got home to LA, I got another letter.

Dear Suzy,

Yesterday we landed in Rome. It is very old, but lovely. You won't guess who I spent the afternoon with. Mr. Goldberg wanted to go to a set where they were filming one of his movies. We watched part of the filming, and I almost passed out because it was so hot with no shade to stand under. I guess Mr. Goldberg just wanted to make an appearance there, because after a few minutes he suggests that we go see some museums and that Demi Moore go with us instead of sitting in the broiling sun. She agreed. Mrs. Goldberg introduces us briefly and she is just gorgeous of course, but from then on I'm relegated to walking behind the entourage with the children.

We went to this incredibly old museum. It must have been a hundred years old, to look at paintings and statues, all very boring. However, I finally saw my opportunity to take some pictures with my instant camera. I'm so excited to send pictures of Demi back to Missoula to my family and friends. Because you know how excited my dad got when I sent that picture to him of me and Quincy Jones, it really made his day. Mom says he's been so proud showing it to all his friends. Anyway, I'm thinking, maybe I can get Mrs. Goldberg to take one of Demi and me together. Well, nix that idea. That would never happen. Nevertheless, I figure a couple of shots of her with my boss would be proof enough that

*I spent the day with her, or rather walked behind her all day.*

*The only problem is that the three of them were walking together and mostly they were stopping and staring at paintings, so the first 11 out of 12 pictures on the roll are the back of her head, as far as I could tell. Then, with only one picture left, she turns to ask a security guy where the ladies' room is. I quickly pull the viewfinder up to my eye. Demi is smiling at me. It's my great photo op. She even preens a bit for me. But just as I'm about to snap the shutter, the security guy rips the camera out of my hand and says, "No fotograhffi in museum," and Demi runs off to the bathroom.*

*I don't think I'll even get them developed. Oh well. Since they're all of the back of her head and her hair is currently bleached blonde, who in the hell is gonna believe it's her?*

*Anyway, hope to see ya soon after I get back. Forget about coming to Rome, it's too hot and dusty, everything's too old and no one speaks English.*

> *Your friend in nanny servitude,*
> *Mandie*

Shortly after they returned, Mrs. Goldberg sent Mandie on a routine errand, to Rodeo Drive in Beverly Hills to pick up some clothes she'd ordered. The tab was $700. Mandie only had $83 in her checkbook so she returned without the goods, and was promptly berated for not having paid for them.

"Mandie. What is the matter?" Mrs. Goldberg wanted to know.

"Mrs. Goldberg, I didn't have the money in my checking account."

"But you know I always reimburse you for it on your next paycheck," she responded.

"I know and I appreciate that, it is just that I didn't have it in my account at the time I was writing the check, and my dad has always told me to……"

Mrs. Goldberg interrupted. "You always need to have enough money in your account to be able to run errands for me."

Mandie said nothing. Her bi-monthly paycheck was $478 after taxes (the first six months it was only $428 because of the half of the placement fee that she agreed to share). Her next paycheck wouldn't be coming for over a week. She didn't want to bounce a check, but she also didn't want Mrs. Goldberg to know she only had $83 left to live on.

When Mandie told me the story, I screamed at her on the phone, "Then tell her to pay you more if she expects you to keep that kind of money in your checking account. Or for that matter, have her give you a credit card for her stuff. This is totally ludicrous."

Why am I spending all this energy being angry when I could be thinking about the situation I chose to be in? I need to stop criticizing Mandie all the time and stop judging our employers. I still refuse to fully embrace my mother's little saying about walking in other peoples shoes, washing their socks, or whatever..... Well, maybe she does have a point. I really don't have any way of knowing why people act the way they do. But it would probably take an act of Congress for me to ever admit my mother was really right about anything. I guess I need to face the fact that I'm not getting a salary for my great psychoanalyzing skills. But, I STILL think my abilities rank right up there with some of the so called professionals.

Goal for this weekend: Try to find a support group called something like: "Women who Love to analyze others too much, When you keep wishing and hoping your employers will see life your way."

CUT TO:

INTERIOR — GYMBOREE - DAYTIME

Two young women stand in front of a bulletin board; the noise of excited children is faint and constant in the background. One of the young women points to a large sign on the bulletin board.

NELLIE NANNY
Uh oh, looks like today's the last day to sign the kids up for the next Gymboree session.
NANCY NANNY
I'm glad you spotted that. Let's call our employers and let them know, I think they are out together.

NELLIE NANNY
Good thinking.

Nancy Nanny asks to use the phone at the Gymboree counter.

INTERIOR — GUCCI — RODEO DRIVE

Two well-dressed, chic women sit in overstuffed chairs sipping coffee. Every so often a Gucci sales person walks up and displays leather handbags to them. A cell phone rings.

SONDRA SOCIALITE

Oh, what now? Lord, it's the nanny again. What does she want this time? Hello? The last day for what? And Nellie Nanny wants to know too? Well, how much does it cost? Hold on.

Women turns to a sales clerk standing quietly before her. I'll take one in the ecru and one in the bone. Not that awful winter white.

Woman turns her attention back to the phone. What were you asking me? Oh right, Gymboree. How much did you say it cost? $103! What? Well, I don't care how many months worth. That's a lot of money for a baby class. I can't make that kind of commitment right now. We're going to have to talk about this later. Fine, I'll ask her.

Sondra Socialite turns to her friend.

Nellie Nanny wants to know if you want to sign Caitlyn and Jordyn up for Gymboree again.

SALLY SOCIALITE

Can't this wait till I get home?

SONDRA SOCIALITE

Tell Nellie Nanny ditto from Sally Socialite. And next time only call if it's something important.

Woman hangs up the phone and turns to other woman.

SONDRA SOCIALITE
Those nannies! Honestly. They'll milk you dry. They
must think we're made of money.

Sales clerk approaches with a shopping bag overflow-
ing with Gucci tissue paper.

SALES CLERK
So that's the two handbags and the wallet. That'll be
$7,500.

SALLY SOCIALITE
Go ahead and put that on my account, darling.

## The Hillbillies Stopped by Beverly Drive

Gradually, my attitude toward my job had changed. I no longer wanted
to be the perfect employee and I wasn't interested in spending all my time
and energy trying to please Julia and Steven. It started to seem obvious that
my take on the world was a galaxy apart from theirs, so I decided to try to
enjoy myself as much as I could during the day, have fun with the staff, and
engage the children in as many activities as they would tolerate with me.
But I was done with being a stress case.

I told myself to stop worrying every morning about whether or not
Julia was mad at me. It seemed that most of the time she was unhappy, and
that I had incorrectly assumed that it was because of something I had done.

Then I started to feel paranoid, thinking about all the phone conversations I'd had with Mandie, as we traded horror stories. Had Julia
ever eavesdropped on my conversations? If so, could she hear what I
was saying through my bedroom door? It seemed like this must be the
reason she didn't seem to like me. Either that or she saw my footprints
on the carpet in her bedroom. Almost every morning I would run into the
master suite after she left the house to weigh myself. Why I didn't buy
my own scale, I will never know. Maybe she was suspicious of what I was
doing in her room.

I decided to test my eavesdropping hypothesis. I enlisted Concetta's
help. I asked her to stand outside my closed door as I sat on the bed and

pretended to talk in a normal tone on the phone for about three minutes. Then I hung up and went and opened the door.

"Well, could you hear me?" I asked.

Concetta proceeded to recite my entire fictional conversation verbatim. We laughed so hard we almost fell backwards down the stairs, thinking Julia might have listened in on last night's giggling imitations of Julia and Margaret (I mean Mrs. Goldberg) with PMS. Then I felt pretty bad. I thought that if I were in her shoes, I probably wouldn't like me the next morning, either.

 Oh my God. Big trouble. Who knows what I've said while Julia's listening? No wonder she's acted so strange around me! Maybe I should wrap a pillow around my head to muffle my voice. One thing's for sure: whatever I say to Mandie on the phone from now on will either have to be censored or said very quietly.

My mother called to tell me that my younger sister, Traci, and her best friend, Nancy, were taking a trip through California with Nancy's family.

"They want to come and visit you when they're in LA," my mother said.

"That's great!" I said. "I'm so lonely for people from home."

"I'm very happy for you honey and Traci's excited too, but I think you should keep a couple of things in mind. Now, you know we love Nancy and her family, but let's face it; they're not exactly going to blend in down there. And you should keep in mind that the Swartz' might not normally come in contact with people who take their road trips in an old truck and camper."

It would have never occurred to me that this could be a problem until she mentioned it, but once she did, I knew I had a situation. Mom was right; Nancy's dad was the greatest guy you'd ever know, and he'd give you the shirt off his back if you needed it. But he *was* kind of like Jed Clampett, only without the millions, even though he *did* live close to an old gold mine near Cottage Grove. I decided to start right away praying that Nancy's uncle wouldn't be traveling with them. He was a dead ringer for Randy Quaid as Uncle Eddie in the *Vacation* movies. Even their dog, Blue, was a character. He could drink more beer than a human, when he had a mind to. Yes, the two cultures would definitely clash.

I stopped and thought more about the Swartz' lives and what they **didn't** experience on a daily basis, protected as they were by wealth and

power. Little things like the signs I had seen all my life when I entered
a restaurant:
- NO SHOES, NO SHIRT, NO SERVICE
- LOGGERS BREAKFAST SPECIAL $2.99

I knew they would never see signs like these, signs that were common in
small towns across America:
- Bonanza Burgers: 5 Hamburgers for $2.99 (10 cents for onions)
- Ten-Family Garage Sale out Lorane Road - Lots of Good Stuff
- Return bottle and pop cans at the back of the store.

And I doubted that anyone around here would think to pick up a
grandparent when they were dumping garbage at the local refuse center
so they could get the 'Senior Citizen Dump Rate.' Come to think of it,
do they even have dumps in LA, or is that just a small town thing?

I decided to stop worrying about the two worlds colliding until the
time came, because I was too busy watching the kids. Still, I did wonder
what they'd be driving and how many people would be piled into the
vehicle. Several days later I looked out the window just as an old Chevy
pickup pulled up out front. I could see Nancy's dad, Gary, behind the wheel.
On the grill was his latest hunting trophy, a large pair of antlers. The
uncovered truck bed was loaded up with suitcases and duffle bags. The
Chevy was towing an ancient camper trailer, a little dented and rusty.

As I ran downstairs I heard the front gate buzzer ring. Julia had
answered it and was now staring out the open front/side door of the house.

"What on earth is that, out on the street?" she gasped.

"Just a sec, it's my sister" I said, flying past her. I ran to the gate to
meet them. Just as I approached, Blue jumped out and proceeded to
relieve himself on a palm tree.

"Sorry, he had to go real bad, I 'spect this neighborhood has some kind
of rules about pets. It is pretty upscale," Gary said. *I am so homesick listening to him, I want to be with 'regular' people again.*

I hugged everyone, especially Traci. I was overjoyed to see them, but I
also knew that Julia was still standing in the door zapping us with her dis-
approving radar. For a moment I got a backbone and sent a silent message
back. *I don't care what you think. Today is Saturday and it is my day off.
I can stand out here all day if I want to.*

I just hoped she wouldn't come closer and say anything to embarrass
them. She'd probably have a nervous breakdown if I opened the gate and

asked them to pull their vehicle in. Traci kept looking at me like, "Okay, now what? Aren't you going to open the gate and let us in?" But I knew I couldn't. We stood and chatted for about thirty minutes. There were lots of stories shared between us all—I was sad that I felt like I couldn't bring my sister and her best friend into the house, and show them where I lived. My disappointment in myself, for still caring what Julia would think of my relatives, over shadowed my excitement about the visit.

I hate seeing the reality of my situation staring me in the face. I can't deny that I am losing my own integrity, because I'm afraid of what they think of me. WAKE UP! I think I am being so noble for honoring my "two year commitment." Ya right!

# Just Another Day in Paradise

When Julia told me that we were all going to Hawaii for Thanksgiving vacation, I started to anticipate my first trip to the legendary exotic paradise with very mixed feelings. Until this point in my young life, vacationing had meant cramming all of us into our family's candy-apple-red-faux-wood-sided station wagon for a ten-hour trip to visit my cousins in Canada. Now that I thought about it, I wondered if my father was at least tempted to sip something other than soda out of his Pepsi can in order to endure the "are-we-there-yets?" and the 100 plus, "Dad, please rewind Elvis again, we want to hear *Jail House Rock." For god sake, I think it was even an 8 track.* Even though a trip to Hawaii with a stay at a posh resort was the fantasy of my young life, I was realistic enough after almost a year with the Swartz' to know that I'd basically be on duty for 192 straight hours (I had counted), and I was not looking forward to being in even tighter quarters than I normally shared with my "family." After my lovely experience in Aspen with the group, I was kind of dreading the trip before it began.

The night after Julia informed me of our upcoming adventure, I decided to work on getting a more positive attitude. I started poking a little fun at my own grumpiness over the news of our upcoming trip. I called up Mandie and told her that she was not going to believe where I was going and what I was going to do. She listened intently while I spun my perfect vision of the eight-day vacation.

"I'll be basking on spun-sugar beaches, with eight nights relaxing on those hibiscus-scented lanai you've heard about." In the version I was creating in my dream-dappled mind, there would be grandparents, aunts and uncles to lavish attention on the kids. The gentle spirit of the island would permeate our hearts, and inner harmony would reign.

"My principle responsibility will be to distribute the beach toys and reapply sunscreen on the kids all day long." Idle images of Polynesian splendor lapped at the edges of my brain—images of hula performances under the torch-lit palms, drinks served in coconuts and a memorable Hawaiian Thanksgiving luau, where I would feel completely at one with the family I was destined to be with forever.

When I described my vision to Mandie, she started laughing so hard that I was actually afraid she'd lost control of her bladder at one point. So I cut my little description of paradise short.

When the time came it was quite an undertaking to get the whole show on the road. Our traveling caravan included Steven and Julia, the three children and me; Steven's parents; his brother, Tim, his wife Kirsten and six-year-old son; and Rick Dyer, along with his date Cyndi Garvey and their four combined daughters. It took two stretch limos, just to get our family to the airport. Altogether we totaled nine adults and eight children. In addition, Steven's friend Al Checchi, his wife, three kids and nanny would be meeting us there and staying with us at the resort.

After we were greeted at LAX, by a professional looking woman waiting at passenger drop off, the limo driver unloaded enough luggage to supply an army division. We were escorted through security, down a long hall to an unassuming door marked "The Captain's Club." I had never known that airlines provide these private little oases for their valued frequent flying passengers. Of course, Steven, his partners, staff and clients combined, must have racked up millions of miles on ACT's American Express card, so they were used to lounging in the private sanctuaries. Steven waved the whole troupe over to the Captain's Club portal.

A stone-faced young woman at the desk stopped us. Airline policy was to allow the frequent flyer one guest, and she was going by the rules. She was firm and implacable with a perfunctory pleasantness that was so calm it was irritating. Steven started arguing his case, but she repeated patiently that this was company policy, with no exceptions. No exceptions? Steven's face began to crawl as if a bug was trapped under his skin. She gave the impression of having weathered a few of these Type A folks in her day. She explained the policy clearly and identically each time, as though her vocabulary were restricted to the airline's script. I recognized the "broken record technique" from the parenting books I'd read.

"I'm sorry, Mr.—" she paused, waiting for him to fill in the blank.

He raised his eyebrows and lowered his face closer to hers. "Steven Swartz," he pronounced emphatically, as though there were not a soul alive who would not recognize his name, with the possible exception of my sister Cindy.

The woman didn't respond. She just calmly kept typing on her computer as she stared into the monitor. I had already learned in my tenure with Steven that there were several things that invariably irritated or angered him. One of them was not being recognized for the powerful man he was. This always seemed a bit of a contradiction, since he hated seeing his name in the papers and went to great lengths to keep his picture from being published. But today was definitely a day he wanted to be recognized.

"Do you have any idea how many frequent traveler miles my company has with this airline?" he smirked, somehow knowing he would be getting his way. I thought about backing him up and I rehearsed my part in my mind: *Yeah lady lighten up, I have a chubby baby on my hip and a heavy diaper bag on the other and I would like to sit down.*

"I'm sorry, Mr. Swartz. I don't know you, and it wouldn't matter if I did because the rules are the rules. You can only have one guest come in with you," she replied with unsurpassed calm. I tried desperately to make eye contact with the poor woman, wanting to affect some sort of facial expression that would tell her that if she didn't change her tune she would be in the unemployment line tomorrow.

From my position just behind Steven, I could almost feel the steam coming off his neck. It was absolutely clear to me that there was no way he was going to allow this irritating little bureaucrat to keep him from bringing his entire entourage into the Captain's Club. We had two hours before our flight.

Once again, I tried to communicate the situation telepathically: *Girl, look at me, LOOK AT ME, can't you see this guy is used to people quaking at the mere mention of his name? There's no way he is going to wait with his wife, parents, children and friends with the riff-raff at the gate.*

Besides, I knew waiting was really only a secondary concern at this point. His ego was far more important right then.

Without saying another word to the woman, Steven turned to Julia and said, "Take the kids and go sit over there. I'll be right back." *Thank God, I can sit down now.* With that he disappeared through the door. By the time he had returned ten minutes later, the woman behind the desk had already been taken into another room by a large man in a business suit and been replaced with another woman with a big smile, who upon Steven's return, personally ushered us into the elaborately decorated club and offered us lunch.

Steven may have won, but the rest of us certainly hadn't. It was beneath his dignity to have to use his sophisticated negotiation skills on an unpleasant encounter with such a nobody, and his mood was not pretty. And when Steven wasn't happy, ain't nobody's gonna be happy around him. The two hours passed slowly.

We were flying out on a 747 jumbo jet. I had never been on a plane so big in my life. Usually when we flew we took various corporate jets. You could have put six of those on each wing of this plane, I swear. We were among the first to board as we were in first class, another new experience for me. It took fifteen minutes for the entire group to get into the cabin. Between all of us we took up a good portion of the first class seating. The tickets alone must have cost almost $20,000. As we all jockeyed for position, the stewardesses helped us stow the carry-ons and find our seats, I could see the faces of the aristocracy already seated, giving us looks of combined disgust and fear. I knew what they were thinking: *How could anyone be so rude as to bring that many children, and so young, into first class? I paid a lot of money to sit here and I'll be damned if I'm going to put up with a bunch of screaming brats.*

It was going to be a six hour flight and several of the children, including Brandon, were already either crying or fighting about something. I wondered whether the young couple just behind us, were settling down for their first flight as man and wife, off on their honeymoon, only to be invaded by the Brady Bunch. I tried to avoid eye contact with them.

First class alone was two stories tall. There was a large circular staircase that led from the floor we were on up to the other. On the second level, there was more seating, a bar and a grand piano. Not that I ever saw it, but that's what Grandpa Swartz reported to me. It was like flying in a house.

I'd never seen anything like it. Right after we got on, Steven, Julia, Rick and Cyndi and all the rest of the adults went upstairs and left me with the various children. When and how had it been communicated to the parents that I would graciously govern *all* the children, I was not aware. It ended up that I got lucky: both Rick and Cyndi's girls were all very sweet and helped me with the younger ones.

The other occupants and the flight attendants all eyed me accusingly. *What gall to bring eight young children on and be insufficiently prepared to amuse them for the duration!* Just who did I think I was?

Who was I? I was the one changing diapers on the edge of the seat, the one wedging herself into the lavatory with a pre-schooler. Three of my little charges cried or screamed when the cabin air pressured their eardrums. Nobody liked their food, and the peanuts were lobbed across the aisles when the flight got boring. One child spilled soda all over another while I was in the lavatory with a third. Pulling down the carry-ons in an attempt to find clean replacements for the shorts that were soaked in root beer took the flexibility of an Olympic gymnast.

I sent out a cry for help, by way of the flight attendant. She delivered the message on her next trip up. Evidently, this was regarded with some amusement by the folks on top. Julia appeared at my side, laughing. "For goodness sakes, Suzy, what are you doing to these kids? Why didn't you come up and let us know if you couldn't handle it?"

After six hours we landed, thank God. Later our entourage met up with Al Checchi's entourage. This included him and his wife and three kids, plus Jenna, their nanny. She was a cute girl about my age, but a lot bolder and wilder, not a difficult feat. I didn't know much about Mr. Checchi other than the fact that he was a bigwig with some airline and Julia said he had more money than God.

While we were checking in at the hotel, Jenna asked me if I'd join her that evening for a night on the town. I wondered what planet she was from. I'm sure I looked at her like I thought she was crazy.

"You get to go out?" I asked incredulously. "I mean, you really get to leave?"

"Of course. I'm off at 6 pm while we're in Hawaii."

I couldn't believe it. I had assumed that her situation was the same as mine since she also was a nanny for three kids of similar ages. The thought of ever being "off duty" had **never** entered my mind. *Okay. You did this* *to yourself. One more example of you not asserting yourself and asking for what you need in order to do the best job.*

"Just ask Julia if you can go with me," she said.

"Are you out of your mind?"

"Never mind, I'll do it," she said, as if it were no big thing. My knees where shaking at the thought.

Jenna seemed so confident and direct when she approached Julia. Julia's cold silence made it clear that she wasn't exactly crazy about the idea. Later, when we were alone, I was told that Jenna's request was impossible to accommodate and I would not be going out that night or any other night. Julia had, of course, pretty much made up her mind about Jenna, and let's just say that the other nanny wasn't on her good list. The next day Jenna raised Julia's temperature a few degrees when she started massaging Steven's shoulders as he sat in a lounge chair. It wasn't like she was coming on to him; she was just treating him like he was her dad, I guess. I thought it was a little strange myself and could see why Julia would be annoyed with her unwarranted familiarity. To top it off, she started telling him he should lighten up a bit, just blithe as you please. Steven was too stunned to take control, for once. Julia didn't say anything, but I can still picture the look on her face. I think the casual violation of personal body space had so shocked her sensibilities that she couldn't begin to formulate words. I didn't think she, herself, would be comfortable enough to touch him like that, without invitation.

The next day Julia made a point of telling me "that girl," which became Jenna's name for the rest of trip, "did not know her place." It made me feel like we were two children living in the 1800's who were not to speak unless spoken to. While she was rambling on, a knock came at the door. It was Jenna. I asked her to come in, and immediately Julia made a quick exit. Jenna and I sat on the bed while I related the story, which started us on a whole litany of comparative tales. Instant nanny camaraderie! It's funny how the subject of money always came up when nannies got together.

Jenna asked, "Did you guys come to the airport in a limousine?"

"Yes," I said, "we always do when we go places as a family."

"Mr. Checchi would never allow that. He made the cook drive us all in the old Suburban; he said a limo was frivolous." *This was the same man who paid for his nanny to fly first class in a 747?*

I laughed knowingly. Oh, so knowingly.

"You think that's weird. Get a load of this. When we got here, Julia made a big to-do about no one using the honor bar. I wasn't even sure what an honor bar was. Turns out there's no honor involved. It's just a refrigerator filled with liquor, cookies, candy bars and other treats. At any rate, under no circumstances were the children and I to eat or drink anything from it. She said she'd buy soft drinks at the grocery store and bring some in for the kids. And yet she has no problem sending the kids' underwear out with the bellman to be cleaned and pressed."

Jenna laughed. I was just getting started. "But get this. The best part was last night after we checked in and I helped Julia unpack, a bellman rolled in this enormous basket of fresh fruit with soft drinks on ice, and an assortment of cookies. When Steven came in and saw it he had an absolute conniption fit." I started imitating their voices as I told the story.

| | |
|---|---|
| Steven: | Suzy, did you order this? Julia did you? |
| | *We both denied knowledge regarding the edibles.* |
| Steven: | I'm not paying for that! Call them to take it back— |
| Julia: | Steven, I didn't order it— |
| Steven: | Well then who sent this? |
| Julia: | I suppose they're going to charge us for this now |
| Steven: | Call them and tell them to pick it up." |
| | *Julia picks up the phone and punches the button for the front desk.* |
| Julia: | Hello. This is Mrs. Swartz in room 77. Would you please send someone to pick up the rolling cart that was just delivered to our room? We didn't order any fruit and we can't be expected to pay for it." |
| | *Silence as she listened for a minute.* |
| Julia: | What's that? Oh, I see...the.... the manager did...... Oh, with the suite. Well then Okay. Just leave it, and tell the manager thank you. And uh ....you have a nice evening as well. |

"Turns out our suites are so flippin' expensive, it's standard to get this assortment of goodies as a gift every other day!"

"Yeah. Us too. Do you believe the service in this place? It's gonna be a blast!" Jenna enthused. From our earlier discussion of evenings off, I doubted that our experiences here would be the same.

My accommodations consisted of a gorgeous two-bedroom suite. Amanda and Joshua shared one bedroom and Brandon and I the other. We were on the ground floor. Steven, Julia, and all the rest had rooms within the luxury hotel, I guess. I never did get a chance to see anyone else's room. Our bungalow was right off the walkway that led down to the beach, so there was plenty of access to the water.

The first couple of days, Julia and Steven would walk up to the large patio door to see what was going on with the kids and then usually take Amanda and Josh down to the beach.

"Bet you never dreamed you'd have your own hotel suite in Hawaii," Steven's brother commented one day as he breezed by. *Yes, it sure is unbelievable.* My room was soon recognized as a convenient spot to drop off a wallet or grab a towel or make a phone call. It was so much quicker to get to my room than theirs. *Sunscreen? Have at it. Flip-flops? Sure, just root around in the pile of them there.* And of course it was easier to just let themselves in through the patio rather than go around and knock on the front door. After all, that might wake the baby. One afternoon Cyndi Garvey came over to survey the crowd of youngsters massed in front of my TV set. "What a great arrangement for you and the kids."

Aloha! I'm more or less in Paradise confinement. I can't go anywhere. I've actually seen Hawaii twice so far, both times from inside a van, when we were riding to a restaurant for dinner. Then back to my room. Brandon hasn't been acting like he feels well, so I take him out in the sun very little. He just wants me to hold him most of the day, and he isn't playing like he normally does. I think Josh and Amanda are having a good time and enjoying playing with their parents.

I'm working my normal hours here, without the weekend off. When I get home I'm going to try to take those two days that Julia 'owes' me and combine them with my normal weekend to see if I can have four days off in a row. I am going to get up the nerve to ask, come Hell or high water!

See, I am starting to have a positive attitude. I'm looking at the bright side: Long time with no days off = 4 glorious days in a row off, when I return home.

## Pacifying the Sundance Kid

One day, the phone rang in my room right after I'd finally shooed out several kids. Brandon was obviously ill and even a little feverish, so I was trying to settle him into a nap. Amanda was in front of the TV, complaining that I'd turned down her *Cinderella* video too low. I was tempted to just let the phone ring, but I picked it up. It was Sarah from the office. "Is Steven in your room?"

"Good guess. I had a crowd of ten here a few minutes ago, but no, he isn't in here."

"There's a message for him. I called his suite but didn't get an answer."

"Okay, I can take a message," I say, transferring Brandon to my other arm while I grabbed for a hotel issued pen.

"No, Suzy, the client wanted to leave it in his own words so Steven would get it straight. He made me write it down verbatim. Listen to this," Sarah explained.

"Wait, do I have to write this down exactly?"

"I'm sorry yes, how are you guys all doing anyway?"

"We'll talk about it when I get home, Sarah," I said sarcastically. Brandon was whimpering now, and I just wanted to hurry up so I could go take his temperature.

"Okay, here goes: Steven, I can't believe you're on vacation again! Isn't this the third one this year? That must be nice." Sarah began

"Sarah, am I supposed to be infusing the anger and sarcasm into the phone message?" At least I hadn't lost *my* sense of humor.

"No, just keep writing. 'Damn it – did you get the Fed Ex package? I want to know what's in that contract, NOW. What the hell is going on there? This is the last time I put up with this horseshit. You tell me you've got this handled – handle it! Call me back IMMEDIATELY.'"

"All righty then, I got it, now what do you want me to do?"

"Wait Suzy, Jason wants to talk to you. We were both here when we got the message."

"Hi, Suzy you have got to make sure he gets this right away, I promised Redford I'd deliver the message"

*Well then, I will get right on this important message from Bob. I could just picture him in The Natural doing that little thing where he sort of bites the tip of his tongue while he touches it to his upper lip and squints.*

"When did he call?" I asked.

"A few minutes ago. Can you find Steven right away?"

"Yes sir, I will. Ya gotta love this work, don't you Jason?" I laughed

The adults were down at the beach. I slung Brandon on one hip and picked up Amanda with the other arm. She didn't want to walk because she said the sand was too hot. We waddled slowly down to Steven and Julia.

After I gave him the message Steven went bounding back to the room ahead of us. I told Julia what had happened and she said, "Oh Redford, he is the worst, just the worst," shaking her head in disgust. *News to me*

I told Julia I thought Brandon was coming down with something. I then casually tried to encourage Amanda to stay on the beach with her mother, so I would only have one potentially sick child to deal with. But, she insisted she wanted to finish watching *Cinderella*.

When we got back to our vacation quarters. Steven was spread out on my bed with the phone to his ear. He had called Sarah and she was patching him through to his client. Steven hadn't received any Fed Ex envelopes that I knew of since we'd arrived, and it sounded like there was a major mess to sort out. I tried to usher Amanda back out the door to the patio, but she began to wail. Steven had been leaning back against the headboard, but now he was leaning forward to brush sand off his legs onto the floor.

*Is he motioning to me to keep her quiet?* That's what it looked like, but that couldn't be it. He has to know there's no way I can control the noise level in the room. When I tried to get her to go outside with me, she just started to fuss more, and then Brandon started chiming in. *No, that's not good; reverse course.* Poor Brandon started to lunge out of my arms for his crib. He really must not be feeling well if he wants to get in his crib. I had to let him lie down. Maybe I can take Amanda out on the patio, yell to Julia that I need assistance, and then run back and get Brandon, before he starts making noise in the room.

By now Steven had evidently reached 'Bob' as he referred to him. He threw himself back on to the pillows to launch into his appeasing talk. He was going to need his full concentration for this. Amanda wouldn't let up. She would not accept my decision that she couldn't finish her *Cinderella* video, RIGHT NOW. I told her I would read a book to her quietly, and she insisted we sit on the bed to start the story. I kept repeating my Amanda mantra: *Please don't have a tantrum. Please don't have a tantrum.* Then I remembered my gumdrops. I desperately searched through my bag for them to use as a mouth-stopper. She took the bait. I juggled Brandon a little in his crib and tried to check out Steven enough to see if he was distracted by the ruckus, without looking at him directly, so he wouldn't get the idea that I was listening in on his conversation. And, yes, of course I was hanging on his every word. Ya gotta be a great multi-tasker in my profession.

I leaned down to Amanda, whispering and crooning, and then I started the story as we were sitting on the bed next to her father. "I promise as soon as Daddy's done talking we will start the movie again. Thank you for being so quiet sweetheart." *Positive reinforcement, Positive reinforcement, don't have a tantrum, don't have a tantrum.*

Steven wound up his business. He smiled and promised Redford that he'd be in touch again soon. He listened to something that made him laugh. He said goodbye and set the phone back in its cradle. Then he jumped up off the mattress and smoothed down the comforter. "Thank you Suzy I appreciate all your efforts, thanks for keeping the kids quiet."

*No, problem, I'm glad it was good for you.*

It felt like the vacation without end. We were leaving to go to dinner one night. I don't know which night; they all ran together. I had made sure the kids were dressed and ready before the van came to pick us up. Growing up in Oregon where it gets chilly at night, even in the summer, I had learned to wear layers and always carry a jacket. So I told Joshua to bring a wind-breaker type jacket, just in case. When we got in the van, I got into the back with Amanda and Brandon. Julia was sitting by Josh in front of us. She asked him, "Why did you bring that jacket? You're not going to need it."

Josh responded with a sick tone, "Cuz Suzy maaaade me," then turned around and stuck his tongue out at me.

Julia didn't turn around. She just shook her head, like she was trying to repel a mosquito. "I doubt you're going to need it. It's 85 degrees out."

"I know, but she maaade me." He flipped around in his seat and made another face at me. It was a bonding moment for the mother and child as they shared a snort of scorn at the expense of the "weather forecasting impaired nanny" in the back seat.

*It's not like I asked him to bring a snow parka. How am I supposed to know it never cools down in Hawaii? I've never been here before. And now that I'm here, I pretty much haven't ever left the hotel room.*

When we were served our food at the Chinese restaurant, I noticed that Brandon wasn't interested in what I was feeding him in his highchair.

Then he proceeded to throw up into my egg drop soup. I cleaned him up, while Steven called for a van to take me and Brandon back to the hotel.

As I stood between his parents seated at the table, Julia reached out to give him a hug and kiss goodbye. I think she felt really bad for him, that he was sick. Brandon turned in toward me. Steven said, smiling at me, "Too bad Brandon doesn't like his Suzy very much."

Julia said, "Huh, what did you say?" He repeated himself to his wife. It made me feel a little better, a little more appreciated, as I left to take him back to the room.

I stayed up most of the night with the little guy until his stomach finally settled down. Eventually I ordered in room service, the highlight of my trip so far. I got to eat in a peaceful, quiet room. Brandon never did improve much—the poor baby had the flu the rest of the vacation. We took him to a doctor the hotel had on staff and kept him on Pedialyte for the rest of the trip. He was beset with diarrhea and vomit the rest of the trip, and I was beset with record numbers of diapers and dirty laundry. He was miserable and I was powerless to help him, and very busy.

The following night, after finally settling down to sleep, I woke up, startled, at two or three in the morning. I froze under the covers, sensing someone in the room other than the kids and myself. I was disoriented, but I had reason to think this wasn't a male burglar. The scent of Fendi perfume tickled the air. Turning very slowly under the covers, I peaked out and there, lying next to me was a blonde woman, sound asleep. It was Julia! *What the hell is she doing in here?*

A hundred thoughts raced through my mind, and I certainly didn't want to wake her with them. Had she gotten drunk and gone to the wrong room? Did she feel terrible for the way she'd been treating me, and had come to make up with me after all these months? Did she and Steven get into a fight? Bingo! That was it. Where else could she have gone, under the circumstances? It made perfect sense.

When the first light of day came, I pretended to still be asleep as she got up and made a hasty retreat. The incident was never mentioned. *Great. Now I've shared my bed with both of them.* We just went on with our normal, excruciatingly strained family holiday.

## Search and Seizure at the Airport

On the return trip we had to go through customs, or at least it seemed like customs. Since we weren't in a foreign country, it couldn't have been.

Maybe it had something to do with gypsy moths trying to hitchhike in on fruit. The fact that I don't remember what they were looking for shows how tired I was. Everyone was already cranky, though I don't know how you can spend eight days in paradise and end up cranky, unless your trip to paradise consisted of one outing to the beach, and one dip in the pool and the rest of your stay in a hotel room.

Of course, out of our army of first class passengers I was the first one in line, with Brandon in the stroller. The inspector was rummaging through my things looking for contraband. Julia and Steven were behind me, about ten people back. The wait was interminable. Everyone was getting crankier by the moment. Mr. Checchi was asking himself, loud enough for everyone in the airport to hear, "What the hell is the holdup?"

I had put two apples in my backpack for the kids to snack on. Once they found the illegal fruit they had to fill out a report and confiscate it. They grilled me for another fifteen minutes about any marijuana, food or plants I might have. Of course, Steven marched up to the head of the line to see what all the ruckus was. I was mortified.

When we were boarding the plane, I overheard Julia asking Steven what had been the hold up. "Oh, one of the kids had put an apple in one of the bags," he explained

I remained silent, fussing over the baby. *Thank God, he thought it was the kids' fault and not mine.* I decided that "honesty is always the best policy" definitely did not apply in this instance.

On the plane ride back, Brandon fell asleep in my lap, so I broke open my backpack, looking for something to read. I had forgotten that I'd brought the latest issue of *Be the Best Nanny Monthly Guide*, the newsletter I now subscribed to. The headline on a first page article read "Traveling with Mary Poppins, Negotiating the Road with Caregiver In Tow."

Caregiver in tow? That's just about how I felt: I was a flatbed trailer, and they were cranking the winch to load me up with a minivan full of kids. I read on.

"To many, bringing a nanny on family journeys would be antithetical to the notion of quality family time. Increasingly, however, many parents are finding a pair of extra hands the best excess baggage they can bring." *Excess Baggage!!!* Make note to call the editor of this newsletter, and give them a piece of my mind.

In the days after our return, I began to notice more and more how miserable I felt. Shortly after the trip, my mother called and innocently asked, "Did you have a good time on your vacation honey? Did you stay in a fancy hotel?"

"I have just spent two weeks with a group of people that never appreciate all that they are fortunate enough to have. They make everything an ordeal, and hardly ever smile, even when they're sitting in the lap of luxury, surrounded by paradise. There was nothing about it that was enjoyable," I snapped. I could feel that I was just about to blow a gasket.

My mom went doggedly on. She mentioned that her friend Earleine had said, "Wow, Suzy sure has it good with all the trips she goes on. Sure must be rough being paid to travel all over."

I went ballistic. "Mom, why don't you give her a rundown—I pack up all the kids, and get criticized for what I choose to pack. I travel with a family that never experiences any joy. Everything in their life is a hassle to them, everyone they encounter is out to screw them over. The kids are crabbier when we're in paradise than when we're at home, since they don't have all the *stuff* they require to be entertained. When they're around their parents they treat me like crap. And they can get away with it. I never know exactly what to do. I just know they expect me to just know what to do." Venting felt good. Good Mom that she is, she just listened.

"I've got Julia saying to me with shock and irritation, 'Brandon still takes two naps?' while I am trying to inform her of her youngest son's sleep schedule. I have the nanny, 'that girl' from the other family snapping back to my employer, 'You don't even **know** how many naps your son takes?' Let me tell you how pleased I was to be put in that position.

"It's all just splendid. Add to that, I'm with two miserable adults that don't enjoy each other's company and its all jjjuuuuuust great. Oh, I'm living inside a fairy tale all right. Just like good ole Cinderella after she married the prince and lived happily ever after. . ." I screamed and slammed down the phone. I decided to call her back after I'd finished venting in my journal.

Boy did Mom's questions bug me. Maybe it was just my exhaustion talking. I get so frustrated because nobody can begin to understand what it's like to live with these people. Most people go on vacation for fun. No, not this family. When the plane landed back home, Julia told me she hoped that Steven wouldn't rush us like he always does. I don't understand why they don't talk about these things.

I'm starting to think I don't want to spend my days with people that don't laugh and joke and enjoy each other. They're uptight and on guard all the time. I want to spend my time with positive, fun people, people that love life and are grateful for what they have. Is there anyone in Southern California like that? I think I am beginning to get a skewed view of the world.

## Hanukkah or is it Chanukah?

"Merry Christmas," I said to Mandie.

"Same to you," she replied.

"What's going on at the Goldbergs? Do they have a tree yet?"

"Oh my gosh, yes. It must be twelve feet tall. And get this: they aren't going to decorate it."

"They're not? So you just have a big naked evergreen in the living room?"

"Only for another day. They hired someone to come in and do all the decorating, not just the tree, but also the entire house. Can you believe it, a professional tree decorator?"

"Yeah, I guess I can believe it. Julia's got the holidays all figured out, too. There's a woman who goes out and buys some of her Christmas gifts and comes back with them all neatly wrapped. Plus, she has a florist come by the house and pick up 20 crystal vases. They take them and come back the next day, each of the vases filled with elaborate fresh flower arrangements. When those die in a week, she repeats the whole thing. On top of that she hires someone to write all her thank you notes. She told me that after Brandon's baby shower the girl that came from the office to write the notes left with carpal tunnel syndrome."

"Their lives really are different than back home," Mandie commented.

"Can you imagine anyone in Montana or Oregon hiring a tree decorator?" I snickered.

I started imagining my little logging community of hard-working men coming home to an interior designer named Pierre, who was gleefully decorating their home in a holiday motif. I could hear the lumberjack saying, "Honey, whadja do with Clyde?" pointing to the spot where his prized elk head had been mounted above the dining room table. "And who is that guy in the living room? I never seen a guy in a pink shirt before!"

Everyone recognizes that holidays can be stressful. In some ways it was great that they could hire people to do all the things they didn't want to do. But the point of doing that, it seems to me, is to free up more time to celebrate with family and friends, not to eliminate the family from the holiday traditions.

When I was growing up, I always had the responsibility of going to the attic to find the holiday decorations. Then, I got to untangle the knot of green wire mixed in with our Christmas tree lights and bulbs. After that the next part of the annual routine could begin. Dad would start looking for that one bulb on a strand of 300 that was causing all the other lights not to work. I tried hard to imagine Julia on one side of the tree standing in a sea of lights and Steven on the other, yelling, "Here, I'm going to jiggle this strip and you tell me where it connects to the other strand of lights, Julia."

Among other things, this time of year took me back to my classes at the Nanny Institute. I remembered the holiday lessons that Linda had mixed in with the subjects of child development, hygiene, etiquette and the rest. One day she had decided to teach us a variety of holiday songs, which she hoped would serve us well with our future charges during the season. I'm not sure why she chose to lead them because she was Jewish, and she didn't really know the lyrics to the Christmas carols.

Her rendition of the twelve days of Christmas was particularly hilarious to all of us. She couldn't get beyond "On the first day of Christmas my true love gave to me...." After that, she would continue humming the tune without words, and gesture to us to fill in the appropriate gift, which none of us could remember either. Was it seven lords a leaping or seven swans a swimming? But she seemed determined that we should have this song on hand for the holiday season.

We had received informal tutoring on many of the Jewish traditions, customs and beliefs; sort of Judaism for Dummies, which I had found fascinating. This had already come in handy from time to time, since Steven and Julia were both raised Jewish. One of the symbols Mary had taught me about was the Menorah, which I thought was the same as a candelabra. As it turns out, I learned, it was exactly that, but a very ancient one from a time before there were candles. Instead of candles, it held eight oil dishes for eight lights, four on each side of one central flame. Mary had said that most Jews light a Menorah on the first night of Hanukkah. I remember hoping that I might get placed with a Jewish family. I had loved the closeness I felt with Mary and her daughters when I participated in the ritual of lighting one candle each night. Not to mention the wonderful food that Mary always served during the holidays.

One Friday night in December, Julia decided to light the candles. It was one of those nights when the kids were being a bit energetic and rowdy. I was looking forward to some peace and reflection when we began the Hanukkah ceremony. But just as Julia lit the candle Joshua began torturing his sister by pulling on her ponytail.

Julia blew up. "Goddamn It! You kids have no respect for anything," she yelled at them. Needless to say, we didn't continue with the lighting for the rest of the nights of Hanukkah. I got the distinct feeling that Julia viewed the whole holiday ordeal as just one big inconvenience. Sadly, her own tradition she was attempting to start with her children hadn't worked out so well either. I started wondering what her holidays had been like when she was a child.

It had already been decided that I would go home to Oregon for several days over the holidays and Concetta was going to go to Aspen with the family for Christmas. I was getting more excited at the prospect of being with my REAL family for the holidays, now that the time was getting closer. But Julia was having second thoughts.

"Suzy, I don't know what I'm going to do. Maria will still be on vacation when we get back from Aspen, and I'll have to let Concetta have two days off, and I won't have any help here on the day we get back."

"I know you want to go home and be with your family, but can you make it back before Saturday?"

I said of course, whatever she needed, and booked my flight accordingly.

Christmas was a much-anticipated event among the staff because it was the time of year that Steven gave out the yearly bonus checks. I knew from my many conversations with my sister and my friend Sarah at ACT that bonuses were the mainstay of ACT employees. Most of them actually made 75% of their entire year's earnings in bonuses. Of course, these were people with six-figure incomes. When Concetta and Maria told me that we would get Christmas bonuses, I got pretty excited. Because I was at the end of my first year, I wasn't sure if I would receive one. Maria told me Steven had given her $10,000 the year before. I also knew that Concetta's check last year was $1,000. I just couldn't wait until Christmas. Like an eight-year-old staring at all the gifts under the Christmas tree, I just *had* to know if I was going to get a bonus.

I was obsessed. I could not get it out of my mind, so I sunk to a new low. While Julia was away I began my search. I looked in drawers, peaked in stacks of mail and in cabinets trying to find a bonus check. No luck. I was just about to give up when I noticed a note to Julia from the CFO of the business, saying, "Please verify these are the amounts we decided on." Attached was a list with the names of each of us on the household staff, and an amount beside each name. Beside my name was $2,500. I could hardly contain myself. This was more than two months pay! I danced around the room waving my arms in the air in an awkward attempt to give myself a silent high-five. Fortunately no one else saw me.

> I did a horrible thing today. I snooped to see if I'd get a Christmas check. And I couldn't believe what I found. They were so generous to me! Maybe they do notice my hard work. Maybe this is Steven's way of showing that he appreciates me. On the other hand, it seems like from the note, that Julia might have had a say in the amount. I wonder whether she'll think it's too much for me, or if she suggested the amount.
> Note to Self: Try not to be so nosy.

I had more time to think several days later, on my way home for an Oregon Christmas, Hansen style. On the plane trip I needed some time with my trusty journal. My conscience was on overdrive.

> I'm feeling terrible. Can't get my misdemeanor out of my mind. Why did I search for the check even though I knew it was wrong? Maybe I have a problem. I never have been very good at minding my own business. I think this all started in the second grade when I used to pick up the phone and listen to what the neighbors were talking about on our *party line*. Maybe I have an undiagnosed compulsion.

I guess Mom knew this about me because I could never find any of my Christmas presents when I went snooping for them. And I looked high and low. When I think back, I guess she had to hide them at someone else's house. Come to think of it, maybe I have some kind of condition, like the syndrome I saw on Dateline last week about a new syndrome called chronic lateism. Maybe I have informationseekingitis.

Note to self: Ask Mom where she hid the presents all those years.

In Oregon my own family seemed like a Norman Rockwell painting compared to the abstract and modern life in LA. We played board games, opened presents, laughed. Very old-fashioned. I decided not to ask Mom about where she hid the presents. I needed a little childlike magic in my life for myself right about then.

While I was there, I went to a party with my high school friends; some of them home for the holidays on semester break from their second year in college. I was beginning to wonder why I hadn't gone to a real school. I fielded everyone's questions about my glamorous job in Southern California.

At the party, I saw my ex-boyfriend, Troy. I immediately forgot everything I'd highlighted in my *Women Who Love Too Much* book, my self-help bible. We decided to "get back together." How I thought this was ever going to work, since we didn't live in the same state, I will never know. Regardless, I was thrilled. Looking back, I can see how needy I was at the time and how much I wanted to have *somebody* that cared about me and I had a history with, in my life.

## Suitcase Packing 101

Before everyone had left for Aspen, I had been given one last official duty, a minor one. Julia had asked me to pack the children's clothing for the trip, including snowsuits. I packed the snowsuits for Joshua and Amanda, but I somehow forgot to include Brandon's baby snowsuit. When we all reconvened at the house after the holidays, Concetta, who had gone with them on the trip, filled me in on Julia's tirade about me when they got to Aspen and they hadn't been able to find Brandon's snowsuit. The first time Joshua saw me, upon my return, he told me how mad his mom was at me. He enjoyed conveying just how worked up she'd become over it. He informed me, triumphantly, that they had to go buy a new suit for Brandon because I fooooorrrrrrrrrtttgot his. He then stuck out his tongue at me, just so I wouldn't miss the point that I was a real loser.

For the first time, I wanted to respond to this truly innocent little seven-year-old by screaming,

*You know what? I don't even care that I screwed up; I don't give a rat's ass if she had to go buy a new one. Big freaking deal, I am not even bothered by my Big mistake. It sure must have been tough to have to be chauffeured into the quaint little village of Aspen. Probably damn near torture to be forced to shop for a colorful new winter outfit, for your adorable young brother. Josh, I know you don't know this, but there are children whose parents work on an assembly line for eight miserable hours to earn enough money to buy them a warm winter coat.*

Thinking about responding with my own juvenile tirade didn't make me feel *good* about myself, but it did make me feel momentarily better. Instead of screaming, I got a grip on myself and told Josh that I was sorry to hear they had to buy an additional snowsuit. Then I calmly went up to my room. Lying on my bed staring at the ceiling, I tried to be honest with myself about my performance on the job. *Was there a time that I was sick and couldn't work?* No. *I was sick several times but I still worked. When I was late to work? I was tardy after my hair fiasco, but that was it. Had I ever missed a day of work? NO! Did I ever complain, or not do exactly what was asked of me? No, I offered to help even when I wasn't asked. Did I say yes to every request they ever made of me? Absolutely.*

Even though I had taken some pre-arranged breaks to go home briefly, I had made up for them when we were away on trips and I didn't have any days off. I had been "on duty" 24 hours a day with less than a 48-hour break on the weekends, for a year. I was absolutely forbidden to leave on weeknights. And yet, Julia still showed nothing but disdain for me. As I lay there thinking, I recognized that I was more than a little discouraged and depressed. It suddenly occurred to me, all at once, that I simply couldn't stay in a place where I wanted to yell at a child who was simply imitating the behavior of his parents.

I can't take it anymore. I feel like I am living in Looneytuneville. Here I am angry and hostile towards a child for not realizing that he lives in the lap of luxury. This is ridiculous. I'm finally losing it. It is none of my business how they spend their money— I did forget to pack the snowsuit, and I am sure it was a big inconvenience to them. Problem is I should FEEL apologetic about it. I DON'T!!!! and I want to scream "GET A LIFE!!!!

You wouldn't know a real problem if it ran over you with an 18 wheeler."

Remember, only 364 days of service left! What was I thinking when I told them I'd stay two years??

CUT TO:

INTERIOR - CONFERENCE ROOM MEDICAL BUILDING - AFTERNOON

Written on the blackboard: Anger Management 101, Mr. Squigmont, Counselor.

There are eight people: seven of them are men, and one is a young woman with light brown hair. Three of the men are wearing U.S. Postal Service uniforms. The young woman is dressed in a maid's black and white outfit. All of the people have deep scowls on their faces. Participants are seated randomly in chairs that form a circle. The counselor is seated in the middle.

                    COUNSELOR
Welcome to Anger Management 101. I will be your counselor for the next three months. My name is Mr. Squigmont. You have all been sent here for the same reason - you are angry.

Counselor laughs at his own joke. Participants scowl at him. Counselor points to one of the men in a postal uniform.

                    COUNSELOR
Let us begin. You.

The man looks around as if the counselor is pointing to someone behind him.

No. You! Please stand up and tell us why the court has sent you to Anger Management.

ANGRY MAN
I beat a guy to within an inch of his life. He stole
my parking spot at Wal-Mart.


COUNSELOR
Indeed, well it's important we are honest and open.

The counselor looks at his clipboard once again.

You there, Ms. Hansen, please tell the group what
brought you here.

SUZY
I was cited for disturbing the peace and harming a government employee. I screamed so loud when I opened my
paycheck, I damaged the mail carrier's hearing. I was
docked $184.22 from my paycheck to reimburse my employ-
ers for some children's clothing. As restitution for my
crime, I have to pay $390.00 for a hearing aid for the
mailman and perform 200 hours of community service at
the school for the deaf, as ordered by the judge.

## Home Alone for Christmas

The next night I called Mandie to find out how her Christmas vacation went. She prefaced our talk with "I know you're really gonna yell at me for this one, since you say that they're always 'one paycheck away from homelessness' when it comes to spending money on me. Anyway, here goes… "Remember Mrs. Goldberg told me I could go home for a few days in December since they were taking the housekeeper with them on their vacation to Aspen? They told me I had to be back on the twenty-third, the day they were coming back. They wanted me to help them get ready to go on their annual 'day after Christmas' trip, and I would be accompanying them. When I was making my plans to go home I told Mrs. Goldberg I could get a less expensive ticket if I stayed over on a Saturday night. She said that this wouldn't work because I had to be back when they returned from their trip. She offered to pay the difference, since I was getting very few days off.

I was thrilled, but when I told her it was $200 more, she said that Mr. Goldberg would *never pay that much*. So I ended up buying the less expensive ticket and planning to stay a shorter time with my family. Then, a few days before I was to leave, they changed their vacation plans and Mrs. Goldberg said, 'Sorry, I guess you could have ended up staying over on Saturday after all,' but she didn't offer to help me change my ticket, and I was too intimidated to ask. Of course I was bummed, but I was still excited to get to go home. While I was there, they called me in Montana and said they were going to stay in Aspen until after Christmas so I didn't have to come home on the twenty-third after all. I guess it was pretty thoughtful of her to at least give me the option of staying home longer."

"Uh huh, so did you?" I said sarcastically.

"I wanted to. But I checked on changing the ticket and found out it would cost $350 to change my return. My family suggested I ask the Goldbergs to help me pay for it, but I didn't have the nerve after she said they wouldn't pay the $200 to change it in the first place. So I decided to just come back, after only three days at home, and miss Christmas with my family. I was in tears on my way back. Christmas Eve and Christmas Day I spent with some surfer guy they had staying at their house, a guy who watches their beach house for them too. It was pretty uncomfortable being in the house with him, trying to make small talk."

I was uncharacteristically speechless when Mandie finished her story because I was furious. I couldn't believe they had the nerve to treat Mandie like an afterthought and ruin her Christmas, and essentially tell her she wasn't worth $200 to them.

My God, do Mandie's employers have a heart? How could they be vacationing, knowing that Mandie was sitting at their home by herself with some stranger, not able to be with her family for Christmas. $200! My God, they've probably spent that much on lunch at some point.

They'll just never see us as valuable. They're simply not grateful that we're taking such good care of their most priceless possessions.

Then I remembered that my monthly copy of *The Nanny Newsletter* had arrived that day. I went to the dresser and grabbed it, fluffed up a couple of pillows and began to pour over it. They always had advice columns, but they rarely applied to my situation. Nevertheless, they were fun to read. I never failed to get at least a few chuckles.

This was the Holiday issue and the story headline was: Ten Great Holiday Gift Ideas for Your Nanny. *Oh, this ought to be good.*

I am quoting: "If you have a nanny that you truly appreciate, now is the time of year to make sure she knows it." *Great advice, but hello, Ms. Editor, your newsletter is sent to nannies, not mommies.* I guess I could accidentally put it on Julia's desk and leave it open to this page.

The article continued: "Here are five thoughtful things you can do for your nanny this holiday season."

1. Leave a handwritten note or poem to tell nanny how much she means to you, your children and your family.
   *Dear Suzy*
   *Roses are red*
   *Violets are blue*
   *We hope you work for us forever*
   *Because it's a hassle to get someone new.*
   *Regards,*
   *The Swartz Family*

2. A full body massage *I won't even go there. I want to have the names and numbers of the parents they think are reading this article.*

3. If you know your nanny like you should, you must also know what she likes to do for fun. Find something special that really says, 'I know who you are.' *They don't even know who they are, let alone who I am.*

4. Give her some extra days off to Christmas shop. If you are able to take time off work during the holidays, share that time with your nanny at this hectic time of the year. *Let's see. Julia will come home at noon today and offer to give me the rest of the day off to shop for my family's Christmas presents.* As I finished reading that one, I glanced out the window and saw three pigs flying by.

5. Give a homemade gift that your child makes especially for the nanny. *Steven and Julia have taken time from their busy schedules to sit down at the kitchen table with Joshua and Amanda to make dough figures together. Once they have lovingly carved the cute little creatures from their vivid imaginations, they slip them into the oven to bake them into tree decorations and then they all laugh together as Steven helps Joshua wash the paint from his*

*fingers. Wait, nightly NBC news flash. . . Hell has finally frozen over. Details at eleven.*

I had to call Mandie back. I couldn't believe there were people who actually treated their nannies like this. When I read it to Mandie that night, she couldn't either. I was beginning to see how frustrated, bitter and angry I was becoming.

That evening was the first time I began to give serious thought to quitting. I'd given it consideration many times before, never seriously because I had agreed on a two-year commitment when they hired me. Now that I could see how resentful I was becoming, I knew I needed to seriously reconsider.

The next morning I decided to actually call a placement agency, just to test the waters for new employment. I was told there were plenty of jobs for someone of "my caliber." The woman at the agency started rattling them off—"I've got an opening with Cybill Shepherd, a nightmare job, I might add. She just fired all of her staff. I also have Zuckerman, he's a producer ... and we just got a call from Shelley Long. You would qualify for any of these positions."

I was told that I could literally pick and choose. When the woman asked me when I could interview, I told her it would be impossible to get away during the week and that I could interview only on the weekends. When I related how difficult my present circumstances were, as far as ever getting time off during the week, she laughed and made light of it.

"Oh for God's sake, just tell your boss you've got female issues and you have to go to the doctor," she offered.

"No. You don't understand. That would be out of the question. If she ever found out, I would be drawn and quartered in downtown Brentwood and, if I lived through it, I certainly wouldn't get a decent reference. I'm afraid that they'll be so angry when I quit that they won't give me a good reference, regardless."

She said, "Oh brother, you're exaggerating. I've never even heard of this guy, and if he's as big as you say he is, than he's far too busy to worry about spending time giving YOU a bad reference. What's he going to do to you?" she laughed.

## Sally Field and My Right Arm

I hadn't yet figured out how to get away or at least how to end my misery, when I got an uplifting call from my friend Tammy, Miss Pollyanna herself.

"Suzy, you're not going to believe it. I'm here. I'm in LA."

"What do you mean?"

"Sally called back on Sunday and said the baby nurse she hired instead of me didn't work out. She said she wanted me to start this Tuesday, as in today. I drove down in my old GTO with my Mom, and I started work today."

"No way, you're gonna be Sally's right arm now?" (My brain had stubbornly clung to the time that Julia had referred to me that way when Sally had called about finding a nanny.)

"Yeah, I'm here now! I was in such a hurry to get here to take the job, I'm driving 95 in the desert. Who knew my car could go that fast? and then we get pulled over!"

"We'll you're preaching to the choir here. The story of my life, so what happened?"

"So mom comes up with the brilliant idea to tell the cop that I'm on my way to be Sally Field's nanny and see if he'll let me off!"

"Just like an a scene out of *Smokey and the Bandit*," I interrupt.

"So I take a chance and tell him, and it works! He even tips his hat and says, 'Well, say hi to Sally for me,' and we went on our way."

"I'm finding out in Southern California that the name-dropping thing with the police works quite well." I commented.

"That's not the best part. You will not believe this. I get here, and I walk in the door, after dropping Mom off at the airport. Sally's just out of the shower, and she's holding the baby. She says she's having a big dinner party tonight, and that's why she needed me to start immediately. People are coming to this party to see the baby for the first time. Sally says, 'Go upstairs and get him dressed in something cute and I'll come and get you when it's time to come down,' can you believe it?"

"She came up to get me about eight, and as we're walking down the stairs she says to me casually, 'I don't think you'll know anyone here tonight except Kurt and Goldie.' I stop walking mid-flight, grab her arm and shriek, 'My God, they're here? Kurt Russell and Goldie Hawn are here?'"

"My God, Tammy," I interjected. "You said that? You can't act like that!"

"Why not? Anyway, Sally says to me, 'Is that a problem?' I went on a long rant: 'Sally, I don't think you understand. Two days ago I am living in my hometown with a population of less than 8,000 people and now, tonight I move into your house, you and Goldie, are my absolute favorite stars; I always go see your movies. You're so great!'"

"I can't believe you said that stuff! I've never been able to be that honest about my celebrity encounters. I've been too scared. I was given strict instructions not to act like meeting these people was anything out of the ordinary." Tammy said that it had been fine and that Sally had been really nice to her about it.

"So then what happened?" I asked.

"I went down and there at the table, along with other people, was Kate Capshaw."

"Oh my God," I gasped. "So, Spielberg was there too?"

"I don't even know. After I laid eyes on Kurt, I almost dropped dead."

"Oh great, so you don't even know who else was there? Well, then what happened? Oh wait. I've gotta go. Brandon's crying. Give me your phone number. Oh never mind, I can get it from Julia"

"Okay...wait. There's more, Suzy!"

"Yes, yes, I know. Welcome to Nanny World."

Tammy ended up staying with Sally for three years. That whole time, Tammy would call me to relate one after another of Sally's expressions of thoughtfulness. Sally left her a nice little note. Sally went out of her way to let her take time off. Sally offered emotional support whenever Tammy felt homesick. Sally sent a car to pick her up at the airport when she returned from visits at home. It was a veritable nanny-employer love fest. I was very happy for Tammy, and I was glad I could give her such a great reference, knowing that she would do an outstanding job. And of course, during my weaker moments, I had a pity party for myself that I had not found a similar situation. I know that bitterness and jealousy are unbecoming personal attributes. Handing Tammy that job lead provided me three years of opportunity to acquire personal growth in many areas.

# But the *Goodbye Girl* had a Happy Ending

It was the second week in January and as disgruntled and frustrated as I was, I knew I would never work up the nerve to actually say the words "I want to quit." I was resigned to completing my tour of duty simply because I didn't want to go back on my original commitment.

I finally decided I needed to call somebody to talk over my situation. Since I was still embarrassed about not heeding Linda and Carolyn's advice, I called Mary, the instructor I had become close to during my education. I knew she would be able to give me some insight on how to handle my situation. She was a great listener, as usual, and we talked for over an hour. It was a huge help. As I was describing my resentment for being stuck here for another year, she said the words that I still remember "Suzy, you didn't commit to stay at this job under ANY circumstances." That really hit me.

The *very* next evening at about ten o'clock I was sitting in my bed complaining to Mandie over the phone. I heard a knock at my door and I knew it must be Julia. I froze, thinking she must have heard part of the conversation. I told myself maybe she didn't, completely forgetting about the results of my controlled experiment with Concetta a few months earlier. Julia hardly ever came in my room. She had mentioned that she always thought it was important to give her nannies privacy, which was something I had always appreciated. I told her to come in, and she opened my door. I was in my pajamas with the covers pulled up.

"I have to go. Julia's here," I told Mandie.

"OH MY GOD, WHY?"

"I'll talk to you tomorrow," I tried to say, calmly.

"WHAT IS SHE SAYING?...ARE YOU IN TROUB....."

"Okay. Bye-bye," I hung up on her mid sentence.

Julia sat on the twin bed next to mine. I could feel my heart racing. *Why in the hell is she in here? What in the world is she going to say to me?*

## What We Have Here is a Failure to Communicate

She began, "Would it be okay if I talked with you?"

"Yes, of course," I responded awkwardly.

"I've noticed lately that you seem to have a chip on your shoulder. What's wrong with you?"

My first feeling was shock: *I can't believe she noticed anything about me. Have I been acting different?* I didn't answer immediately because she didn't pause. She clearly had more to say.

"You know, I was pretty disappointed in you about the snowsuit, because I asked you if you packed all the kids' snowsuits and you said yes. Then when I told you it wasn't in the suitcase later, you didn't seem to even care about your mistake."

That split second, before I had a chance to prepare my thoughts, I just blurted out, "I'm not happy here. I've been thinking about quitting, that's what's wrong with me. I work nearly 24 hours a day, I can't even leave the house in the evenings and I don't want to keep on doing this. I have no life other than work."

Julia looked stunned beyond shock. There was an awkward silence as she sat there, scowling at me. Her chest was heaving with labored breaths. I felt myself cringing. The lump in my throat must have been the size of a baseball. I wanted to put my hands over my ears, fearing her anger.

"What do you mean?" she said with a disgusted expression on her face, not waiting for me to answer. "What exactly do you think a nanny does, Suzy?"

I came up with the brilliant line: *Well, I think some of them work 9 to 10 hours a day,* but I didn't have the nerve to open my mouth for fear of what else might come out.

"I've been thinking of quitting," I muttered sheepishly, in case she didn't hear me the first time.

"We do a lot for you. I don't think you understand that."

"Julia, I am very appreciative of *everything* you've done for me..." She rolled her eyes, as if to say, yeah right, I don't believe you.

"I feel very bad and I'm sorry, but I'm just not happy," I said pathetically.

She started using her sarcastic tone, "So what are you saying? You're just going to leave tomorrow."

*My God. I could never do that to the kids.* "No, of course not. I'll stay until you can find someone else."

"This is just like you. I tell you something I don't like about you, and you just up and quit."

*Where the hell did that come from? Just like me what??? As if every time I was reprimanded I had threatened to quit? I have never mentioned ANYTHING ever about leaving here.*

She concluded our little conference by saying, "I wish I would have known you were going to do this before we gave you that Christmas bonus." With that, she let out a deep stage sigh, stood up, swirled around and left the room in a huff. I didn't fall asleep that night until three in the morning, worrying about what she was going to say to Steven. I half feared he would be knocking on my door any minute.

When Steven got home that night, I broke out in a sweat. I could hear her downstairs talking to him, something she had never done before. She was always in bed when he got home late. I couldn't hear what they were saying, only their voices going back and forth.

I hardly slept the next two nights. I knew I would need to talk to Steven, and I had begun rehearsing the scene in my mind, playing both characters. I knew he was going to erupt like a volcano. I heaped guilt on myself by the shovel-full. I wondered if I should give the Christmas bonus back. But my biggest worry was about the children. My relationship with Brandon had sustained me. The kind of love I had experienced for him was the reason I had wanted to be a nanny in the first place. I had a great deal of love and affection for Amanda, a lot of sympathy for Joshua's angry behavior and a love for him that he couldn't ever truly let in. But, Brandon had opened his heart to me, as I had to him.

I began to think about the impact my departure would have on him. After all, I was his primary caregiver. I was the one who'd made him feel secure and who met his needs. He was the only one in the entire family that laughed, really laughed, not a baby giggle either. His was a big hearty belly laugh. He was the only one that was truly happy and content. But the saddest thought that crossed my mind was that I wouldn't be missed. There would be yet another nanny after me. Would Brandon even know I ever existed, a month from now? I was going to be a blip on the radar screen of his life.

> I'm so miserable. I want to be me—I am tired of not reacting like a normal person. My usual excitement about things is gone. Today when I talked to Magic Johnson, the whole time I was thinking that this should be a fun moment in my life. But NO. I can't express those kinds of feelings around here. I can't express much of anything I naturally feel here.
>
> The stress is not worth it. The money I make is not worth it. To give up the feeling of joy, is not worth it. And yet I'm so scared I'm going to wimp out when Steven finally confronts me.

## Some Men You Just Can't Reach

In the days after our first conversation, I had thought about my decision, like he had suggested. It seemed like my obsession to be the best caregiver I could possibly be had sustained me for an entire year. My only real nourishment had come from my own deep need to be a part of helping to grow healthy, happy, well-adjusted children. Outside of my work I hadn't found anything fulfilling in their world, and in my job I had stopped trying to do my very best. I knew that I was emotionally drained and miserable, so I had to leave.

I braced myself for the next conversation. I knew there were two choices. If I stayed, he would be happy. If I left, I would suddenly become the worst nanny ever. I remembered how easily he had intimidated poor Maria all these years, every time she wanted to move out of the house.

I knew he wouldn't like my answer. I had to stand up to him. I rehearsed in my mind an answer to every objection he would make. And I dreaded the inevitable confrontation.

A few mornings after our first talk, he came into Brandon's room while I was getting him dressed. He politely asked me if I had reconsidered my decision to leave. He repeated that he had always loved my work and that he didn't want me to go. The more he talked, the more afraid I became that I'd back down. He wasn't the type of man who was used to taking no for an answer.

He repeated his request for me to stay until after the Aspen trip, or at least until after Julia returned from her vacation at The Golden Door spa. *That means I'd be here another two months! I thought.*

I just hung my head and said, "No. I really do want to give my notice. Mr. Swartz, I'll stay for four weeks," I said, as I repeated my offer from the earlier conversation.

"I'm not happy here, and I don't think it's fair to the children to be around them when I feel like this." I explained.

"Oh Suzy," he rolled his eyes and used the most condescending voice possible. "Brandon is just a baby. He doesn't know the difference. And Amanda and Josh are too busy to know the difference."

I didn't answer. *You can't hit any lower, can you?*

"Don't you think that's pretty egocentric of you?" he asked. I wasn't positive what the word meant. *Note to self: Get to college soon, girl!*

Suddenly, I saw him as he really was. A sad, pitiful shell that in reality had nothing but things. I looked into his eyes as his words flew by me and drifted away. My mind raced. You say your children are the most important things in the world to you, and I know you believe that with every fiber of your being, but those are empty words. You're no more connected to them than you are with your wife. All of this is just another picture, like the ones hanging on your walls. A seemingly ideal life, a position of great importance, lots of money and power, a beautiful home, three adorable children and a wife who would do anything for you. But none of it goes beyond the depth of a single brush stroke. There's nothing there, only a very thin veneer. Nevertheless, like a talented artist, you've made it appear that there is depth to the scene.

When he realized that I wasn't going to change my mind, his face grew ugly. "Do you plan to work here, in this town...as a nanny?" he said with a smirk.

"Um, yes, I think so," I said, shocked at his question.

"Hmm, we'll see," he said, chortling. He had become the Grinch himself. With that he turned in his $2,000 suit and walked half way down the hall. He then barked out "This has really fucked up my week!" to the staircase.

At that moment, as sad and as frightened as I was by the words out of Steven's mouth, as painful as the experience was, I realized I *did* have an inner strength that would see me through it. I tried to reassure my numb, shaking body that I had made the right decision. I finished dressing

Brandon and took him in my room to play. I didn't want to go downstairs. I was too scared to face Julia.

An hour after Steven left, Julia appeared at my open bedroom door. I handed Brandon a toy train and looked up at her. "Steven just called and he wants you out of the house, immediately!" I stood up silently and walked toward her in shock.

"He doesn't want to have to see you when he comes home," she snapped.

"Um..." my mouth was dry I couldn't form any words.

"Was it really that bad living here?" Julia asked in a horribly disgusted voice.

I started to answer her and she cut me off.

"Oh, never mind. You're going to leave anyway so it doesn't really matter now. I just wish I would have known that you were going to quit, before I gave you that Christmas bonus." She repeated to me for a second time.

I considered offering to give it back. Instead I pleaded, "Julia, I would still like to continue seeing the kids." She cut me off with...

"No, I don't think so. I don't think that is a good idea. I think it is just too confusing for the children, it just wouldn't work."

With that declaration she walked out of my bedroom. My heart sank. I didn't want to believe what my ears had just heard. I guess I had always known, on some level, that this would be my ultimate punishment, if I chose to leave. Maybe it is part of why I had stayed up until this point.

I was devastated. I walked over to my little Brandon, playing innocently on the floor. I couldn't believe that I might never be able to see him again.

I tried to get my thoughts together. I didn't know what to do first. *Does this mean I stop taking care of the children and pack my stuff?* Cindy could help me settle down and give me advice. So I called her at the office. "Cindy, Julia says I have to move out right now, what do I do? Do I keep taking care of Brandon while I'm packing?"

"No, you don't. Just start packing."

"I have several car loads of stuff to take to your house; how am I going to do that all by myself?"

Cindy was probably thinking, *To my house - oh great, that's all we need, one more permanent resident and all your crap.* But what she calmly said was, "Can I come help you after work?"

"No, he said I have to be out before he gets home. Can't you come help me now?"

"No, I can't. I'm working." Now my sister's strong work ethic, the one I was so proud of when I got her the job, was backfiring on me.

"Can't you tell them that you have to leave to do one of your I-9 form things?"

"No, Suzy, I can't do that. What if Steven was to show up while I was there?"

"Alright, fine," I answered. "I have to go so I can get started. I don't have a key to your apartment so I'll just have to pile it all up in the hallway until you get home to let me in."

"Sorry, Suzy, but I have to go. Dan Gibbons the CFO is walking up."

I walked downstairs with Brandon in my arms, hoping to God I wouldn't see Julia. When I went into the kitchen Maria was standing there with her boyfriend. I said, "Can you watch Brandon? Julia said I have to get out right now, and he hasn't had his breakfast this morning."

"Yees, I know. I heared," she said. "Heere, give me dee baby. Don't worry I feed him."

I couldn't say much without my throat constricting.

"Thank you," was all I whispered. I hurried back upstairs. *How was I going to do this? I had no boxes and a lot of stuff.*

It ended up taking me about four hours to fill garbage bags (the cheap kind, not the ones used for the trash compactor, of course) with all my worldly possessions. I had to make several trips in the car to Cindy's apartment, so it took quite a while to get everything out.

Concetta was off that day, so I wasn't able to tell her goodbye in person. I hugged Maria. We both cried, and she just softly said, "I so sorry. You know how dey are."

Amanda and Joshua were sitting at the dinner table, eating a snack and watching TV. I knelt down next to Amanda and said, "Honey, I have to go, but you can call me anytime. I'm leaving my sister's phone number with Concetta and Maria, and whenever you want to talk to me you can call me."

"Where are you going?"

"I'm going to live with my sister," I answered.

"Why? Why are you leaving?" I was at a loss. *What could I tell a four-year-old to help her understand?*

Joshua interjected, "Yeah, I know you're leaving. My mom told me that my dad's really mad at you."

I chose not to respond to that invitation, and I hugged Amanda for as long as she would let me. Next, I went back in the kitchen and hugged Brandon one more time while Maria held him, and then I went to Joshua and hugged him and told him I was sorry I had to leave him. He didn't hug me back. I didn't know then that I would never see him again.

Until now I had no idea how terrible it would feel to leave the kids. They didn't talk about this at nanny school. There's such a strong sense of loss, like I'm losing my own family. Steven and Julia just don't get it. They don't have any idea how this could affect Brandon. I was his primary caregiver for over a year, then one day he wakes up and I'm not there. I don't know if I want to find another nanny position. I don't know if I can go through this again. It's too hard.

Note to Self: Call nanny school and tell them they need to prepare students for this.

After the numbness wore off, in the days following my eviction, I started to worry. I knew that Steven and Julia were angry, and I kept replaying in my mind his threat that I'd never work in this town again. I told myself to get real. Would Steven really spend his precious time answering calls from some random stay-at-home mom from Santa Monica, calling to inquire about his former nanny? And what could either of them say about me? I could hear Julia now, telling on me: "She let the kids watch too much TV and one time she threw butter at our son."

Nevertheless, I still worried. What if the busiest man in Los Angeles felt motivated to concern himself with his ex-nanny's business? Something about the way I'd seen Steven do business cued me to the possibility that this could get ugly. I had a strong feeling that he wasn't going to let a "little girl from Podunkville" say NO to him without making sure she experienced the consequences.

I called back the women at the agency, the one who had previously suggested that I was making "too big a deal," out of the fear that my employer would be angry with me after I quit. She was thrilled to hear that I was available and booked me for an interview the very next day.

When I got there I discovered the parents who were nanny hunting, were writers who had made their reputation by writing for *The Golden Girls*. The mom, who was pregnant, recognized my name right away.

"Oh, I've already heard about you, Suzy."

*Uh oh.* "Oh, really?"

"Yes, you're the great nanny. You're the one who diagnosed Steven Swartz's youngest son with meningitis."

*Excuse me?* There isn't much that's missed in Hollywood. Except for the truth, which would make the story much less interesting.

"Oh that. I didn't actually diagnose him. In fact..." She cut me off.

"Yes. Steven's our agent," she said beaming at her husband, conveying the message: *This is great, Steven only settles for the best, so this girl must be outstanding.*

This wasn't looking too good. Not only did these two essentially work for Steven, but there was also the small matter of the location, which happened to be ten doors down from my former residence. *I ask you, in the huge metropolis of LA, what were the statistical chances of that?*

"Tell us about yourself," she continued.

I mumbled something. *Why bother? You're not going to hire me after Mr. Superagent gets a hold of you.*

I knew Steven would tell them not to hire me, but what possible explanation could he find? Maybe that I quit after I accepted the Christmas bonus check. Of course he could always tell about the time I tried to wear that hideous jumpsuit that made me look like I was an exterminator. I could hear it now: *I thought she might try and wear it in on the plane and I'd suffer a severe blow to my public image; she simply doesn't have good sense when it comes to fashion!*

The interview went well and I could tell they liked me: they gave me a tour of their elegant home, which had been featured in *Architectural Digest,* and then showed me the room I would live in. When they walked me out to my car, both smiling from ear to ear, they said they thought I would fit in perfectly with their family.

As I started my car, I told myself that I had just been paranoid. It apparently hadn't bothered them at all that I'd worked for Steven. The more I thought about my previous concern, the more I convinced myself that "Mr. Almighty" might not even bother to take a call at his office from a couple seeking a reference.

But it turned out my fears had been justified. The next day the woman from the agency called and told me very nonchalantly that the couple I met yesterday had decided to "pass on me." It was as if they were playing Monopoly and had just drawn the "take a ride on the Reading Railroad card" and I was still stuck in jail waiting to roll doubles.

"They're *PASSING* on me! I told you!" I reminded her. "They must have talked to Steven."

"I checked it out, and you're right about that," she said calmly, "but I've talked with Steven at length today and I think I managed to work a deal with him." *Oh really? I can tell by your voice he has you running scared, lady.* "I can send you on *any* interview I want, as long as it isn't with someone who works in the entertainment industry." She said this as if it was just a minor detail in their agreement, the part where she had agreed to cut out 90% of the population that might have a job available.

Okay, I wasn't just paranoid. Now I know I have a real reason to be worried. That agency lady, Miss "I've-never-heard-of-him-you're-just-exaggerating" sure did change her tune today.

I might as well just pack up right now, but then how far does his influence reach? If I leave here and go back to Oregon to start college, is he going to call the Dean and say not to let me in? Stop thinking that way. Now you really are getting paranoid.

Note to self: I have got to find out why everyone is afraid of him and takes his word as the gospel.

The next day, reality was really beginning to set in. I interviewed with a couple that had never worked for or with Steven, but they did know him socially, just like everybody else in town. Despite a great interview that ended with smiles all around, two days later they called and declined.

I knew that a person with my experience was in great demand in Southern California. The majority of wealthy people were seeking a child-care giver who was intelligent, hard-working and devoted to children. But the unspoken, "non-politically" correct reality was that they also wanted someone who was not overweight and did not speak English as a second language. It was starting to look like the word from the Swartz' had more power than my qualifications as a nanny school graduate, a native speaker of English and someone who naturally loved caring for kids. It was clear that Steven didn't mind at all giving his valuable time to make sure that I wasn't hired. If I wasn't going to work for him, I guess he didn't want me working for ANYBODY.

CUT TO:

INTERIOR - OFFICE - DAYTIME

Attractive man seated behind large desk. Phone rings. He pushes speaker button.

           RECEPTIONIST
Sir, I have Cher on line 3.

           MAN
Tell her I'll call her back in half an hour.

           RECEPTIONIST
Yes sir.

Phone buzzes in again. Man hits speaker button.

           RECEPTIONIST
Sir, I have Jane Fonda on line 6.

           MAN
Tell her I'm in a meeting.

           RECEPTIONIST
Yes sir.

Phone rings again.

           RECEPTIONIST
Sir, I have a Mrs. Larison on line 1. She says she is interviewing your former nanny and would like to get a reference. I can take a messa......

           MAN
There's no one I'd rather talk to. Put her right through.

CUT TO:

EXTERIOR - CITY SIDEWALK - DAYTIME

It's windy and snowing, blizzard conditions. A woman who looks too young to be homeless is dressed in rags and pushing a shopping cart. She has a tattered shawl pulled over her head. All the passersby are bundled up. Woman approaches a newsstand. She looks up at copies of The Oregonian lining the newsstand walls.

                    YOUNG WOMAN
Oh my God. How long is he going to beat that drum? All right already. You won.

## LOS ANGELES SUPER AGENT FIRES NANNY: VOWS "SHE WILL NEVER WORK IN THIS TOWN AGAIN!"

Scene ends with girl pushing cart off into the distance.

# TAKE TWO!

## "I NEED HAIR AND MAKEUP NOW!"

# Sleeping with
# the Enemy

The more I dwelled on Steven's blackballing me, the angrier I grew. How could he possibly justify his behavior in his own mind? He had begged me to stay, telling me how much he liked the care I gave the kids and yet here he was warning everyone what a terrible nanny I was. If I was so unfit, why did he want me to finish out the year? How much harm could he do? I was pretty nervous when I looked at the evidence so far, maybe he really did have the power to keep me from working.

Since the good ole placement coordinator, Ms. "I Have Worked a Deal with the President of ACT," wasn't returning my phone calls, I decided to look elsewhere for a referral. I took my resume to a placement agency called Malibu Mommies. Maybe this agency would be a little more understanding of my situation. Malibu Mommies sounded like a wholesome and friendly place. I told them up front about my tenure with the Swartz' and the whole business with the reference. Surprisingly, Malibu Mommies lived up to my hopes; they said that they'd be willing to work with my situation, because they had seen it happen to many other nannies.

To my great relief, two days after I applied at the new agency they called me saying that they had an actress who was okay with the fact that Steven wasn't going to give a glowing report of my tenure with him. I wondered who could have that kind of independence in this town. I showed up for the interview at a home off Pacific Coast Highway in

Malibu, on a quiet little street with a front gate and a hedge all the way around the property. After I pushed the button and was let in, I drove up a short driveway to a large but unpretentious home with a huge front yard.

Barefoot, the owner of the home opened the door seconds after I rang the bell and greeted me with a hardy handshake. "Welcome Suzy," she said, in a familiar husky voice paired with a big smile. There I was, warmly shaking Debra Winger's hand!

Before she even interviewed me, she showed me around the house. Although I had never seen her big hit *Urban Cowboy*, I loved *Terms of Endearment* and I had watched the Academy Awards the night she was nominated for best supporting actress. When I'd seen her on the big screen, I had a feeling she might be a "real person" who really wasn't affected by fame. When we finally sat down, I discovered my intuition had been right. She offered me tea, and I explained about working for Steven for the past year and his unhappiness with me. She said she was okay with that, and said she'd tell the nanny agency she didn't need a reference from him.

She had already called all my references from Cottage Grove and the practicum families I had worked for. She was just as genuine in person as she was on the screen, and I couldn't help noticing how unassuming her home was. There were no Chinese artifacts glued to tables or famous paintings on the walls. She told me she had an alarm system, but she never used it.

## A Nanny and A Mommy

I soon learned that Debra was one of the few clients in ACT's history who had jumped ship. Since I knew from personal experience how much Steven hated the word no, I could only imagine how he reacted when she told him she was leaving.

"I like Steven, but I couldn't continue to work with him. It was as if I knew my boss was dumping toxic waste into a playground; I couldn't sit by silently and do nothing." She didn't explain what the toxic waste was, and I never said a word about my time with the Swartz', except to say how hard it was to leave the children. Steven's response to her quitting, she later told me, was to threaten to tell the media she was pregnant. She had recently had a miscarriage, and she had been very upset after that. She had decided to wait a little longer, to retain a little privacy, before she was willing to divulge her second pregnancy to the public. Steven had gone right for her place of vulnerability. I've wondered since then if he had anything to do with her not getting a lot of big parts or publicity after that.

Debra had a nine-month-old son named Noah. She said that her husband, Timothy Hutton, was currently in Baton Rouge working on a new film. She told me that I would be going with her on an extended visit to the set in a couple of months. Timothy and her friends had insisted she hire a nanny because Noah was up most nights and she was exhausted. Debra didn't really think that she needed a nanny because she was home all day. By now, it seemed like a foreign thought to me, the idea that a woman wanted to take care of her own child by herself. She told me she had hired a baby nurse for a short time after Noah was born, but it hadn't worked out. By the time the nurse figured out that the baby was awake and crying in the middle of the night, Debra had already been in his room comforting him for five minutes. So she had let her go after two weeks.

Debra and I were comfortable with each other right off the bat. During the interview, she even asked me if I would be interested in reading scripts for her, just to give her an idea of what the story was about, since her agent sent her so many. I was thrilled with the prospect of doing a secretarial/assistant task, and told her so. She told me before I left that she wanted me to start right away, so we made arrangements for me to move in. I was given a nice bedroom and bathroom on the bottom floor with an enormous bed that sat so high off the floor I nearly had to get a stepladder to climb in.

This time, I was determined to assert myself regarding my salary. Debra asked me if I thought I should be paid less than I was at the Swartz' because I was now only taking care of one child. I had never thought of it that way. Then she said, "Or do you see the pay as compensation for your time, regardless of the number of children you are caring for?" I was amazed by her clarity and her concern for me. I told her I didn't want to make less than I did at my last job. Then I blurted out, "I want to net $400 a week." Why I threw in the net thing, I have no idea. And I don't have a clue how I came up with a raise of $100 a week. I guess I thought I was done being taken advantage of, so boy oh boy, I was going to be paid well this time, to work 24 hours a day. Of course I didn't bother to ask IF I was actually going to be on call 24 hours a day. I also never brought up the issue of a contract *again!* I was too embarrassed to, since she seemed so casual about everything and easy to talk to. I thought she might be offended by the formality and think it was unnecessary.

I love Debra! She's so cool, so completely REAL. And she lives and works in this town. Amazing. I embarrassed myself once again. When my interview with Debra was over, I realized that I would be working about half the time I did before, and yet I'd be making more money. Maybe I drove too hard a bargain. It isn't her fault that I've been a doormat. She shouldn't have to "make up for it." She said we could work it out with the money, so maybe it doesn't matter to her. I have high hopes that this will be a great working relationship.

Mom had to call me tonight to tell me she ran out and rented *Black Widow*, since Debra was in it, and then she proceeded to give me a blow-by-blow of the movie. Finally I had to cut her off and tell her it really wasn't necessary for me to know the plot. I informed my mother that I wasn't going to be given a movie trivia quiz to get the job.

Note to self: Try not to be so hard on your mother. She deserves to have a little fun with your Hollywood connections. That's more than you can say for yourself so far, but things may be looking up.

## Life with the Urban Cowgirl

My sister was more than happy to help me move all my stuff from her cramped apartment into Debra's house. Not only was Cindy sharing the place with her two original friends, but also, one of the girls had taken in Pedro, a sweet fellow employee who was down on his luck. He was living there part-time. In addition, I had invited Troy to move down since we had, against my better judgment, 'reunited' when I was home at Christmas time. So, he took up residency on my sister's couch while he looked for a job.

Working for Debra was the polar opposite of working for the Swartz'. For one thing, she loved being a mom so much that she spent far more time with Noah than I did. The plan was for me to start getting up in the night with him so that she could get some much needed rest. Noah was very bonded to his mother, and he wasn't too sure about this other person living in his house and coming into his room in the middle of the night. So, we worked on getting him used to me when he woke up in the middle of the night. I'd stand in his room in the dark of night while she tended him, trying to get him 'used to me.' Now, here was a professional nanny dilemma. When

I was up at all hours of the night with Brandon, no one else was ever up, so it didn't matter what I was wearing. It now seemed inappropriate to report to work with no bra on. I'd have to write to the National Nanny Protocol Agency and see how one handles themselves in this type of situation. They have to have a section on what to do when you have to stand next to your employer in your pajamas, while maintaining a professional appearance.

One of the first mornings I was at Debra's I answered the phone and a male voice said, "You must be Suzy."

"Uh, yes I am."

"Oh, hi! This is Tim calling from down in Louisiana."

"Oh yes. How are you?"

"Doing great. I'm so glad you're there. Debra didn't think she needed anyone. But I know she's getting tired with Noah getting up so much in the night. And I wanted her to have some help while I was gone. I really miss those two."

"Yes, I'm hoping Noah will become comfortable with me so that I can get up in the night with him instead of Debra"

"So, I look forward to meeting you, when you all come down here," he said cheerfully.

"Yes, I guess so, it was nice talking to you and I hope I can help Debra get rested up. Let me find her for you, so you can talk to her."

A cordial conversation. One marriage partner concerned about the other. There was even an indication that they valued the child-care giver. It was freaky. Abnormal. It had taken me just one short year to reach this level of cynicism.

In addition to my help, Debra had a cook and a housekeeper. A few nights a week the cook came over to make dinner. The rest of Debra's meals were prepared ahead and put in the freezer with heating instructions. She made the most awesome, 1000 calorie-a-slice cheesecake. Debra loved it. She told me that when she was preparing for a movie it wasn't allowed in the house. As in, everything that was high calorie was banned from the premises. But since she had just finished a film, the no sweets rule didn't apply and she liked to indulge herself.

I didn't mind helping her out a bit. I didn't feel like I had to sneak, like when I ate the homemade cookies at the Swartz' house. After Maria had found out I was eating so many, she had restricted me to two a day. If I exceeded my limit, my "chocolate chip punishment" was to help her make another batch. Remembering this made me miss the Swartz' staff and children so badly that I made a note to myself reminding me to put it out of my mind as much as I could. It hurt too much.

Debra was a principled person, and I soon found out that she was well known in Hollywood for not being willing to play the game. Later, when I got to know her better, I found out that she had moved to Israel when she was just sixteen to live in a kibbutz. After she came back, she got a job at Magic Mountain, where she was in a serious accident that left her in a coma. She was partly paralyzed and blinded in one eye for several months. She told me that this had given her time to think long and hard about where her life was going, and that's when she had decided to become an actress. She seemed very thoughtful about how she wanted to live her life and I could see why.

Debra seemed to take things like the environment very seriously. She wasn't into being politically correct to fit a label. She based many of her personal decisions—what she bought, where she shopped, what they ate—on how it impacted the planet. She used cloth diapers. She said she'd once used disposable diapers on Noah when they flew somewhere. When he got a horrendous rash, she researched what the absorbent material was made of and vowed to never use them again.

Debra said that her cook had previously worked for Steven Spielberg, and she said how funny she thought that was. I didn't get it. She went on to say how she thought it was all her karma, to have these people come to her, people that had been previously employed by someone she'd had problems with. I hadn't known she'd had a falling out with the famous director. What's not to like about her? I wondered. I never asked her what the problem was, but the cook's stories about Spielberg's child made Josh sound like an angel. I didn't really get what she meant about karma, but it was kind of weird that two of the people in Hollywood that she had trouble with, had essentially sent her their cast-offs.

I like it here with Debra, but miss the kids so much I can't stand it. It's almost harder to call Concetta and ask about them than it is to have no information. I dreamed last night that Steven and Julia said they were sorry and asked me to come back and visit the kids.

Note to self: get some hobbies. Buy a book on deciphering dreams.

I hadn't been working long at Debra's when I got a cold. She said that this would prevent me from getting up in the night with Noah, and that I would need to rest and take a lot of vitamin C. I couldn't believe my ears for more than one reason. First, it blew me away that she would even notice that I had a cold. Second, I couldn't believe that she would suggest I lighten my workload so I could get over my minor illness quicker. I immediately called Mandie to report that my new employer had noticed I was blowing my nose a lot and was concerned about me getting enough sleep. She laughed heartily into the phone, and then she complimented me on the little comedy routine that I was trying out on her. To this day, Mandie still thinks that I made up the story just to get a reaction out of her.

This place was in another galaxy altogether than the one I inhabited previously.

## They Never Show This in *People* Magazine

One morning Debra abruptly announced that Timothy's mother was coming to town for a visit to see the baby. She asked if I would go and pick her up at the airport. Debra called her mother-in-law and told her that I would be wearing a flower so that she could find me. We found a very pathetic looking small flower in the yard and pinned it on my jacket so she could spot me. Debra said anyone would have to be leaning right up against me to see the wilted thing, and we both laughed about it.

I set off to LAX in my car to retrieve her. The flight was due in at American Airlines at noon, so I arrived half an hour early and found a safe parking spot. I wanted to have plenty of time to locate her arrival gate. I still hadn't met Timothy, but I knew how cute he was from having seen him in pictures. Since Debra hadn't really given me a description of what his mother looked like, I figured I'd just look for the cute family gene when I got to the gate. Between that and my little flower, I figured I wouldn't have a problem.

At 11:45 I was standing at the gate ready to scrutinize every woman over the age of fifty as they came out of the tunnel. At 12:15 the plane arrived and I stood smiling, looking to catch the eyes of any women who might fit the part. On that particular flight there wasn't one woman who acted like she was looking for ANYONE, so I asked the attendant at the gate if there were any people left on the plane. She said no.

Apparently either I'd missed her, or she'd missed the plane. It was now nearly 12:45 so I used a pay phone and called Debra, only to get the answering service. She never answered her phone, preferring her privacy. Instead, she'd just call in whenever she felt like getting her messages. The voice at the answering service asked who was calling. I told her I was Debra's nanny and that I was at the airport. I asked her to try to ring through to the house.

The operator came back after a minute and said no one answered. I was stunned at how easy it actually was to get through. Here's a very well-known actress with an answering service that believes anyone who calls and wants them to ring through to the house. What if I were a reporter from the Enquirer? I decided that the hard part about contacting celebrities is that you can't get the phone number in the first place. I wasn't surprised when she didn't answer. Ever since I had lived there, I had never actually heard the phone ring at her house, unless it was Timothy calling. Maybe he has some backline special number, I thought.

The next American flight into this gate wasn't for another two hours, and I realized that I could easily spend the entire day waiting right there. I called the answering service back ten minutes later. This time the operator told me to leave a message and she would see if she could get it to her some time today. All righty then. Sometime today would be great for me!

"Tell Debra her mother-in-law did not get off the plane. Find out if she called," I snapped into the receiver. The operator, sensing the frustration in my voice, patched me through to Debra.

"Hello, Suzy. Where are you?"

"I'm at the American gate. She wasn't on the plane."

"That's odd," she said.

"Wait. Wait a second. Maybe this is her. She might have gotten past me and..." I put my hand over the phone and squinted to see a woman with large brown eyes and light brownish-gray hair, talking on the pay phone next to me. Debra suggested saying her name to see if the lady would turn around.

"Uh, what is her name?" I can't believe I forgot to get that tad bit of information before I left the house. Debra told me, and I proceeded to call it out, only loud enough not to embarrass myself.

I called out, "Maryline, Maryline." The woman was oblivious to me.

I spotted another possibility. "This might be her. This woman's a classy dresser, with beautiful skin and silver gray hair," I reported into the phone. No answer, just an immediate throaty laugh.

"Oh no, Suzy, I don't think she's the one, keep looking." "Why don't you call me back in ten minutes? I'll call her house and find out what happened."

Ten minutes passed. Once again, I got the answering service to patch me through.

Debra answered. "You're right. Her husband said she didn't get on that plane, but she'll be on flight 456. It's due in at four. Do you mind waiting?"

"Oh, uh no, um, no problem. I responded in a tone that was definitely lacking in enthusiasm.

"When did she plan to notify you of her change of plans?" I inquired. *That's real considerate. She missed the plane and she doesn't call anyone to let them know. Doesn't she realize that someone is here waiting for her? Maybe she just thought there was a limo on call.*

Contrary to popular belief, movie stars don't always send limos to pick up people at the airport. Most of them have important people picked up by their employees, in their personal cars. Well, except for Sally Field, who has the heart to send a limo for her beloved nanny. I began my new mantra again: Bitterness is not becoming, Bitterness is not becoming, Bitterness is not becoming.

When the four o'clock flight de-planed, this time there was no mistaking Timothy's mom. I knew from Debra's description that she was the lady with the big black purse. Let's say she looked like she had lived a very full life.

"Hello, Mrs. ..." Oh crap, I don't know her last name. I know Debra said she had been married several times so I'm sure it's not Hutton. So I just kind of mumbled and went on with my introduction of myself. "You're Tim's mother, aren't you? I'm Debra's nanny, Suzy. So nice to meet you."

"Yes, dear. Can you carry that bag for me?" She pointed toward the floor, leaving my outstretched hand floating in empty space. I looked down to see an enormous red leather bag. She must have smuggled a body in that carry-on, I thought. Then I lifted it. *My God, what's in there? Maybe she brought her team's bowling balls along to share.*

"We'll have to go to baggage claim for the rest," she said as I struggled toward the elevator with her. I wondered how long she planned on staying. When the baggage delivery belt started moving, she pointed out one suitcase after another.

"Grab that black one, that's mine. Oh, oh, that big one with straps, that's mine too."

After I'd pulled four large suitcases off the conveyer belt she said, "There. I think that's it. Where are you parked?"

"Uh, maybe I should go get the car and bring it up to the terminal," I replied.

"Good enough. Why don't you hail that skycap? He can bring these out to the curb," she told me. As I made my way back across the parking lot I looked back to see Mrs. "Formerly Hutton" sitting atop the pile of luggage, lighting up a cigarette and taking a deep drag.

When I finally did make my way around the big horseshoe shaped version of destruction derby that serves arrivals and departures at LAX, I managed to squeeze into a spot near my future passenger, who had lit up a second cigarette. *Oh my God, what am I going to do? She's not planning on smoking in my car, is she?*

Even though I'd been in LA for over a year, and I'd made a lot of progress, I still hadn't learned to be very assertive about anything that involved confrontation. I even took the change out of my ashtray when she lit up her third cigarette. I immediately rolled down my window. She left hers up. Keeping my window down was all I could do for the looooooong ride back to Malibu, to manage my growing nausea. She was a chain smoker, yellow fingers and all, probably forty years into her habit.

When we got back to the house, after helping unload a year's worth of luggage, I raced back out to my "used to have that new car smell" car. I rolled down the other window, put one fan in the front seat and one in the back. I wiped down the ashtray with a rag soaked in Pine Sol, left the doors wide open and kept the fans running until it was time to go to bed that night.

Several days later Debra announced she was going out for the evening for the first time since Noah's birth. This triggered a memory of another nanny I had met who told me the sad story of an actress she worked for who had left her newborn baby in a nurse's care to go off on a six-week vacation. Debra took a different direction, as she did with most things. She was seriously devoted to Noah, and she treated this first separation almost ceremoniously.

So I was on duty that night, with Maryline as my sidekick. For some reason this was a big deal for me, as well as for Debra. I felt the gravity of the trust placed on me as she separated from her baby for the first time. All right, the seasoned nanny was, in fact, a nervous wreck. I'd fed Noah finger food before, but never a bottle. What would I do if I spilled the six ounces of precious breast milk she had pumped? There was no formula in the house. I was beginning to see why the other name for mother's milk is liquid gold. No way was I going to interrupt Debra's first evening out, no matter what.

The first Feeding Ceremony commenced. When I finally managed to defrost the bottle and bring it into the living room intact, Mrs. I-Still-Had-No-Idea-What-Her-Last-Name-Was sat in a large chair near the fireplace, cradling Noah and staring at me. Did she sense my trepidation? Was she judging me? Carefully, I put the bottle down on a table beside the couch. Then I crossed the room and reached out for Noah, silently. She held him out to me as if to say, are you sure you can handle this?

As Noah relaxed in my arms and smiled at me, I picked up the bottle. This anxiety is ridiculous, I thought. When I finally eased the bottle into his mouth, the baby had an "all right already give me the damn thing" look on his face. He sucked furiously and I began to relax.

After a few moments, the silence was broken. "Don't you think you should switch sides?"

"Excuse me?"

"That would make it more like you were Debra, and she was switching boobs," Maryline offered. I knew Debra took breastfeeding seriously because she had joked with me that she was planning on weaning Noah when he was eighteen, so her mother-in-law did have a point.

I didn't want to switch sides since making any move at all might jeopardize the cargo and the irreplaceable fuel. I was shocked that he had taken it so well, considering he had only taken a bottle a few times in his life. Should I risk it? I did...Thank God he wasn't fazed by the breastfeeding fake out and he drained the bottle. The ceremony was complete; the spell was lifted; and joy filled the room. Maryline beamed, Noah gurgled gently and I was so happy I almost wept.

Debra came home much earlier than expected. She was really bummed. Some teenagers had thrown bubblegum into her hair from the theater balcony. She thought it was another karma thing, a sign that she shouldn't have gone out and left Noah. A lot of things were karmic to her. Maryline, who was an expert at removing gum from hair, got out a jar of peanut butter to help out. Debra said that when she reported the incident to the manager, he had brought the little juvenile delinquents out to the lobby. She wasn't sure that they knew who she was. She thought maybe they had chosen to do it to her because they recognized her and thought it would be funny. I reassured her that it probably wasn't personal and that it was just some random act by thoughtless kids. I felt bad for her that her big night out was cut short, but she was relieved that Noah had done so well.

One of the best things about getting to know Debra was that I could so easily identify with her. When I thought about how attached I'd gotten to Brandon, I knew that one day I would be just as fanatical a mom as she was. And then there was another little commonality. One day when we were driving home, we passed a California highway patrolman on a motorcycle. She mentioned that she'd better slow down because if she got one more speeding ticket, she was going to have her license suspended. I had known before that we were kindred spirits, but this cinched it. Now that's my kind of gal: one misdemeanor away from public transportation.

> I am so relieved that Debra is one of those "what-you-see-is-what you-get" kind of people. I think living with her will change my lack of assertiveness. She knows what she wants in life and she's determined to be the best mom she can. She doesn't care at all about looking glamorous, either.

One day I discovered I had a complete ant infestation under the carpet next to my bed. It was creepy. There must have been a large hill of them somewhere in my room. As I was falling asleep, I kept feeling their little feet and I'd swipe them off. There wasn't anything else I could do but vacuum them up because Debra didn't allow the use of any insecticides. She said the ants were harmless, and she didn't want to use poisonous chemicals in her home. I decided she was right, so I learned to co-exist with them, sort of. I developed a routine. When I'd see that they were crawling up the wall, I'd squash them. Then I'd pull the carpet back and get the vacuum and suck them all up. I'd run it back and forth over the wood strip with metal staples that held the carpet down until I got every last one of them. I lay in bed at night imagining they were all finding their way out of the vacuum and mounting a furious charge back to their place of residence. It was a slightly twisted Cinderella special. The delightful, industrious animated ants would find a hero in Debra, while I would definitely be playing the part of the evil stepmother.

Debra wasn't a clotheshorse. Sometimes she would wear her pajama bottoms and a T-shirt around all day, or she'd just throw on a sweat suit when she went out. Her attire never got much fancier. One afternoon after she got dressed, she asked me to go with her to Beverly Hills and when I saw her I actually thought about declining. Then I realized I must have been looking at her the way the Swartz family did at me when I wore that ridiculous white jumpsuit. She looked like a gypsy in a three-tiered skirt, each tier a different color. The bottom one had a row of dingle balls hanging from it. It was purple, red and green and her top was something orange that you'd normally wear only to the breaking of a piñata. She was comfortable with it, but I was on the alert. I wanted to send a recon to wherever we were going to assure there were no photographers from *People* magazine. Then again, maybe she was just creating her own style.

I still didn't get why these people with glamorous wardrobes would ever leave the house looking like they shopped at Goodwill. I never did figure that out. The funny part was, before we left for Rodeo Drive, she asked her dear friend and me if it matched okay. I didn't answer, as there was no way around this one politely. Her friend said it looked fine. I was thinking, I hope for God's sake we don't run into Mr. Blackwell himself, because this one outfit alone would seal her spot on his Worst Dressed list. But this was what I loved about her. She didn't care what people thought.

## Do You Have to be Pregnant to do This?

When we were walking on the sidewalk looking in all the expensive stores, she went up to one, the kind you have to ask permission to gain entry. She peered in the window and the sales lady acted like she didn't see her. Debra just laughed and said, "She has no idea who I am, she isn't going to give me the time of day." She made a funny face in the window and we just laughed and walked on. It was so much fun to go places with her because I could just relax and enjoy myself.

Debra wanted to do everything related to taking care of the baby. Only once during our shopping day did I stay outside with Noah and the stroller while she made a quick run into a store. When she came out she said, "My, Ma'am, you sure have an adorable child." To which I said, "Oh thank you, Ma'am-many people say he looks just like that actor Timothy Hutton." We both hooted and strolled on. Her friend that was with us, was probably fifteen years older than Debra. She was a writer, and she looked like someone I knew. The more the three of us talked, the more I learned about her and it began to dawn on me why she looked so familiar. She was a child-care expert who had written several books, and she was also a consultant for Jane Fonda and her pregnancy workout video.

Suddenly I realized where I'd seen her. I remembered when my friend Amy and I started a workout program our sophomore year in high school. We were bound and determined to tone up our bods. The only problem was that the only workout video around her house was her step mom's. Since she had recently had a baby, the video was for expectant mothers, led by the star of *On Golden Pond,* herself. So there we were, using Campbell's Tomato Soup cans as weights, doing deep knee bends, "feeling the burn" through our leg warmers along with the twenty bulbous women following along in the studio in their horizontal striped leotards. I wondered how much these poor women were being paid to participate. When I looked closer at Debra's friend I realized we'd been in the same video exercise class. She had been in the group, right alongside Jane. I had only seen her two times, since that was how long our exercise regimen lasted. I guess you just never know when you're going to bump into someone you once shared something meaningful with.

I sometimes forget how different it is here than in the rest of this town. When I look around me, it seems like most people's lives are more like the Swartz'. Debra told me today about this actor friend of hers (she didn't say who it was) who was so caught up in the business of being a star that at one point he realized he hadn't even seen his child in five months, let alone spent any quality time with him. He left the house early in the morning and came home late at night every single day. His child was never awake when he was home. How do you forget to see your own child?

## An Officer and a Gentleman

"Suzy, would you like to join Tony from MGM and me? We're going to have a Debra Winger slide show."

"Sure. What are we going to watch, your vacation pictures?"

"No. These are the studio cuts they've sent over. You can help me pick out the worst ones."

Like many actors, Debra didn't much like to watch her own movies or even look at the slides. She never felt she had done as good a job as she could have. I could relate to that.

"Go ahead, Tony, crank it up."

"Hate it. I'm not in character," she said to the very first one.

I smiled.

"Ohh-h-h, look too fat. Out."

God, she was a rail.

"Too tired. Look at the luggage under those eyes."

So far they had all looked good to me. I thought she was a doll.

"Ah. That's a keeper," she said. "What do you think, Suzy?"

"Uh, I like it. You look happy and full of energy."

"Right. Good one, Tony. Keep it."

And so it went until we'd gone through a hundred slides and ix-nayed what seemed like half of them. I hadn't seen much difference in most of them, but then, they weren't mine. If they had been, I probably would have burned them all. I was every bit as self-critical as she.

"Ya know, Suzy, those pictures remind me of Richard Gere."

"Why is that?"

"I go through this process after every movie. When I did the selection of slides for *An Officer and a Gentleman*, I noticed that a lot of them were missing. "Anyway, when they showed Richard the slides, he chose the ones he liked, throwing out all the good ones of me before I had a chance to look at them. Later, when I was driving down Sunset Blvd., and I saw the billboards I could only laugh because the shot they used was a great one of him, and I, of course, looked like a bag of wallets."

"I never did get along with Gere. He seemed arrogant to me. The love scenes were an expression of our tension. Talk about tense—well, they just expressed a whole lot about our relationship."

Her voice trailed off as she walked to the other side of the room. I made a mental note: Sounds like I missed something. Go see movie again. I had thought that they had liked each other in the film. I guess that's why they call it acting.

## Jack Nicholson's Words of Wisdom

When it was time for the Academy Awards nominations, Debra showed me the nomination packet she got in the mail. She cast a vote for Timothy's movie, *Made in Heaven*. She was probably one of very few. She told me that Jack Nicholson had given her a piece of advice when she'd been nominated for *Terms of Endearment*: If you don't vote for yourself (or in her case, her hubby), how can you expect anyone else to vote for you? That's good, I thought. *I should* be voting for myself more often.

Noah was a very sweet baby. He was inquisitive and he loved to go outside. Debra said it was great that his name started with the word no, because she didn't like the thought of saying "No" to him. When he would get into something or drop something on the floor, our first impulse would have been to yell "No." She wanted him to have a "Yes" attitude toward life. So she said his name worked well because if we accidentally started to correct him, we could say, "No No No No-ah."

Debra spent nearly the entire day with Noah and when I tried to take care of him at night, he only wanted his mom. She and I decided not to upset him by having me tend to him in the night. Debra seldom went anywhere during the day. On the rare occasions that I did take Noah for walks, Debra wanted to come as well. I was beginning to feel like a third wheel on a bicycle.

One afternoon the three of us went to a park in Malibu. After we'd been there a few minutes, I put Noah in one of the swings and began pushing him gently. He began to laugh and giggle. Debra must have thought that this might be as much fun for a grown-up, so she climbed into one of the "adult" swings, kicked off her shoes and began pumping and laughing, thrusting her legs into the air to gain momentum. Just then a man walked up to us and said, "Hello Debra."

I glanced over, and there was Jack Lemmon standing near the swings in a pair of shorts, a golf shirt and tennis shoes. I recognized him right away since I had seen *The Odd Couple*, one of my dad's favorite movies, about twenty times. When Debra introduced me to him, I gulped and shook his hand and smiled. He said, "Can I buy you two a falafel?" I was too embarrassed to say I didn't know what a falafel was, so in unison Debra and I said, "Yes. Thank you." I just hoped and prayed that whatever the thing was, it didn't have mushrooms on it.

As we were eating these odd concoctions that appeared to be the Arabian equivalent of a taco, I spotted someone else I recognized. "Oh my God," I leaned over to Debra, "that's Steven's brother's wife. What do I do?"

"Just act like you're having the time of your life," she laughed.

The sister-in-law walked toward the swings with her son, Max. I gulped, caught the thoughts that were swirling around my head and said, "Hello, Kirsten," as casually as I could.

"Oh, uh, hi, Suzy. What are you doing here?"

"Oh, I work for Debra now," I pointed and smiled. "You know her, don't you?"

What was I going to say: How 'bout those Lakers? Bet you've heard all about how horrible I was for quitting. I kept thinking about what she was going to report to Julia. She was probably going to break her ankle running to her car, to relay the news that I was now working for the original mutineer from the ACT ship.

I voiced my fears to Debra, and I could anticipate her response even as I was telling her. For the second time that day, we spoke in unison: "So what?"

So What! So What! So What! So What! As long as I could remember to say that, Steven and Julia lost their control over me. I was voting for myself, starting now. The time with Debra had gone a long way toward healing the hurts I had brought with me when I had taken the job.

### Mission Impossible Nanny Style

I hadn't talked to Concetta in awhile. It had been too painful when I called shortly after I left, when she described how Brandon looked around the house for me and wandered in and out of my old bedroom.

After I had spent some time with Debra, I was ready to call Concetta again.

"How are the kids, how is everyone doing?"

"Oh, Suzy. It's you! You should hear how they're talking about you around here."

"What are they saying?"

"Julia and Grandma Swartz are saying bad things because you are working for Miss Winger. I can't tell you the horrible things they said." *I didn't really want to know. I could just imagine.*

"Amanda has had me try and call you many times at your sister's, but there's no answer."

My heart sank. On the one hand, I was happy that Amanda had asked to talk to me, but on the other that meant she did in fact miss me. It hurt to know that I was another loss in her short lifetime. I gave Concetta my new phone number I had installed in my bedroom.

"Concetta, how's Joshua?" I inquired. "You know Josh is Josh, he will always be the same." I was so sad that neither Concetta nor Maria was able to understand the reason he was so difficult. In a way, I had participated in confirming the belief he held that if you start to love someone, they leave. And now that I was banned from ever seeing the children, there was no way to show him that I did still care about him, that I saw more in him than a defiant little boy. As far as he knew, I never loved him enough to ever call or visit.

Then the conversation took a turn for the better.

"Would you like to see Brandon?" Concetta blurted out of nowhere.

"Oh God, I'd love to!"

"Steven and Julia just left for Aspen last night. I could sneak him out and meet you at the park. Maria will stay with Joshua and Amanda, so they won't know," she said in a conspiratorial tone. I would never have brought up the subject. I couldn't imagine what Steven would do if he ever found out that I'd sneaked out with his son.

"He hasn't been himself for weeks since you left," Concetta continued. "He's walking now, but he still seems so sad. It would do him good to see you."

She was breaking my heart. "Don't tell me any more, Concetta. Please." I missed him so much that my throat constricted, trying to hold back tears. As much as I wanted to see him, I didn't know if I could do it. No matter how long the visit, I'd just have to leave him again. I paused and caught my breath.

"Let's do it," I said emphatically. From there we hatched a simple plan and I met them the next afternoon in the park that I used to take Brandon to often. I got there before Concetta did and I sat waiting, gently gliding in a swing, anticipating. Then her car came up and parked in the distant lot. Concetta got out, came around and unfastened Brandon's car seat and lifted him out to the ground.

I could see that she was telling him I was here by the way she whispered to him and pointed to me. Little guy. So cute. So innocent. He craned his head up, looked around and finally fixed his eyes on me. I stood up. When he saw me, he toddled off across the grassy field straight for me. He threw his little arms around me and squeezed me with all his strength, not uttering a sound.

My heart felt like it would collapse in on itself, aching - yet joyful. How could it be possible to feel all these things so strongly at once? I had guessed it would be hard, but I had never even had an inkling it would be this hard. I squatted there, holding him for a long time. When I pulled away slightly to look at his beaming face, tears dropped off my cheeks onto the collar of my blouse. I wiped my eyes quickly.

Concetta and I embraced silently.

"Suzy, I didn't tell you, but I'm the nanny now. When you left Julia asked me if I wanted to quit doing the housework and start taking care of the kids. I jumped at the chance. I knew it would make you happy," she said. "Plus I get to wear regular clothes now. I don't think Julia likes it, but I told her that the other nannies didn't have to wear a uniform."

"Oh, Concetta. That makes me feel so much better-for both of you." I hugged her again.

I picked up Brandon and put him in a swing as Concetta and I continued. She was so happy that she didn't have to spend all her time cleaning and that she could wear her own clothes. And I had already seen how much she loved Brandon and how she cared for him on my days off. I knew Brandon was bonded to Concetta, and Amanda was very attached to her too. I was so relieved that he was being cared for by somebody he was comfortable with, and that he wouldn't have yet another person coming into, and then leaving his life. And even though Joshua had always been hostile to Concetta, even more than he was with me, I was glad he didn't have another new person he felt he had to put his guard up against. This was the best situation possible for all three of the children. After that weekend, Concetta and I had a few more clandestine meetings, but I knew that Brandon's young memory of me was slipping away. He was becoming used to Concetta. He was forgetting me.

Today tore me up. I love that little guy so much. And even though I don't have to worry about him anymore, I still have a big hole in my heart. Maybe I should just go home. I don't want to get attached to another child because it hurts so bad when I have to leave. I feel like I'm holding myself back from giving

Noah the love he deserves. I don't feel good about myself for holding back my emotions and not getting as close to him.

I had been having such a good time while I was at Debra's that it took me awhile to understand what was really going on with her. I began to realize that I wasn't really needed at all there, and I started to feel guilty about the amount of money she was paying me. I decided I needed to talk to her. Fortunately, she came to me one day soon after I figured this out and said that she realized that she didn't really need anyone to help take care of Noah, especially fulltime. She said she just wasn't the kind of person that would give time with her child away to someone else just because she was paying for it.

I was glad to have the chance to tell her how bad I had felt for being paid so well for so much less work than I was used to. She said not to worry about it, but she thought it would just be best if she went to Baton Rouge and took the housekeeper with her to help with Noah. She said that when she had met me she had liked me right off, and she even enjoyed the karma of living with yet another cast off. She added that she would be happy to give me a good reference. Then she was gracious enough to offer to let me stay at her house while she went to visit Timothy, so that I could look for another job. I remained there for the next two weeks, enjoying the quiet of the house. I once again started looking for a new position as, what else, a nanny in Hollywood.

During my time off at Debra's I had a chance to call and see how Tammy was doing. Every time I had spoken to her, she had told me she was thrilled to be working for Sally and Alan. The last time I had talked to her, she was so excited because her name was going to appear in *Cosmopolitan* magazine, because they were doing an article on Sally. Sigh.

When I wasn't envying her, her upbeat positive attitude always made me smile, so I decided to give her a call and see how she was doing.

"Hi, Tammy. How are you hon? What's the latest with you? Go on; share with me your latest tale of nanny bliss. I can take it."

"I got to fly on the Concorde; I brought some pictures back for you."

"Of what?"

"I took a whole roll of film of the interior of the plane. Every time Sally and Goldie turned their backs, I took a picture. I wanted to send some to my mom to show her what it looked like. I even took a photo of the hors d'oeuvres. I've never seen butter before in the shape of a swan."

"Oh my gosh, I was going to call you an idiot till I remembered when I was in Hawaii I took a picture of my room service trays! I felt like a knight at the round table-there were so many silver serving trays. Even my pizza had one of those huge covers you see in the movies, and it came with cloth napkins." We both laughed.

"Yeah, our idea of fancy dinners was when we used to hang out at the old Pinocchio's pizza parlor in town after football games," Tammy said. "I miss the times we had there."

"And I really miss the pizza," I whined.

"Gotta go," Tammy said. "Sally and I are off to go shopping."

"Great! Have a wonderful time!" I replied with a forced cheerful tone. I was thinking that it was a good time to hang up anyway. If I had to hear one more time about Tammy's wonderful life I was going to have to go borrow one of Noah's pacifiers to soothe myself.

My personal life wasn't going so well either. My impulsive idea to have my bad-boy boyfriend move down hadn't been my best idea ever. Now that I had Troy back I didn't really want him. He'd been in LA for three months and still hadn't come up with a job, or the ambition to find one. To be honest, he was the kind of guy that looks a lot better in his own habitat. His rugged good looks and casual style belonged in a small logging town, not in Southern California. It seemed like everything I had wanted in my life hadn't really been what I thought it would be once I got it. And that made it hard to decide which direction to go next.

By the time Debra returned home, I still hadn't decided what the next episode of my Hollywood drama would be. I wasn't sure I even wanted another role as a nanny. Since I hadn't made any life-changing career decisions yet, I had to move back in with my sister, in the Brentwood box. Her apartment was bursting at the door jams. And Martha was still sleeping in the closet. Michelle had now taken in another co-worker who slept there off and on. Troy slept on the living room couch and I slept in a sleeping bag on my sister's bedroom floor-five, sometimes six of us stuffed into a 500 square foot box. We were packed in as tight as OJ's fingers in the infamous glove. When my mother came to visit awhile later, we had to go to Futon's R Us and rent something for her to sleep on.

It was a huge mistake to talk Troy into moving down here. Back home I always thought he was the love of my life, but now it's clear we don't want the same things. Maybe I should just break up with him and then move back home. Of course, then he'd end up going home too which would increase my chances of wimping out again. Knowing me, I'll just end up getting back together with him for the 86th time.

Why do I feel compelled to stay and take another nanny position? I know I don't ever want to get attached to any children like I did with Amanda, Josh and Brandon. I have to decide soon, since I need income for my car payment. I feel at a loss. I knew I should have taken the SATs when I had a chance.

# My Interview with a Set of Chairs

*A*fter I moved into the apartment, I decided to get serious about finding a job for both Troy and me. I was still revising my resume, and at the same time I took on the impossible job of trying to get Troy to write one of his own. I decided to just ignore the voice in my head that said, *What if Steven still doesn't give you a good reference? What are you going to do then?*

On a Friday afternoon I went to a new agency that I found in the phone book under Domestic Placement Agencies. It was named after the founder, June Art. When I met with the owner, it occurred to me that the same Ms. Art that greeted me had probably opened the doors in 1936. She was still going strong placing domestic help in Beverly Hills. The room smelled as musty as the elderly woman seated behind the desk looked. I introduced myself and sat down, sliding my resume over to June, who peered at it over a pair of granny glasses perched on the end of her nose.

"Hmmm," she muttered after giving it only a cursory glance. "I think I might have someone for you right away," she said without even glancing up at me. "Sit down over there," she said motioning to a waiting area behind a partition, while she buried her nose in a Rolodex. She dialed the ancient black rotary phone, which had probably been installed the same day she opened.

"Hello. This is June Art down at June Arts," she said to someone. There was a brief silence and then June spoke up again. "I think I have someone for that position you called me about....Yes, uh... let me check," I heard her say. Then she stood up came to the other side of the partition, gave me one long look head to toe and went back to the phone. "Yes, she's attractive. Can you hold a moment," she said cupping her hand over the mouthpiece and rolling her chair out from behind the partition.

*Now what's she going to say about me? On second thought, she's Not drop dead gorgeous so it shouldn't be an issue with your husband making a pass at her, like he did with the last girl I sent you?*

"Can you go over to Paramount Studies right now, dear?"

"Uh, yes, yes, I suppose so. How far away is it?" she didn't answer me, and rolled her chair back to her desk and finished her phone conversation.

"Okay then, right away." With that she banged the phone down.

She emerged from behind the partition and handed me a slip of paper with the directions and the name, R...something, something, Pe...something, something, something, written on it next to the words, "set of chairs." Poor old June's handwriting was little more than a scrawl so I was completely bewildered. Was I going to be a nanny or a furniture mover? I thought I'd made my career choice clear to June, but then she looked nearly 95 years old and she hadn't spent much time reading my resume. Perhaps she was placing me as a "domestic house manager."

"Ms. Art. Uh, I can't quite read what you've written. Does this say set of chairs?" "No dear." She laughed and coughed. "It says, set of *Cheers*, you know *Cheers* the TV show. You're going to talk to Rhea Perlman, my dear." "Don't worry. The studio isn't far, dear. I'll show you how to get there."

June hadn't even checked my references, and obviously the person who she was talking to hadn't asked either. *So that's gonna help me a lot, once I mention my little "reference problem," so much for a second interview.*

I'd never been on a movie lot or seen a TV sit-com set, or even met an actor from such a popular TV program, so I decided to drop off the resume, just for the adventure of it.

Once I left the agency, it occurred to me I'd brought Mr. "Why Do I Need a Job When I'm Living with Your Sister for Free?" with me. I had never guessed that they would send me on an actual interview the first minute I walked in the door. There was no way I was going to drive on to the Paramount lot with Troy in the car. Did I mention that he was a fourth generation lumberjack? Troy regularly used the wrong tense of the verb, which drove me crazy; I was constantly correcting him. He truly believed that ain't was an actual word, because they used it on his favorite TV show, *The Dukes of Hazzard*. I will never know why I didn't just leave the poor guy alone and let him live his life and forget about trying to convince him that the WWF wasn't real.

He *was* muscular and handsome. However, his entire wardrobe consisted of T-shirts, faded 501's, tennis shoes and several baseball caps in various colors. Occasionally this ensemble was complemented with a pullover zip-up "hickory shirt" (if you don't know what that is, don't ask). His signature accessory was a faded circle on his back left jean pocket. This coming-of-manhood logo had been permanently imprinted on all of his Levi's by carrying and sitting on a can of Copenhagen chewing tobacco 24/7. His jeans still showed the white faded circle outline right down to the detail of the letters, C O P E N H A G E N. He had been dipping snuff for so long, that even when the can found its way to his left front shirt pocket, the ring remained.

I made the mistake of telling him that I was going for an interview after I dropped him off at the apartment.

"Hell no, you ain't droppin' me nowhere. I wouldn't miss this for the world. I'm here in Hollywood, I might see some movie stars."

So he stayed in the car and when we pulled past the guard at the big wrought iron gates that had the majestic words "Paramount Studios" emblazoned across the top, he started fidgeting in the seat like a kid on his first trip to Wally World.

"Do not move!" I said emphatically, pointing my finger at him like he was a forlorn dog being scolded to stay. "I'll be back as soon as I'm through."

"Who're you gonna see?" he said, not moving an inch.

"Some people on a TV show," I answered. "Now promise me, Troy that you will not get out of this car."

"Oh my God," he said, holding his hand over his mouth. "You're gonnna see Sam Malone? I gotta come."

"No. If you move from this car, I will never speak to you again. Just sit here and look out the window. Sooner or later some movie star is bound to walk by." I checked my hair in my hand mirror once more, pulled and smoothed my skirt and began looking for the *Cheers* set.

I could feel its energy the minute I walked in. Everywhere there were people scurrying about impatiently. Just before I stepped through the door marked "Quiet. Cheers taping," I glanced over my shoulder to see Michael J. Fox talking to another man. *Wow! Alex P. Keaton. I love that guy.*

Oddly enough, I'd never been a big *Cheers* fan, though I was familiar with the players. I knew that Rhea played a waitress on the show. When I got inside, it was dark and I asked a man where I could find Ms. Perlman. He pointed to a set of bleachers where the audience sits when the show is taping. That day, Ted Danson, Kelsey Grammar and the others were rehearsing. I looked into the uppermost row of seats and there, sitting by herself, apparently going over lines in a script, was Rhea. I introduced myself and she smiled pleasantly, giving me a quick head-to-toe scan. Our meeting was brief. She told me that she and her husband had two daughters who were three and six, and they already had a nanny. They were hiring someone for the baby, who was six months old. Then she asked me if I wanted to meet her husband.

I liked Rhea immediately because she was easy to talk to. I could just tell that she would be great to work for. I was feeling very good about this. But then, as we walked up the stairs, behind the set, I was jolted back to reality when I realized I would have to tell her husband about my employment with Steven. I was sure Debra would give me a good word, but I knew that Steven would be my downfall. Rhea hadn't asked about any previous employment or even looked at my resume. I could have been the nanny from the *Hand that Rocks the Cradle* for all she knew. She probably thought that all the background checks had been done by the agency that she had paid to find me.

Well, I got the shock of my life when she opened the door into a very modest room with a couch and chairs. *Would have been nice if Miss Senile June would have been less worried about me winning a beauty pageant and more concerned about informing me that Rhea's husband was Danny DeVito!* I'm sure I was gawking, but I tried to use some of the composure I had learned at the Swartz'.

I could tell right away that Mr. DeVito was as pleasant and kind as he'd always seemed, underneath it all, on screen. I had always liked him, even when he played the bad guy. He was quite relaxed, although interviewing a twenty-year-old nanny would hardly seem to be cause for anxiety. He just had a laid-back presence. I extended my hand, told him my name and then started in, "Mr. DeVito, I have to tell you about Steven Swartz," before he'd even had a chance to take his hand back.

"Steven? What about Steven? He's our agent," he said smiling.

*Okay, I might as well get up and leave right now. Let's stop wasting our time.*

"Uh, he's pretty upset with me," I blurted again, wanting to grab the words back.

"Were you fired?" he asked

"Well, technically I quit. I gave him a month's notice, but he wouldn't take it. When he asked me to stay longer, I just couldn't, so I said no, and he wasn't really very happy about it."

Mr. DeVito smiled, and then he laughed. "Oh, I can see that. Steven does not like anyone telling him no," he said as he wagged his finger back and forth in warning. "I'm not worried about Steven, so don't you be. We will decide for ourselves."

Then I got a huge surprise.

"We're about done here, so you can just follow us over to our house," he suggested. I still hadn't been asked for my resume or references.

"Sure, I'd love to see your place," I said. Then I remembered that I had Paul Bunyan in my car and he hadn't shaved.

"Oh. I forgot. I've got my boyfriend in the car. Could I come by tomorrow?" I quickly suggested.

"We wouldn't think of it," he said, smiling and putting his arm around Rhea. "We'd like to meet him."

*Sure you would. But I don't want you to witness my great judgment in men. Oh my God. What am I going to do? One look at Troy and he'll think I just fell off the turnip truck.*

When I got to the car, Troy was still sitting there in a tank top that looked a size too small, with a Chicago Bears logo on the front. I started yelling at him to take the can of chew out of his back pocket so we didn't look like a pair of complete rednecks.

"Suzy, you're never gonna guess who I saw while you were inside-Robert Blake! Do you believe it?" he enthused.

"Any chance you have a collared shirt in the trunk you might be able to put on, before I go on this interview?" I asked, already knowing the answer.

We followed Danny and Rhea's old BMW to their home. When we got there, I convinced Troy to stay in the car, and I streaked into the house.

They introduced me to the older children, and then Rhea showed me to the baby's room. This was the room I would be sharing with the baby, sleeping on a twin bed next to him, she explained. She apologized for the accommodation, explaining that Danny's mother and sister were coming soon from New Jersey for an extended visit and they would need the guest bedroom. We had a pleasant conversation and I left my resume with them and thanked them for their time. They told me they would call me that night with their decision.

And they did. Danny called my sister's apartment to say that they indeed would like to hire me, asking if I could start the next morning.

When I arrived at 7 am, the family was asleep. I stood in the slate-rock entryway while Danny finished a phone conversation he was having. I soon realized that he was talking to Debra. So they must have looked at my resume after all. He spoke as if they were old friends; this encouraged me.

Danny seemed to be chatting about his latest film, and she was apparently updating him on what Timothy was doing now. I stood there awkwardly, not knowing whether to sit down, stand until he was finished or to pitch in and start cleaning the kitchen. It was such an uncomfortable feeling. It passed through my mind that this was the problem with my career. It was always so hard to know my place and what was expected of me. It occurred to me that this problem wouldn't be solved by new circumstances. Here I was getting an opportunity to work for a family just like I'd been looking for. It was a family that seemed a little more "normal," one that would possibly appreciate my efforts, and I just didn't feel as happy about it as I should.

Suddenly Danny looked up from his phone conversation and smiled at me winningly. He looked nothing at all like the bad guy characters that had made him famous. It seemed possible that, just like at Debra's, I might be a real person to this family; not just a milk-server, burper and stain-remover. My mind kicked out an old phrase: *Watch out what you wish for. You just might get it.* I was wrestling with myself over whether I should join yet another family or pursue the dreams that were starting to form in my head.

My dreams got postponed. I spent the day getting unpacked and finding my way around, but my heart (and head) was someplace else. The first thing I did in my new room was jot down the thoughts that had been bugging me.

I'm angry with myself for questioning my good luck. This is just the kind of position I've been looking for, but somehow it doesn't feel right already. Maybe I'm selfish, which isn't always a bad thing.

I keep on thinking about this idea of becoming a nurse-midwife. I would like to plan to go to college. In the meantime, here I am with two kind people, and they want me to help them care for their baby. How bad can that be?

## Life with Louie and Carla

Being a part of Danny and Rhea's family life turned out to be even better than I expected. They were public people who had busy lives working and raising their kids, but they did it well. They doted on their children and each other. Just being around them made me feel good. I started to see that things were turning around for me. I could already tell that I really was going to be a big help to them.

Their house in the Hollywood Hills was unassuming. No long driveway with iron gates at the entrance: you just parked on the street in the older neighborhood and walked from the sidewalk through a gate into their courtyard. Lisa, the other nanny that watched three-year-old Gracie and six-year-old Lucy, had been with them for three years. She had her own exterior apartment. She was into the grunge scene, which seemed odd, given Danny and Rhea's demeanor. Lisa was nearly six feet tall and as thin as a breadstick with jet-black dyed hair, a navel ring, occasional black lipstick and matching toenail polish. She also had something stuck through one eyebrow. It looked like a safety pin. I was kind of worried about her getting tetanus.

Although I shared a room with the baby, I had his bathroom all to myself. Jake was a sweet baby, and he took to me immediately. He really looked like a miniature Danny, except he had lighter hair that stood straight up on his very round head. He giggled a lot, and was rarely ever fussy. It was lots of fun to care for him.

Rhea and Danny seem like such real people, and they're fun-loving. This could be just the kind of situation I've been looking to find. Jake is a doll, too, but I'm aware that, no matter how much I enjoy him, I seem to be guarding myself. I just don't want to repeat the heart-wrenching experience I had leaving Brandon. So I'm caring for Jake and giving him lots of kisses and love, but I'm determined not to fall in love with him. Now I really have empathy for why Josh didn't let new people get close to him.

Every day Rhea and I went to Paramount Studios with Jake, where I hung out on the set of *Cheers* and took care of Jake while I watched the rehearsal. The first day I arrived they were all sitting at a long table right in the middle of the bar area that was the center of every episode. I was surprised at how casually they dressed. Most of them looked like they had just rolled out of bed. When Rhea walked up and introduced me, they all said, "Hi, Suzy," in unison.

Ted said, "Did you come from that Baby Buddies agency? That's the one we always use." I said I didn't and just smiled. *Some things are better left unsaid, like my mom used to say.*

Rhea showed me to her dressing room. Nothing fancy. In fact, the stairs leading up to it were kind of like what you'd find in a warehouse. The long hallway upstairs led to different rooms, one for each of the actors. Then at the end of the hallway was the little sitting room where I had met Danny on my first interview.

Jake and I set up camp upstairs. I took him for walks outside on the studio lot. At first it was quite entertaining. I had never been on a set while actors were rehearsing, and I found everything fascinating. Four days a week, the entire cast and the writers would come together around 10 am. Rhea said it was a real problem getting everyone there on time, including herself. The director had tried everything to get the cast to be prompt. They had even gone through a period of time where they had donated a certain amount of money, for every minute they were late, to a charity. But according to her, that hadn't seemed to make a difference. She said the problem was that a few of them would be there ready to rehearse and then someone would be missing. Everyone would get tired of waiting, and then a couple of people would go do their own thing, like make phone calls. When the person that was holding everyone up arrived and was ready to start work, they'd be missing one or more of the other cast members. They often engaged in that frustrating cycle during the first part of rehearsal every day.

When they were reading the script at the beginning of each week, they didn't even do a walk-through. They all just sat at the table reading their lines, ad-libbing and changing lines to make them funnier. The oddest part was that all the writers would laugh out loud at their own jokes. It seemed to me that if you had written the line, it couldn't be all that funny to hear it read by a character. But they all seemed to really enjoy themselves, and I loved all the laughter.

On Fridays, there was a full rehearsal for the live taping that night with an audience in the stands. From the bleachers, it felt as if I were spying on a family that lived in an odd dollhouse. There were lots of cameras, and none of the rooms actually had four walls, and of course there was no ceiling. Guys straight out of the Mr. Universe contest, I swear, rolled the cameras and cameramen around on some kind of platform on wheels. I couldn't help but notice, again and again, just how buff those guys were.

One of the many things I learned by watching the rehearsals was that they tried to avoid wasting any of the actor's valuable time. So when they were doing the final rehearsal with the cameras and deciding just how the lighting should be, they used stand-ins. These people didn't look like the characters, but it was important that they were the same height so they could adjust everything correctly. Each of them wore cardboard signs, hung around their necks with string, labeled WOODY, KIRSTIE, etc. They called the stand-ins by the actor's name instead of their own names. Sometimes they would literally have to stand in one place for an hour while the cameramen got their angles and the action was going on around them. Once they got everything perfected they would call the actors to come and recite their lines, standing on the X marked on the floor for that scene. Whenever I felt unimportant in my job, I thought about these guys.

About a hundred people would attend the final taping, which combined an enthusiastic audience with opening night jitters, even though the same scene had been rehearsed many times before. As the cameras rolled, people stood to the right and looked into a monitor, watching the action that was going on just a few feet away to see how it looked on the television. After each scene, the director and some of the writers discussed their thoughts with the cast. They needed lots of breaks to match the right props, from books to mugs of beer. Each one was painstakingly scrutinized and rearranged. They also had to move walls around because the set next to the bar scene acted as almost every other room you saw, from the pool room to Rebecca's office to Carla's house. When the scene changes were lengthy, they sent in the stand-up comic who had warmed up the audience and entertained them with one-liners, magic tricks, songs and free chocolates.

One morning I rode with Rhea and Kirstie to the set in Rhea's station wagon. Kirstie had slept over the night before. Sitting beside her in the station wagon, I noticed that she probably hadn't had her roots done in awhile. It was neat seeing Kirstie, who always looked so put together on television, look like such a regular person, flaws and all. I was glad to see that she was real, not just a TV star with a fake expression and a permanent tan. Danny and Rhea had a lot of friends like that. It seemed like the nice ones stuck together in Hollywood. The DeVitos were always really generous and kind, taking in actor friends who were down on their luck, getting them parts in movies and even lending them money. They had a lot of faith in people. I admired that.

Life with the DeVitos was definitely different than living with the Swartz'. For one thing, theirs was a happy house. I could tell that Danny and Rhea were really in love because they were always so playful with each other. One day while we were driving to the set, Rhea's car phone rang and she pushed the speaker button.

"Hello."

"Hi sweetie," I could hear Danny's voice.

"Hi, Dan. What's up?"

"Are you on the way to the set?"

"Yes, dear. Why?"

"I'm just driving the ole Pontiac. Man, this thing is great! And I was just sitting here thinking about how much I'd like to jump your bones in the big back seat of this ole' thing. You know what I'd like to do...?" He giggled.

"Danny, you're on the speaker phone and Suzy's sitting right here, darling."

Silence.

"Oh, sorry about that, Suzy," he giggled again. The line went dead.

Rhea laughed and explained that he was driving her car, the first one she'd ever owned as a teenager. This interaction was typical of the two of them. They saw the fun and nostalgic value in something like a first car. I started thinking that I should have kept my first car, a '66 Mustang, the one my understanding parents let me paint hot pink. It was amazing and inspiring to be working with two middle-aged people who would even think of fooling around in the back seat of a car, like two sex-starved teenagers.

## A Place Where Everyone Knows Your Name

Instead of having several live-in people, most of the Devito's staff went home at night. They only had one housekeeper during the weekdays, and she had a hard time keeping up with the busy household. But I don't think Rhea ever cared that her house was far from immaculate. Being with her children was all that really mattered to her. They also had a cook that usually came in to just make dinner each night and serve it. The cook was from Oregon, and it was fun to visit with her about life at home.

During the week, there was a guy working there to do jobs that Danny needed done or to run errands for any of us in the house. He was in his mid-twenties, he was so funny that conversations with him kept me laughing for hours. One day he told me about trying to be a sperm donor when he was hard up for cash in college, but the clinic had informed him that none of his ever "took" so he wasn't able to continue donating. There was an awkward silence for a minute. "Oh my," was all I could come up with. Then I started laughing hysterically. He didn't seem to mind.

They also employed a house manager who mainly did things for Rhea. She handled everything that average people would take care of in their homes. Everyone helped out with the kids, making lunch when necessary or picking them up from ballet lessons. They had lots of vehicles and everyone seemed to take turns driving whatever was available. The newest automobile was at least five years old. While I was there, though, they did get a new Land Cruiser to haul the kids around in. I'm pretty sure that it was the first new car they'd bought in a long time.

When Danny's mother and sister came out from New Jersey for an extended stay, I was delighted. While they were there, eight people were sleeping in the five-bedroom house. During the day there were thirteen of us running around, so it was cozy. His sister, Angie, was so much fun that she made my free time go by quickly, playing cards and sharing stories. Angie was shorter than Danny, and his sweet mom looked like she was about 4'9". I was the same height as Rhea, 5'3". I was taller than Danny and the rest of his family.

Angie shared wonderful "Danny stories," as she called them. She said that he used to cut hair for her in her salon, for extra money. In fact, he was still the one that would cut his daughters' hair instead of taking them to a salon. Angie told me that when Danny had first come to Hollywood and only had two bus tokens to rub together, he would ride the bus all over Hollywood just to get some sleep at night. When things got really bad, he would call Angie and ask for a few bucks to tide him over. She would always send money to him when she could. It was obvious that they both dearly loved their elderly mother. It seemed odd to hear about Danny's former life, given his fame as an actor. I guess, like many so-called overnight success stories, his was years in the making.

## Spa Karma

One weekend, I planned a special Saturday for myself. Wised up by past fiascoes, including the acid face peel and the alien straw antennae perm from my first year in LA, I decided to indulge myself with a facial and wax job at a deliciously overpriced salon on Rodeo Drive that Rhea's house manager had suggested. I had an inkling of trouble the minute I walked in. A large Russian woman with a mustache greeted me at the door, speaking in an accent so heavy I could barely understand her. At that moment, I began to suspect that this might not be as relaxing as I'd hoped.

"Vee start vis zee arms." She looked like one of those Soviet weight lifters in the Olympics and I'm not talking about the female ones. I had gained a modicum of courage since my first spa visit. But I knew I was still too timid. And until this Saturday I hadn't realized just how easily intimidated I still was by a new situation.

I have been having my eyebrows waxed since I was about twelve because that's the only way I can keep from having one big uni-brow across my forehead. I had never had my legs waxed, and I thought it would be a treat not to have to shave for weeks, maybe even months. I had decided to have my underarms done as well, so I wouldn't have to worry about shaving, since I was out in the pool practically every day with the kids. I had envisioned a fairly simple procedure, the kind of waxing where they actually cover your legs with warm wax and then when it cools, they peel it off. I knew it wouldn't be painless, but I expected a lengthier version of what I was used to with my eyebrows. After some minor discomfort I would have silky smooth legs, and then I would be treated to a soothing facial.

I had been looking forward to this relaxing Saturday outing. But, as usual, it didn't happen exactly like that.

"You sit dair," the Russian matron grunted, pointing to a long padded recliner, not unlike a dentist's chair or some other instrument of torture.

"Here, poot on zees. I be right bock." She handed me a sleeveless tank top, which I dutifully put on. Then I reclined in the lounge.

In about three minutes the woman returned with her sidekick, another large Russian woman. Together they looked like a WWF tag team. *Why exactly did we need two people for my waxing and facial?* "Raise arms pleeze."

I hesitated because I was embarrassed to raise my arms and expose my European-style pits. I had figured beforehand that I needed to grow the hair out somewhat, or the wax wouldn't have anything to attach to. I hadn't shaved for about a month.

"Come, come. Vee don't have all day. Raise arms pleeze." I raised my arms, exposing my extremely hairy underarms. "Owweeee, yew shafed, tisk tisk!"

She then slathered a heaping spatula full of hot wax on to each underarm. "Ah-ghuu-u-u-!!!!" The wax congealed immediately and gripped my skin. My arms froze into a permanent two-fisted declaration, as if I'd just crossed the finish line with a world record time in a marathon. The pain was excruciating. I imagined hot bacon grease might feel like this if anyone were stupid enough to pour it into an open wound. I started hyperventilating.

*Oh my God, she hasn't even begun the process of peeling the wax off and I'm already in enough pain to qualify for the* ER.

When she finally did pull it off I nearly passed out. I swear she ripped off three layers of my skin. I yelled out like a wounded animal.

Another woman came charging into the room with a look of total confusion and dismay.

"Vhat is gowink on in heear?"

The large Russian woman responded nonchalantly, "She shafed," as if to say, 'she made her bed, now she has to die in it.' The third woman looked down at my bleeding armpits and shook her head with thinly-veiled disgust.

"Vell, yes, she shafed." "Come on less go, dare is noting wee can due for heer" with that she grabbed the 'assistants' arm and they left the room. *Hey, guys. I'm not from another galaxy. Last I knew, most American women shave the hair on their bodies.*

*So much for coming to a "hoity toity" salon. They must only see clients that can't be bothered with such trivial matters while showering. What do they do, routinely have all their body hair removed professionally on a weekly basis?*

"Now vee do duh legs," the lone torturer said, as she applied and pulled thin strips of something that looked suspiciously like those fly-catching strips that you hang in a horse barn. At this point, I was squirming on the lounge, splayed out like a fish that was about to get filleted. I started groaning before she started slowly pulling off each strip, my fists still clenched high in the air, armpits still decorated with Kleenex to stop the bleeding. As she pulled the strip off my shinbone, I vowed right then and there never to give birth if there was any chance it could be this painful. When she told me to turn over so she could do the backs of my legs, I gasped, "No thank you. I just need the front done. No one really sees the back."

Thank God I hadn't come in for a bikini wax. I never did get the facial; I was in too much pain and I couldn't afford it. She charged me $125. More than the standard waxing price, she said I had taken her twice as long as a "ragulur clieent" and she had great difficulty working with coarse hair that had been previously shaved, so she had added a surcharge.

I wonder what Debra would say about my karma today. Did I deserve this torture because of my sarcastic attitude toward my poor unhygienic classmates in nanny school? See if I ever laugh again about someone's body odor. This is the only plausible explanation I can come up with for my bizarre experiences regarding any type of 'beauty' treatment I attempt to receive here in LA.

## Where was Richard Simmons When I Needed Him?

After a couple of months watching the Cheers set on a daily basis with nothing to do, the excitement wore off. My only entertainment was going down to the buffet table that was set up every Friday for all the crew that came in for that night's taping. I think they chose the cuisine with the requirement that it have the highest fat and calorie content possible. Ruffles potato chips with ranch dip, every kind of donut imaginable, cheese rolls, Cheetos and my personal favorite: an assortment of mini candy bars. Of course, I filled my plate throughout the day, mostly out of boredom.

At one point, I had been back to the table so many times that the lighting guy said, "How many maple bars have you had?" I was humiliated. The next time I went down for a plain cake donut, having eaten all the maple bars. I made sure that the idiot who had nothing better to do with his time than monitor my excessive food intake wasn't looking. I had been able to eat exactly what I wanted all my life, and I thought it was ridiculous to ever deprive myself of something that tasted good. Of course, a 110-pound teenager whose baby fat had been left far behind hatched this theory. Unbeknownst to me, I had been putting on weight for awhile. One morning I casually got on the scale and realized I'd gone from a respectable 114 to an inflated 139, a lot of weight on my small frame. Even though I was no longer a stress case, the boredom of routine and my growing unhappiness with my life was starting to reap consequences. *Egads.*

I thought that the evil dryer had been shrinking all my clothes. Now it's official; there is a weight conspiracy against me, and it has been plotted by the inanimate objects in this home. They must have called a meeting. Their mission, no doubt, is to make me think I've gained weight. I just know that stupid scale upstairs has got to be completely inaccurate as well.

What the hell is going on here?

Note to self: Maybe I shouldn't have been so quick to dismiss the comments about the maple bar by the security officer.

Action that needs taken: Stay up late and try to find that Richard Simmons Deal a Meal infomercial to see how much it costs.

One afternoon shortly after this discovery, I went into the kitchen when no one was around. There on the counter sat a very beguiling bag of Mrs. Fields cookies. This was extremely unusual because Danny and Rhea always ate well, avoided red meat and didn't have sugar in the house for the kids. But then *she* didn't seem to have a problem with food. I took a peek around the corner. "Danny," I said loud enough for anyone to hear. No answer. The coast was clear. I opened the bag quickly, my eyes still darting about the room. Inside were six large, thick, sugary cookies-two chocolate chip, two peanut butter and two snickerdoodle. I grabbed one, closed the bag snuggly and ran upstairs to my room. It was the snickerdoodle, the largest of the six, and it tasted like heaven. I decided I'd indulge in just one more.

I ran back downstairs, listening for footsteps on the way, and opened the bag. I took another one and retreated once again to my room. I repeated this scene four times until there was only one cookie in the bag. You'd think I would've eaten that one too and thrown away all the evidence. I just didn't have much experience at this.

I went upstairs to my room. As I was licking my thumb of excess chocolate, I heard the house manager in the kitchen yelling, "Who ate these cookies? I bought these special for Rhea," to anyone listening. I went out into the hall, where I stood next to Lisa, who was thin and tall and didn't look at all guilty. We both pled ignorance. I turned immediately to check for evidence of crumbs on my shirt and then retreated again to my room, where I made an entry.

I'm pathetic, a caricature of the frumpy nanny. Still wearing the official nanny uniform of California, T-shirts and shorts, I guess the extra adipose tissue has kind of crept up on me. And to top it all I have Tammy call me with an update of her great life. She spent her 21st birthday on the movie set Of Steel Magnolias. Sally was kind enough to have the whole cast and crew surprise her with a birthday song serenade. I will be repeating the following sentence in my mind until it is the truth. I am not bitter, I am not bitter, I am not...

Top Priority: Buy Geneen Roth's book, Feeding the Hungry Heart, this Saturday. On second thought, buy the companion book, Breaking Free From Compulsive Eating.

Note to self: Buy Rhea some more cookies.

After the television season ended, I didn't really have anywhere to go during the day. I let Troy, who had finally found a job, drive my car all week so he would have transportation. I was that grateful that he had a job. But I had given away more than just my car; I realized. This was just another example of the ways I had given up on myself. I had stopped wearing make-up, and in the morning I usually just slipped into the clothes I'd worn the day before, unless they were filthy.

Sometime after I had noticed the weight gain, Peggy, the house manager, saw a picture of me, one of those glamour shots I had taken only a few months before.

"Who's this? Is that yo-o-o-o-u-u-u?" and then looked me up and down as if to say, *How is that possible?* Peggy had never been all that kind to me, but this topped the scale, so to speak,

"Maybe you should wear this much make-up more often," she said, laughing quietly to herself.

I wanted to answer, *Ya know, I was considered a hot number back in my day. Oh my god, my day.... was only a couple of years ago. I have to put myself back together. I already look like a haggard housewife and I'm not even married.*

Danny wasn't doing a film at the time, although he was constantly working on stuff for his production company and had scripts lying around the house that he was reviewing. He had already completed *Romancing The Stone* and *Ruthless People*. He was nostalgic for his buddies on *Taxi*, so once in awhile he would come in and pick up Jake and me and take us to lunch in the commissary and then take us home. One day when we were leaving he surveyed the Paramount lot and said, "Wow, I spent a lot of years here."

I just loved the way that this family really enjoyed every moment of their lives. They were hardly ever in a hurry. But just being around them wasn't enough. I kept thinking about all my friends who were moving along with their lives, in college, making future plans. And I knew I wasn't getting any closer to where I wanted to go in *my* life by staying here and working as a nanny. As I read the self-help books about weight, I knew that this was a big part of the problem. My heart was hungry.

## I Don't Want to be in *Back to the Future*

Rhea was about to turn forty and she was looking great. When she wasn't working out at the gym she would go to the studio on the lot and work out with a personal trainer. Danny was planning a huge surprise party for her in their backyard. I knew it was going to be a big production. The other nanny, who was more hip than I (as if that would have been difficult), knew all the latest music because she went out to nightclubs and parties in LA. She suggested that Danny have a local band play for the party, one she'd heard at a club and thought was very good. Danny said he'd never heard of the Red Hot Chili Peppers and didn't think he could risk having a no-name group for this special occasion. He looked at me and asked my opinion; I nodded in agreement and said that I'd never heard of them either. This bit of advice, combined with my great recommendation to

Mandie regarding that no-name caterer Kevin Costner, gave me a batting record of 0 for 2.

Several nights before the surprise party, I was in Jake's room when I heard Danny's voice coming from the room next door. I heard him call Steven by name, so naturally I stood at the door of my bedroom to listen in on the conversation. From what I could gather, Danny had never called him for a reference when they had hired me. I guessed that he had meant it when he told me that they'd just try me out for themselves.

The two of them must have been discussing a business deal, and then Danny got quiet. I froze. For all I knew, Steven had purposefully tracked me down and called Danny to try and get him to fire me. I heard Danny say, "I know. Wasn't that a coincidence? Rhea found this nanny and she used to work for you... Huh-uh." There was a moment of silence as Steven said something then Danny replied, "Oh, so you'd pass on this one, eh?" as if he was still in the interviewing stage. "Yes, okay. Okay. Got it. I'll talk to you later." He finished with, "Thanks for the tip, Steven. I'll let Rhea know."

Enough time had passed since I had left the Swartz to gain some perspective. I was starting to wonder if I might have been able to leave on better terms with the Swartz family. Steven had said that he valued me. What would have happened if I had tried harder to make things work out? I kept wondering if I had made a mistake by leaving. I still hated confrontation, but maybe I could have talked to him like he was a real person, not a mogul. Maybe if I had gone to him and told him what was bothering me, that I thought Julia didn't like me, things would have been different. I was starting to think that I shouldn't have seen the situation as black and white-stay and be unhappy, or leave. Maybe I could have worked something out. I had almost forgotten all the bad times as I was caught up in the nostalgia and the guilt over leaving the Swartz children.

I'd been doing a lot more thinking about myself since I had gained weight. I now saw that I had been a little depressed ever since I had left the Swartz. I'd started journaling more. It was really helping me to figure some things out.

It kinda seems like the deal with the Swartz was as much my fault as theirs. I never set any boundaries with Julia. By never requesting what I needed it just made it easier for her to ignore the possibility that I had any needs at all. I settled for what they gave me, rather than asking for what I needed in order to be a good caregiver.

Why wasn't I clearer about what I wanted when Steven talked to me at the end? I probably just thought about Maria, who never seemed to get any change she wanted. I never even attempted to tell him what I was so unhappy about. I guess I was waiting for him to ask, like a victim of circumstances. Maybe I really did have other options than just giving my notice.

This was so hard to admit. Here I was at a good nanny job, and I had carried my past with me. This could be another reason for my depression.

The house manager had invited Troy and me to Rhea's birthday party. I was sure it was going to be a dressy event. I knew that getting Troy to wear something I deemed appropriate would be about as challenging as convincing my dad, when I was a teenager, that I was going to the drive-in with a group of friends and we were really going to WATCH the movie.

I finally managed to find a jacket, white dress shirt and tie for him to wear. The last time I had made him wear a tie was our homecoming dance, and he had stuffed it in his pocket ten minutes after we had arrived at the gymnasium. After arguing at Nordstrom's for half an hour about buying some dress shoes, we went back to my sister's to get ready for the big party. I pulled out my ole stand-by black dress, once again, but I couldn't get the zipper zipped. I decided there was no way I was going to get the dress on without busting a seam, so I gave up. I just couldn't chalk it up to the dry cleaners shrinking my all-purpose garment anymore.

I heard Troy in the living room telling my sister, "Suzy just doesn't think my Nikes go with these khaki pants." I rolled my eyes in irritation. Why didn't I just admit it? I was dating Jethro from The *Beverly Hillbillies*. I threw on something of my sister's that was a cross between a skirt so short a hooker might wear it and a white jacket that made me look like I belonged in a medical office. My sister, ya gotta love her, normally doesn't own any clothes that are in fashion for the current decade. This was no exception, but I didn't have a choice.

We arrived at the party, where several valets were waiting to park our car. I stepped out and pulled my knit skirt down for the eighteenth time while my sidekick fidgeted with his tie as if he had a noose cinched around his neck. It was just getting dark as we entered the outside gate, but I could clearly see that we were the only ones dressed up. The rest of the guests wore shorts, golf shirts and sleeveless blouses; all pretty casual. Once again I'd forgotten about chic-casual LA style. After he'd gotten a gander at the crowd, Troy turned to me with a knowing smirk and hastily bid adieu to his tie and coat and rolled up his long sleeves as if he were Popeye the Sailor.

Looking around the patio, I could see that all the *Cheers* people were invited, as well as Marilu Henner, Tony Danza, Michael Douglas... and, oh my God–the last person on the face of the earth that I wanted to see–Steven Swartz. My first thought was that he had tracked me down. He was still in his office uniform. I didn't see Julia anywhere. I kept looking over at him and he kept looking back in my direction. I was thinking really rational thoughts like *maybe he doesn't recognize me,* or *maybe he doesn't remember me.* In the meantime, as he kept looking directly at me, I made sure I kept enough bodies between us so that I wouldn't have to talk to him. Finally, with a sigh of relief, I spotted him making his way toward the valets. *Thank God,. He only stopped by to make an appearance.*

CUT TO:

EXTERIOR - ABANDONED WAREHOUSE - DAYTIME

A sharply-dressed businessman stands in shadow, talk-ing heatedly to a rough-looking man dressed in black and leaning against a black Cadillac.

Business man keeps looking around making sure nobody sees him as he hands off an envelope.

                    BUSINESSMAN
Everything should be in there. Just find out where she's working that's all I need. There will be extra money in it for you, if you find out by tomorrow.

                    GUIDO
Do you want me to rough up her boss a little? Do you want me to break her kneecaps?

BUSINESSMAN
No, just get me the information, I'll take care of the
rest. And remember, we never met.

GUIDO
Of course, Uhhh...Mr. Smith, yes of course sir.

Guido clambers into his black Caddy and the businessman gets into a sharp-looking brand new BMW. Guido
dials his cellphone.

GUIDO
Hey Al, yeah it's me. I don't know who this girl is,
but she must be pretty important. I don't know! A
celebrity, a dignitary, somebody big. We're getting a
lot of dough to do this quickly and quietly. I want you
to handle this personally. There will be a little something extra in it for you if it all goes down without
anybody knowing, or anyone getting hurt. I need the
job done by tomorrow. Yes, tomorrow! How the hell am
I supposed to know where to find her? That's your job.
Start by canvassing the parks in Beverly Hills and talk
to some of the other nannies.

Seeing Steven at the party last night was pretty weird.
I'm actually getting paranoid enough to think that he
might have been following me. I was glad that he left early.
The struggle with Troy getting ready for the party just
brought it home that we're different, even though I wasn't right
about the dress code. I can't shake knowing that we're not
headed in the same direction. Seems like the most loving thing I
can do for him is to let him go, so that he can find someone who
appreciates him just as he is. There's just no way I'm ever going
to be excited about the monster truck rally coming to town. I keep
trying to mask his bad-boy scent in cheap cologne. I'm pretty
sure he's sick and tired of my constant nagging and complaining

about him doing pretty much everything wrong in my eyes, anyway.

Note to self: Get out that book about Women Who Love Too much and find the chapter about how to get out of this. And then take the advice.

## Hung Out to Dry

Weeks after the party, the house manager mentioned that Steven told Danny that I had left them "high and dry." I really lost it.

"High and dry!" It was hard to keep my voice from shrieking. "What the hell is he talking about? I tell them I'll stay for four weeks so they have time to find someone and that control freak is so angry that I won't stay the year that he makes me leave the same day. And I left THEM high and dry!!!"

My worry had changed to anger, and I was finally getting really ticked off at Mr. Most Powerful for the first time since his little campaign started to not let me work as a nanny again.

"What else did they say?" I saw a little bubble of spit fly onto the house manager's blouse.

"Uh..." She started; too scared to answer me, for fear I might really lose it. Casually, as if it were nothing, she said, "uh, just that you were a terrible slob."

"Oh yeah, that's me, throwing my dirty laundry over the banister and leaving it in the foyer for weeks on end. I also left banana peels between the couch cushions. It was just horrible. Julia had to go behind me with a broom daily. Just call me Pigpen. That house was immaculate every minute of everyday. I never even saw a dish in the sink. I was a wreck if I rinsed my drinking glass out and had to set it on the counter until the dishwasher stopped running."

I fumed about it all day long. *Where the hell did the slob thing come from? How pathetic to say that, just because that's the only negative thing he could come up with.* Then I remembered one Monday morning when I had just gotten back from a visit to Oregon. I was unpacking my suitcase and I had dirty laundry everywhere. My sheets were off my bed, my bathroom had make-up strewn all over the counters, wet towels were on the floor and Brandon's toys were all over my room. Steven had walked in to tell Brandon goodbye. I remembered being mortified when he walked in. I just knew he would be horrified that my room was such a mess. Steven laughed and said, "Don't worry about it. Looks like my college dorm." So, there you have it, all my dirty laundry was out and evidently it was still drying in Steven's mind.

The next day Tammy called to let me know she was back from her trip to Aspen. She wanted me to know that she got to see Concetta and the kids because Sally's family had gone out to dinner with the Swartz'. I was so excited to hear any update.

"How were they, How did the kids look?" I grilled her for every possible detail.

Even though Tammy had stayed with me at the Swartz for a couple of days when she'd come out to interview, Julia hadn't recognized her at first. When she had made the connection, in the middle of dinner she gasped, "*OH*, you're *HER* friend!" She had pointed her finger at Tammy, as if she were a plague-bearing rodent. The kids had looked up at her, and then at Tammy, in alarm. It was as if she had figured out that Tammy was a part of that "nanny mafia" that's responsible for so much trouble in Hollywood.

"That Suzy," she fairly spit. "She left us high and dry!"

According to Tammy, she had continued with disparaging remarks and finger-pointing while Sally and Alan attempted to steer the conversation away from the topic. As soon as they got into the car, Sally had made it clear to Tammy that they had attended the dinner for business reasons. She apologized for the uncomfortable incident.

"I'm sure that your friend is a very nice girl, because she helped us find you" she said. There's a good reason people really, really like Sally Field.

## Should I Stay or Should I Go Now? Should I Stay or Should I Go Now?

My mother called to say she was coming on a visit. Ever since she had found out how well Danny and Rhea were treating her daughter, she had become a big fan of theirs. She had subscribed to *People* Magazine, which she read with a sharp eye out for any mention of them. I teased her that her real motivation for the visit was to see them, not me. But in my heart I knew that if I were a nanny in North Platte, Nebraska she'd be out to see me, just the same. That's just how my mom is. But she was probably a lot more excited by the prospect of meeting my famous employers than she would have been to visit me in Nebraska. When she arrived and we walked up to the door together I felt an unfamiliar urge to protect the poor star-struck dear. I wanted to give her a hug. Instead, as daughters will, I hissed instructions for her not to embarrass me.

Rhea welcomed my mother as if she was an old friend. No fuss, just an easy warmth and instant familiarity. Within a minute or so my mother was loosened up, completely in her element, just talking about kids with another mom. Rhea told us that Danny and the girls were watching TV in the office and suggested that we check in on them. We peaked in the room to find Danny lying on his belly on the rug, one elbow propping up his chin while he swatted his free arm at the kids climbing up on his back. I said "Danny, this is my mother."

The kids looked up and greeted her, Danny called out "Yeah, hi!"

Rhea frowned in the doorway. *"Danny*, its Suzanne's *mother."*

He jumped up and flashed that big, sheepish, "whaddayagonado?" smile. "Sorry, sorry," he apologized as he extended his hand to Mom. "I thought you said 'this is Mariah.' "

My mom was charmed down to her toes. She still enjoys keeping up with Hollywood in the occasional copy of *People,* but there's an annual issue she dismisses as a waste of time. For her there's never a contest-it's Danny DeVito, Sexiest Man Alive.

My Mom is just so crazy about the DeVitos, and they seem to be returning her affection. I don't have a clue about how to deal with this. I have a good job. But I'm still tired of being on call every minute of every day. I'm thinking that I'm just not cut out to be a nanny any more.

The very next morning, the issue came to a head. I was still sleeping in Jake's small bedroom in a twin bed just five feet away from his crib. He was a fitful sleeper, and when he wrestled his bedclothes into a knot during the night, I'd always drag myself out of bed to untie him. Every time he shifted, I'd jolt awake, wondering if he were about to wake up and if I should get a bottle warmed up before he really started crying. That morning he woke up at 5 a.m. on the dot, and as he made disgruntled noises I ran downstairs to get a bottle ready. When I returned to the room, Jake was already letting out little cries of distress, so I lifted him out and held him in the rocking chair until he was finished drinking. He was falling into a fragile doze as I lay him back down in his crib. I was relieved that I'd be able to crawl back into my warm bed for another hour, but just as I had snuggled down he started fussing again. I knew that sometimes he'd just fuss a bit and then fall asleep, so I didn't get up and get him out of his crib. Instead I did something I'd never done before and just put my pillow over my head. I was startled when the light went on and I looked up to see Rhea standing in the bedroom door, "Why is Jake crying?" she said. It sounded like an accusation.

"I just gave him a bottle," I said sheepishly, "I think he's going to go back to sleep."

"I don't think he's tired," Rhea said, taking Jake into her arms and making some cooing noises at him.

She didn't say anything more to me as she took Jake back into her bedroom, but I felt horrible. Not only did Rhea think that I didn't care about her son, but for a minute there she had been right about that. I had cared about my sleep more than him. I was wracked with guilt. *What kind of a nanny ignores a crying child just five feet away from her?*

I thought about what had happened. I had been awake most of the night, making sure that Jake was okay and that he didn't cry too much and wake the rest of the house. But no matter how many times I had gotten up and comforted him I still couldn't give him enough attention. Then it occurred to me that this was part of my job description. I wasn't his mother, who could just ignore him and go back to sleep. I was his nanny. I could see that I was simply becoming resentful of taking care of others. It was very clear to me at that moment that I just didn't want to focus on taking care of someone else all the time any more.

I felt so crappy about what I had done, I wanted to make it up to Rhea. Instead of taking advantage of the extra hour of sleep, I got up, straightened out Jake's crib and went down to the kitchen and unloaded the dishwasher. At least this gave me some time to think, I couldn't shake the feeling that I just didn't want to be a caretaker anymore. There was so much I needed to do for myself.

These thoughts got me to thinking about my relationship with Troy. When I had met him, I had thought that this was the man I was going to marry. Absurdly, I had stubbornly stuck to my plan, although I had realized a long time ago that Troy was not the knight in shining armor for me. It seemed like it was the same thing with my plan to be a nanny. When I had decided to leave home to work in LA, I had made up my mind that there was no sense in going if I didn't commit to at least five years. This would give me enough time, I had figured, to really experience California and come home a worldly woman.

When I had gone on vacations as a child, I always wanted to come back different; taller, more confident or with an exciting adventure or two in my journal. But it hadn't happened that way. I had always come back just the same. As I thought about it, I finally felt like I was growing up because it hadn't taken me five years to realize that I didn't want to be in LA any longer. If that was true, why was I just mindlessly going along with my first plan? I thought that maybe I should leave LA and let Troy pursue his life that would include monster truck rallies.

While I was going about my childcare duties that day, I kept wondering how I could tell Danny and Rhea that I wanted to leave. They had been so nice to me. I could still hear my mother going on about what down-to-earth people they were and how lucky I was to be working for them. Leaving the Swartz' and finding Debra and then Danny and Rhea had just given me a new perspective about what I really needed. Now it seemed like I had to make things happen if I wanted them to be different. I was beginning to see that it was time to do what I knew in my mind and heart was right for me. I think that day I realized that up to this point in my life I was waiting for someone else to ask me what I needed. I could see that now I was ready to make the major switch from child mentality, where my parents met all my needs, to being an adult; taking care of myself and making my own life choices.

I wanted to just go for a drive, but my Mom and Troy had taken my car the previous day so that they could go sightseeing while I worked. I wouldn't have been able to leave the kids anyway, but I was frustrated to be stuck there, miserable, with no way of getting out to clear my head. It was another sun-drenched day in California and I took the girls out to the backyard to play in the pool while Jake was taking a nap. After spending twenty minutes searching for their swimsuits, which they had worn the day before but had wrapped in towels and left under their beds, and then locating their alternate suits and beach ball, floating frogs, towels and all the other pool necessities, I was ready to just collapse in the sun and relax.

I was just settling down in the lounge chair when the girls decided that I needed to be the referee for their water fight and soaked me to the bone, as an invitation. I heard the front gate buzz and my Mom and Troy sauntered into the backyard. They were joking about how Troy had wanted to pan for gold at Knott's Berry Farm but didn't find so much as a flake.

"I think they don't have any gold in that tub at all," Mom laughed, as I stood there dripping. Then she started to tell me about visiting Tammy at Sally's, commenting about how she had such a wonderful job "almost better than yours," she smiled, "And she's so appreciative that you got her that job interview."

Mom had held the baby and had taken pictures. To top it off, she'd eaten lunch with Tammy and Sally. She was on cloud nine. She said that Tammy had wanted to come to Knott's Berry Farm with them, but she was packing to go on another trip to Aspen with her employers. This time, though, she was going to have some time off to enjoy it while she was there.

"Sally and Tammy get along so well. Tammy seems to just love her job," Mom said, "and why not, with such a gorgeous little baby and such a beautiful house?"

That did it! I was already mad that I had never been to Knott's Berry Farm, or to most tourist spots in LA for that matter. But here was my Mom, telling me about how much fun she had at Sally Field's without me; how she had wished Tammy could have come with them to the amusement park. *What about me? I never have any time off to enjoy myself. And here they are taking my car without me!* I couldn't help myself. I started yelling at my Mom and Troy, accusing them of trying to make me feel bad and leaving me stuck behind these black gates with no way of getting anywhere.

"To top it off", I said quietly so that the girls wouldn't hear, "I don't even like being a nanny anymore, but neither of you know me well enough to even notice."

Mom was appalled by my outburst at first, but when I dissolved into tears she realized how serious I was. She said that if I wasn't happy there maybe I should just quit and come back home. She said that she'd even help me look for a new job there if I wanted, or I could apply to college. She was so calm even after I had yelled at her that it made me calm down too and I started to think reasonably about the whole situation. It wasn't Danny and Rhea who were making me miserable; it was my own desire to do something that was closer to my dreams. The next night, after my mother had gone home, I had a long date with my journal. I had a whole lot to get clear about.

# ☆ You'll Never Nanny in This Town Again

Okay. It's clear now that I have to quit the whole nanny stint and start making plans for my future. Something else is clear: these plans just don't include Troy. I saw today that I'm really not even mad at him for not seeing how miserable I've been. I've just come to expect that he'll never know what's going on with me. I'm starting to want more from a boyfriend. I want someone who'll share my dreams. He might always be my "hard habit to break" but I'm tired of not being able to talk to him about what's really going on in my life.

Simply by deciding to leave I had a surge of excitement for what lay ahead. It was time to think about college. But how was I going to tell this to Danny and Rhea? Not only had they been wonderful to me, but also I had come to adore the whole family. Deep down I knew that I had to take the leap and show that I'd learned something from the last year. This was my chance to practice the assertiveness I knew I'd need in my life as a grown-up.

The opportunity presented itself sooner than I expected. A few mornings later Rhea asked me to accompany her and the kids to the park. When we got there we took a stroll on the manicured green grass as the kids played close by on the jungle gym. Rhea suddenly turned to me saying, "we're so happy with you and I know Jake loves you." A few months ago, I would have given anything for that kind of appreciation, but now it made me instantly uncomfortable. I knew that if I didn't have the nerve to tell her then, I would get in even deeper and it would be even harder to break my commitment.

I took a deep breath, and everything I'd been thinking came pouring out in one long speech. I explained that they were the best employers I'd had. I said that if I'd worked for them first I'd probably be there forever, but I had come to them already burned out. I said that a 24-hour a day job didn't give me time to figure out what I wanted to do with my life, but I thought I wanted to go to college. So I had to leave. But I promised her that I would absolutely stay as long as they needed me until they found someone else, and I offered to contact the nanny school and see if there was anyone there to fill the spot.

In the days and weeks that followed, Rhea and Danny still treated me well, although they seemed a little more business-like with me. It was as if they had already started to cut me out of their hearts, just as I had learned to do with the Swartz children. I kept calling the nanny school, but for two weeks I got no response. It seemed like the pool of nannies had dried up just when I needed a replacement. Finally, after biting my nails to the quick, I heard back from the school about a possible candidate. I told Rhea that there was a new person at the school who might work out for her and Danny. She called right away to get a reference, talking to my instructor friend Mary.

After that, she came back to me and said that Mary had recommended the new girl but that she had said "This girl is no Suzy." She smiled and patted me on the shoulder as if she were truly going to miss me.

That's when I realized that I had actually made a small impact there beyond my normal nanny duties. Danny and Rhea must have liked me from the start to take me in, even knowing about my little "reference issue." And even though Danny had listened patiently to Steven, he had never treated me any differently after hearing that I had left the Swartz' "high and dry." Even now that I was leaving them, the subject was never brought up. The biggest compliment they gave me was one day when Danny said to me, in a contemplative moment, "I guess ole Steven was wrong after all." I said "thanks" and smiled. I have never forgotten those words.

When the new girl came for her interview, Rhea asked if I would help evaluate her. We sat down in the sunny breakfast area, where not long ago I had eaten all of Rhea's special cookies. I wracked my brain for the right questions to ask, ones that would bring the girl out of her shell and reveal everything to us. *I should have written something down*, but I saw that Rhea was doing the interview off the cuff as well. We talked to her a little about her background and history, which seemed solid enough. She didn't have a ton of experience being a nanny, but she had gone through the program without any problems. I wanted to warn her about getting too attached to the children you cared for, the one topic they had missed covering in nanny school, but I couldn't say anything with Rhea next to me. During one of Rhea's questions the girl said that she didn't think she could make a blanket statement that she "loved children" because she had to meet the child first to know.

Later, when Rhea asked me how I thought the interview went, I said "I wasn't sure about this girl." I figured that someone who wanted to be a nanny, to work 24/7 with kids of all ages, should be able to say she loved children. "It just seems odd coming from someone looking to be a nanny" I shared.

Rhea told me to go ahead and keep looking. I had contacted the local placement agencies also, but none of them had any promising applicants either. I wished that I hadn't already gotten Tammy a job because then I wouldn't have to feel so bad about leaving. I would know someone great was replacing me. But Tammy was still happily settled in her job, and I still hadn't found a replacement. Finally Rhea said that she was going to go ahead and hire the girl we had interviewed, since there didn't seem to be anyone else.

It wasn't until I started packing that it hit me. I am really leaving. I was frustrated by not finding a good replacement, but it kept me from thinking too much about how I felt. I've been in a happy limbo where I could fantasize about college and home without feeling the pain of leaving yet another job. I'll never find another family who'd be this nice to me. Oh my gosh, I'm probably never going to be a nanny again.

# FINAL TAKE

# ☆ You'll Never Nanny in This Town Again

# Return of the Hollywood Nanny

## Part I

I had been back home for just a few months when I got a surprise. One morning I answered the phone to Rhea's voice. I almost didn't recognize it because she sounded so sad. She said her gut told her something just wasn't right with the new nanny. Jake was crying a lot and didn't seem nearly as happy as he had been with me.

"I'm going to have to let this girl go," she said. "Is there any chance you could come back for awhile, and go with the kids and me to visit Danny on location?"

I agreed, Jake's behavior was out of character, because he'd always been such a content baby. Then I said that I'd fly back down and work for them again, at least until they could find someone permanent.

I called Mandie, who was back home in Montana, as soon as I flew into LAX to give her an update on my never-ending nanny life. Mandie had given her notice at the Goldberg's about the same time I had left the DeVito's and we hadn't had a chance to talk since. I was anxious to hear what had been going on, and how her departure from the Goldbergs had gone. Mandie had sat in on the interview process like I had. She told me about the horrible interview she and Mrs. Goldberg had held with a nanny wannabe. After the interview was over, Mrs. Goldberg had asked Mandie what she thought of the new candidate. She had replied that the girl wasn't too bright, as far as she could tell, trying to sugar-coat how completely clueless she thought the girl REALLY was. Mrs. Goldberg had simply replied, "I don't need a rocket scientist. I just need a nanny" and proceeded to hire the girl.

As it turned out, the kids couldn't stand Miss "Not the Brightest Bulb on the Tree." The Goldbergs ended up not being too fond of her either, so Mandie said that she was also going to have to go back soon to pinch-hit until they found someone qualified. We laughed that we were both never going to escape nannyhood at the rate we were going. I promised I would call her when I was done with this tour of duty and said that I missed our nightly phone chats.

The next call I made was to Concetta. Before I could even say anything, she suggested we meet at the same park we used to sneak to. "I'll bring Brandon and we'll have a quick visit," she said.

It had been seven months since I'd laid eyes on Brandon, and when I saw him in the playground I couldn't believe how much he had grown. He was almost a toddler. No longer a baby, as he had always been in my eyes. When he saw me, he immediately threw his arms around me, and we hugged for a long time. My throat started to form a familiar lump. On the one hand, I was overjoyed to see him, but the meeting was bittersweet because I knew that this might be the last time. He was now old enough to talk, and soon he'd be at the age where he'd report things back to his parents.

I sat on a swing with Brandon on my lap and Concetta took our picture. Brandon looked at the camera with such innocence and the biggest smile, with those wonderful chubby cheeks. I looked a little like someone whose puppy just died. When I returned home, I had the picture blown up into an 8x10 and framed it. It had a special place on my dresser for many years.

After our swing, Brandon played in the sandbox with some other kids while Concetta and I sat together on the edge of the sandbox, just two of many nannies at the park that day.

"I miss Brandon so much," I said. "It's like I've lost a part of me."

"I know you do," Concetta said, patting me on the arm. "He misses you too." *I wondered if he really even remembered me.*

"Take my word for it; you're one of the best things to ever happen to him. He is such a sweet little boy now. I think he'll always remember you in some special way." Concetta was so kind. She always knew just what to say. The belief that she was right has given me comfort for years.

It was good to be back with the warm, friendly DeVito family. I had missed them, especially Jake and the girls. This time, with Danny's sister and mom back in New Jersey, I could stay in the guest bedroom. Jake had no trouble warming up to me again. I felt like I was in a different emotional space with this nanny round because I knew it was temporary and I was excited about the nursing program I had applied to.

Part of the reason that Rhea had wanted me to come back for awhile was so that I could help her out on an upcoming trip. She and the kids were flying to Santa Fe, New Mexico, where Danny was filming a movie.

"With your help, we'll make the best of it," Rhea said. "Gracie's ears always bother her on planes and it's no fun for her to fly. I have a feeling she'll have a hard time."

This turned out to be an understatement. But she wasn't the only one having a hard time. Rhea sat with the girls, four rows back, where Gracie screamed her head off for nearly the whole flight. The other first-class passengers kept huffing, mumbling and turning around. It was as if they thought screaming babies were only supposed to be part of the *coach* experience. Jake, who was on my lap, was good as could be, but the man next to us didn't think so. His expression and body language said that he was disgusted to have to sit near a baby. It didn't help that Jake kept grabbing at the guy's food and trying to crawl over to the lap of this perfectly groomed, and fairly pissed-off, stranger.

Behind us, people had recognized Rhea, and they kept violating the first-class sanctum. Although the stewardesses tried to head them off, some passengers sent their kids up to get autographs: "Daddy told me to tell you he watches your show all the time." After awhile, first-class started to look like a kindergarten class.

Finally, we reached Santa Fe and Danny. He and Arnold Schwarzenegger were filming the movie *Twins*, which wasn't filmed on a set but in a real town outside of Santa Fe. Even I thought it would be great fun working on location, but I hadn't given much thought to the weather. It was hot. No, that's not strong enough. It was a sauna. I couldn't figure out why they chose New Mexico because the script seemed to have absolutely nothing to do with any particular city.

We settled into our hotel that first day. I shared my room, which was just across from Danny and Rhea's, with Jake and a port-a-crib. The girls had a room connecting with Rhea and Danny's. This time I wasn't just

Jake's nanny; I was helping to care for all three of the kids. As soon as we were settled, Rhea, the kids and I went down to the set to meet Danny and go to lunch. When we got out of the elevator in the lobby there was a blonde woman who was about 6 feet tall and as gorgeous as any super model. We exchanged hellos as I was trying to maneuver the stroller out of the elevator.

As we were walking away the woman said, "Rhea? Aren't you Danny's wife?" Rhea smiled and nodded, like the woman was a fan. This was a routine thing we heard everywhere we went, and we always tried to keep walking. I had learned to do that when I was with them and they were recognized. Otherwise, it was very hard to get away. I had taken on Danny's mantra when we were out in public, *Keep Moving, Keep Moving.* Anyway, the blonde woman said, "I'm Kelly Preston. I'm playing Arnold's girlfriend."

**Cut!** *You are playing the part of dating somebody who's over forty? Are you even of legal age? And, come to think of it, why haven't I ever seen a movie where John Travolta has the hots for Betty White? Oh yeah, it's only men in Hollywood who are ridiculously mismatched with younger women.* I told myself to get off my own personal little soapbox and act nice.

The cast and crew were working intensely to make a quality picture while staying under budget. Everything seemed very professional and smooth. The local townspeople, however, weren't accustomed to seeing movie people. When the cameras, trailers and big-name stars arrived there was mayhem throughout the town. The residents turned into an excited mob. It was downright scary.

When we first went out to the set, one of the security people told us they had already had trouble with the number of people that had gathered around the set. So when Danny made his way over to us, he said we had to start walking right away. They were supposed to be giving us two bodyguards to help escort us to lunch. All of a sudden, I felt like I was in the mosh pit at a rock concert. I had Jake in a little stroller and I couldn't even move him. Teenagers were grabbing at him saying, "Is that Danny DeVito's baby?"

We finally got some security guys to help escort us to the restaurant, but in all the commotion Gracie lost Rhea's hand and started crying out. Suddenly she seemed way too far away from the group, and there was a huge ocean of fans between us. I was the closest to Gracie, so Rhea took the stroller and said, "Grab her!" Then I pushed through the crowd and scooped Gracie up. It was a weird feeling, having all those people so close to you but ignoring them and not making eye contact. I was just pushing through, as if we were of a different species. And yet it was the only choice.

Finally, we retreated to a small air-conditioned restaurant. They had reserved a separate room for us. A guard stood at the front and informed the owner that there would be no autographs signed. The other restaurant patrons were not allowed in the room. Jake started getting fussy after we sat down and ordered. I told Rhea I'd take him out and walk around in a part of the restaurant that I could see through the window of our private dining room. I walked into the bar area which was empty except for a bartender who looked like he was in his mid-twenties. He was drying glasses. We exchanged hellos, and I perched on a little couch so Jake could look over the back, which he found entertaining.

After awhile, the bartender said, "You want to see something, you have never seen before, in real life?"

*Oh great this guy is going to break into a bit from* Cocktail.

"You're not going to believe this," he said, "but if you look right there through that window into that room, you can see Danny DeVito. He's here filming a movie."

"Naw! Really?" I said.

"I think he's filming it with Arnold Schwarzenegger," he said, looking all proud of himself.

"That's what I heard too," I said.

"And did you see his wife? She's that one from *Cheers*, I think. What is her name on the show...Karen or something? No, it's Carla. You know the one that's always such a smart mouth and has all those kids."

"Oh yeah," I said. "I never really watched that show much, but I think I know who you're talking about."

"Yup, we've been getting more movie stars in town lately to do films," he said, as if he were personally responsible for the location contract with Warner Brothers.

"Oh really?" I said. I looked through the window, and I could see that our food was served. I decided to go back with Jake and see if he would sit still for a minute while I tried to eat. "Nice talking to you," I said as I walked out.

"Hey, you know what? This is going to sound weird, but your baby kind of looks like ole Louie De Palma, himself, I used to love watching *Taxi*" he chuckled to himself.

I turned back around with Jake over my shoulder. "You're not the first to notice the resemblance," "It *is* kinda uncanny, isn't it?"

For the next five days we tried to avoid the blistering heat. We played in the pool, stayed in air-conditioned places and most of all tried to stay out of the public. Poor Danny had to be in the heat for hours. I never realized how long one short scene you see in the final movie really takes. The actors and actresses retake and retake and retake the same scene, over and over; stifling heat and all. Whatever it takes to get the shot perfect. Guess that's why they get paid the big bucks.

It's time to leave AGAIN. This attachment detachment really sucks. Rhea and I had fun with the kids while Danny was working. I'm glad she called me to come help her. Danny and Rhea's generosity, as usual, was overwhelming. *Twins* sounds like a funny movie and Schwarzenegger is such a nice guy. I hope the movie does well. I hope I keep in contact with them so I can see the kids once in awhile as they grow up.

I'm excited and a little nervous to go home and start college. It's just a few days away. What a change that will be. I haven't had to study in several years. Well, come to think of it, I really never have studied before. I now know that becoming a nurse and working in the field of labor and delivery is my true passion. I knew I should have taken advanced chemistry in High School.

The next day, I flew from Santa Fe to Portland. I was days away from starting my first year of nursing school. My life as a nanny was finally over.........well almost.

## Part II

It was summer, three years after I had finished being a nanny. Life was good. I was in a great nursing school at a private college in Portland, and for the last six months I had been dating a great guy. He was a family friend of Mary, the nanny school mentor who had always been a phone call away when I was in LA. She had set us up on a blind date. My old boyfriend, Troy, had joined the armed forces. I was still in touch with his family, who I had always adored. Every once in awhile I would call for an update on him. I was glad to hear that he was doing well, but my heart had definitely moved on. Like Troy, Hollywood seemed to be a million miles away.

Out of the blue, Rhea called my parent's business. Anita, the office manager, answered the phone that day.

"Hi, this is Rhea Perlman. I'm looking for Suzanne."

"Oh my God, oh my God. Hold on! I'll get her mother."

"Anita just about fell off her chair," my mother told me later. "She was so excited."

I was excited too. I hadn't seen or talked to the DeVitos in so long. Rhea sounded the same as always. She said they were going on a working vacation, followed by a real vacation, and their nanny was not able to go. The main event was a trip to Hawaii. Would I be able to go with them? The dates worked great with my school schedule so I didn't have to contemplate it long. I would miss my new boyfriend, but I thought Hawaii deserved another chance. This time I'd be going with people I really liked who would share in the joy and challenge of traveling with kids.

A couple of days later, Rhea called back and said that their back-up nanny changed her mind and was going after all. I tried not to show my disappointment, but I think she must have sensed it because she sent me a huge bouquet of flowers with a note that said, "We will meet again. Thanks for being so great."

Two days later, she called again. Sheepishly, she told me that the back-up nanny had backed out again.

"Would you still consider going?"

"You bet!"

One of my first thoughts was about my nanny friends. I wondered what was going on in Mandie and Tammy's lives. *Wait until I tell them I am back at it AGAIN!*

Next thing I knew I was flying back down to LA, to continue my 'care-giver of children' saga. Maybe I never *was* going to leave nanny life behind.

Rhea said we wouldn't be leaving for Hawaii for a couple of days. I settled in at their place, and just like the last time, I wanted to call Concetta immediately. It had been two years since I'd spoken to her. I thought how grateful I was for that one night, so long ago, when Steven had generously given Concetta and me his tickets to the Lakers' Game. Long after leaving this family and the kids I'd come to love; I would record the Lakers games in an attempt to catch a glimpse of one of the children attending with their dad.

It was the only way for me to keep up with them, to see how they'd grown. Many times I'd seen Steven and Julia in the courtside seats. She looked as beautiful and stunning as ever. Many times I was able to see Josh and Brandon for a split second. Of course I longed for more, but I was thankful for the small opportunity, the glimpse into the children's lives. Now that I was there in LA with my hand on the phone, I was petrified to call. I didn't even know if Concetta still worked for the Swartz', but I decided it was worth a try. I was scared about who'd answer, so I had my story all ready.

A woman answered, "Hello, Swartz residence."

"Yes, may I speak with Concetta please?" I said, my voice shaking.

"And may I ask who's calling?"

"Uh, yes this is Cassandra with Robinson's department store and I, uh, have a question regarding her statement."

"Hold just a moment please."

*Oh great...Now I'll be stuck in Purgatory forever because of my blatant lie.*

"Hellloooo?" Concetta said. *I loved hearing her voice.*

"Hi Concetta, its Suzy...the nanny."

"Soooozy!" she yelled.

"Oh my God, is anyone right there? Who's standing next to you?" I didn't want her to get in trouble.

"It's okay," she said, "they're gone to New York."

"Who was that that answered the phone?" I asked.

"It's Mrs. Swartz' new secretary who works here at the house. You know how it is."

"Oh yes, dear, I know. That's good for you; no more phone messages." We both laughed. "Anyway, how are you? How's Maria? How are the kids? Oh my gosh, how big are they now?"

"Brandon is so big you wouldn't believe it, Maria is fine"

"Please tell her I said hello and that I miss her."

"She's off today but I will, when I see her. I can't wait to tell her I talked to you."

"Are you still the nanny? Did they ever hire anyone else?"

"No, I'm still the nanny and I get to wear whatever I want." She laughed, and I laughed too.

"Oh I am so glad; I wish I could see the kids." I couldn't keep from saying what I knew was never going to happen.

"I know. They're too old now, though, and you know they'd tell."

"I know, Concetta. I was just wishing."

"Guess what, Suzy!"

"What?"

"I'm pregnant!"

"Aghhhhhhhhhhhh!" I screamed. "No way, you're kidding. Really?"

"Yes, I am," she answered, a touch of pride in her voice.

"Did you get married?"

"No, it's my boyfriend Juan's baby."

"Oh my gosh...How far along are you?"

"Oh, maybe four months."

"What are you going to do? Are you going to bring the baby to work?"

"I don't know. We'll see. Mrs. Swartz has been very nice to me."

"I'm so glad," I said.

Then I asked, "How are Grandma and Grandpa Swartz?"

"They're the same, you know. Listen, Suzy, I have to go," she said. "The kids just got home from school."

"Okay. But, quick, give me your phone number at home."

"I just moved to my cousin's and I don't have it. You'll have to call me back."

"Okay." I could hear the kids in the background.

"Please give the kids a hug from me."

"I will. Bye, Suzy!"

"Bye!"

When I hung up, I started sobbing and I couldn't stop for a very long time. I knew that I'd never see any of them ever again.

I went downstairs to try and forget about my phone conversation. I was pleasantly surprised by something really sweet, this note I saw on the dinning room table. I remember it said something like this:

*Dear Danny and Rhea,*

*During this time of year we think of all the things we are grateful for and we realize that we are more fortunate than most people. We live an extraordinary life and have all the comforts we could ever wish for. So, instead of buying gifts for our friends, we have donated money in your honor to a children's charity.*

*With love,*
*Arnold and Maria*

It was the first time since moving to Los Angeles that I had ever known celebrities to acknowledge that the lives they lead are very different from the majority of the American public. My suspicion that Maria Shriver was a person of character was confirmed, and I felt hopeful that all the high profile people weren't like I had decided they were when I worked there before.

Danny and Rhea knew that I was only going to be with them for a short while this time, and they sure made me feel appreciated. Even though I still worked every minute of the day and never had any "off" time, I loved being with them because they made me feel like I mattered. They introduced me to their celebrity friends, invited me to their parties and took me around to famous places. One day we took a tour of Cecil B. DeMille's house, which was for sale. We stopped by on a whim, like it was a garage sale; only it was Old Hollywood they were selling, room after gaudy room of it.

The first stop on our way to Hawaii was San Francisco, where Danny was on a month-long shoot. The location was great. We tried to do some sightseeing, but nearly everywhere we went, crowds formed around us. Sometimes it made us laugh, like the time we were going to dinner on Fisherman's Wharf and a guy with a Bronx accent yelled over to us, "Hey, Louie! Everybody tells me I look just like you!" I thought "everybody" must be blind; the guy was about 5'10" and 250 pounds.

Most of the attention we got wasn't the least bit funny. Mobs of "adoring" fans clamored for autographs. They wanted to take pictures or ask inane questions. Once, on a ferry across San Francisco, a group of kids and their "chaperons" surrounded us, sticking their hands in our faces and insisted on autographs. Rhea said no, that they were on vacation and she wouldn't be signing anything. Normally, she was pretty accommodating, but she just didn't like when fans demanded things of her. In a short while, the crowd grew rowdy. Gracie, Lucy and Jake were frightened and there was no way off the ferry. So Rhea finally agreed to sign a few autographs. That seemed to calm the "fans" a bit. What annoyed me most was that the parents didn't do anything to stop their kids. In fact, they were in on the mayhem too.

Things were much calmer on this set than we had experienced in Santa Fe, a couple of years before. On outside shoots, the police and members of the film crew kept the crowds at bay. I was happy to be nearby watching the filming. I especially liked watching the little boy, who played one of Danny's sons. He was that adorable kid in *Kindergarten Cop*, who said, "Boys have a penis and girls have a vagina." He and the other kids in the movie would play with Lucy and Gracie during their time off.

One day, the girls said, "Daddy, can't we be in the movie?" Then Jake chimed in. "I want to be in it too." Danny agreed to let the kids appear in the film, but then Rhea said, "If Jake's in it, then Suzy has to be in it too." Rhea asked if that was okay with me. I said, "sure."

I was sent to Hair and Make-up, certain that they'd transform me into a glamorous starlet. Wrong. They put me in a horrible 70's outfit-brown cords, rust-colored top, and a flower-power headband. Worst of all they brushed my hair all straight, and parted it down the middle, one of my pet peeves because it makes my forehead look like an eight ball. I tried to roll up my sleeves, just a small attempt to look better, but the wardrobe lady came rushing over to me, saying, "No, no, no. Roll those back down. You look too hip, they didn't do that in the 70's."

My part wasn't exactly a speaking role. The kids and I were to appear in a crowd scene among the many people watching a puppet show. We were all supposed to yell, "We want the clown! We want the clown!" As far as I was concerned, in my 70's get-up I was the clown. I had a feeling that my fifteen minutes of fame was not going to pan out too well for me.

## Just Another Day in Paradise

It's true that Danny and Rhea were kind, regular people, but they also liked to live well. After filming in San Francisco we took one of the studio jets to Hawaii. It's a little different than a commercial flight: no shoving carry-ons into overhead compartments, no squeezing past people to get to your seat, no lines for the bathroom.

Before the plane took off, the pilot came over and introduced himself to us. He was around fifty and he looked to me like someone's dad. The stewardess stood behind him, smiling. She was 25ish, blonde, thin, and pretty. I had seen a lot of women with cookie-cutter good looks just like her in LA. They weren't stars, they weren't loaded, but everywhere you looked they were orbiting the rich and famous. You saw them as often as you saw BMW's on the freeways. They were just part of the landscape down there. This one's name was Cindi.

"With an *i*," she said first thing.

She told us she was a big fan of *Cheers*. She said she loved being a stewardess. She shared a lot of things with us, a whole lot of things. Pretty soon we realized that she was a total yacker.

"You're so funny, Rhea-can I call you Rhea?" and "Hey, Rhea, what's the real Sam Malone like? Are you friends with him? Is he so hunky in person?"

Rhea smiled and nodded. It was the same smile-and-nod combination she always gave to people who bugged her right off the bat. Usually it made them go away and stop asking questions or making stupid comments or kissing her butt, but this one didn't go away. She didn't get it. Pretty soon we were snickering and rolling our eyes whenever Cindi with an 'i' walked away. What else could we do? We knew we were stuck there in the overly friendly skies with her for the next three hours. It could have been worse, I guess-she did keep bringing us things, like delicious cheese and crackers, and coffee. Normally I didn't drink coffee, but the plane ride was making me tired and this stuff was delicious. The kids were all sound asleep, so Rhea and I thought we'd enjoy some peace and quiet.

No such luck. Part way into the flight the plane started experiencing turbulence, so Miss Cindi strapped herself into a seat across from us.

"Hey Rhea, I have this great recipe for spinach dip. I got it out of a magazine. It's for fancy dinner parties. You take one package of frozen spinach, two cups of sour cream. Or is it one cup? Wait, hold the phone, I think it's a cup and a half! Nope, nope, I remember now, its two cups..."

We looked down at our magazines, trying to ignore her. It didn't work.

"Hey, Rhea," she said, "I wouldn't have thought you'd be like you are, after watching you on *Cheers* and stuff, but you seem really classy. I guess we have that in common, cause people tell me I'm classy too. It's important to be classy, especially in a job like this. I meet a lot of big famous people. Hey, you know who else is classy?"

Rhea shook her head.

"Actually, a lot of people," she said. "But mostly," she tipped her blonde head toward the front of the plane, smiled and kind of wiggled in her seat a little bit. "You know. Don't you?"

"I'm afraid I don't," Rhea said. She nudged the side of my foot and I tried not to laugh. I was beginning to wonder if Cindi with an 'i' had been hitting the hard stuff in the back of the plane.

"You know," she said. "The big guy."

"God?" Rhea said.

Suddenly I started to laugh, almost spitting my coffee all over the perky stewardess.

"Nooooo. You're funny. Not God. I mean yes, of course God is classy and all, but I'm talking about him, you know, the pilot. Bud."

Rhea used her nod-and-smile combination again.

"This is some turbulence," I said, trying to change the subject.

"Don't worry," our lovely stewardess said, "Bud can handle a lot of bumps and movement. Hey, you guys," she said. Her voice got softer, "Can I tell you something secret?" She looked at the cabin door again then back at us. "Bud and I are having a thing."

"An affair?" I said.

"Well, yes, technically ... but I hate to use that word because, I mean, what Bud and me have, it's special. Oh God!" she said, looking like she'd just ruptured something. She brought her hands up to her chest and bit her lip. "We're like so, we're like so ... *in love!* There, I said it. But it's true. He's leaving his wife and everything."

Rhea nudged my foot again, and I put my hand over my mouth to stop myself from laughing out loud. Rhea had so much more control than I had. *How was she keeping it together?*

But Cindi wouldn't let up.

"Hey, Rhea," she said, poking her on the shoulder with her index finger. "I've been meaning to ask you... do you know Kevin Costner?"

"No."

"Oh. That's weird. Well, anyway, I was thinking your kids could play together. He was on here with his kids and they're like the same age as yours. You should call him."

"Thanks, but I don't know the man."

"You *don't,*" she said, looking completely baffled. "Oh! Well, I do. Just call him and tell him you know me. We flew all the way to London together. I don't think he'll ever forget it."

Just then, Rhea started pretending like she was coughing. I pretended to look for something in my pocket book.

"So, you gonna call him?"

"I'll give that some thought," Rhea said, coughing harder.

"Can I get you something for that cough?"

"That's okay," Rhea said, holding her head down toward her lap.

Finally, Miss Cindi Clueless went and sat in the back of the plane with a romance novel, so we got a nice long break from her. All that business with Kevin Costner got me thinking about when I first moved to LA and gave Mandie the great career advice not to take the job with that guy who said he was in the movie *The Untouchables*.

Later, Cindi with an "i" came back. She fluffed our pillows again and gave us chocolate mints that she assured us were very classy.

"Like I was saying," she said, as if there'd been no break between the last conversation and this one, "that Kevin Costner is a real Mr. Nice Guy. Also, he's hunky. Not that I'm looking." She pointed toward the front of the plane with her head again. "I mean, why would I, right? I've got my own hunk in the cockpit. But seriously, Rhea, Kevin's kids are little *darlings!*"

"How's his nanny?" I said. I think I was getting wired on coffee and those classy chocolate mints.

"Oh," she said, looking completely confused. "I don't know."

She walked away again and Rhea said, "Okay, you sneak. What was that all about?"

I told her the story about Mandie's job interview.

"That's too hilarious. But what the heck was he doing living in the Valley with only one bathroom?"

"That's the funny part," I said. "I thought for sure he was a big nobody, because he was down to one bathroom while his house was being remodeled. Because of all my great knowledge and experience, with the rich and famous, I assured my friend that there was NO Hollywood star that could get by with only one bathroom, for ANY length of time."

Rhea laughed so hard she almost spit her coffee out.

Hawaii is amazing! A real paradise. I have watched movies in my room, eaten Butterfingers out of the honor bar., Which they seem to re-stock every time I leave the room. It's so great to be able to reach in and have a Butterfinger whenever I want.

The Mauna Lani Bay Hotel is to die for. Oh my God! I've never seen such a beautiful place. I'm in the main building, in a huge suite with a balcony and everything. Rhea, Danny and the kids have a house with a private pool a short walk from here.

The beaches are spectacular, and it's so warm out! I went and bought a new swimsuit first thing. When I got back to my hotel room, there were a dozen roses from Wes, my new boyfriend. What a surprise! I miss him more than I thought I would. I really like this guy.

Mom called this morning to see how the trip's going. She was going on and on, saying she saw my hotel on *Lifestyles* with Robin Leach. She asked if there were a lot of famous people here, and if I have my own butler and pool. And, do they serve margaritas right on the beach? I went, Mom, did you forget about the time change? It's four in the morning here. She quickly hung up and I went back to sleep.

I woke up missing Wes, so I called him. I was just going to talk for a minute, but next thing I knew, I was on the phone for half an hour. I couldn't believe it when I looked at the clock. I love it here, but I can't wait to see him again.

The rest of the trip went quickly. I loved swimming with the girls at both the pool and the ocean. For once we weren't mobbed and Rhea and Danny could relax and just be real people. When it was time to leave, I made a sweep of my room, in case I left anything there. I set the envelope that Danny and Rhea had given me to leave for the maid on the bed. Next I headed over to their private house, to help Rhea finish packing up the kids. When I got there, Danny was seated at the huge marble dining room table saying, "Okay. I see. Uh huh." And a man from the hotel was standing behind him, waiting for his approval of the bill. When I glanced down at the table, I saw twenty-five pages of charges. Then I saw the bill for my room. On the front page it said page one of eight, and the total in the bottom right-hand corner was so high that I'm embarrassed to think about it, even today. I saw the words "Movie Rental" and realized that all those movies I'd watched, and half-watched before getting bored, weren't free at all. How was I supposed to know that they charged for them? I think they needed a clearer warning on the information channel. I felt like an idiot.

Then I remembered the phone calls to Wes, and all those trips to the honor bar. In retrospect, I'm willing to bet those were the priciest Butterfingers on record. I stood there with my bag beside me, feeling sheepish.

Danny said to the guy, "What's this one?"

"I believe Room 368 was your room?"

I wanted to crawl under the dining room table.

I stood there, expecting Danny to question me about my bill. But he never did. He paid the man and slipped him a big tip too. Still, I felt guilty. I walked over to the table.

"Danny, I'm sorry about all that, I didn't realize..."

"All what?" he said. "Don't worry about it. We're just glad you came with us"

Luckily there was time on my flight home from Hawaii for writing in my journal. At first I was consumed with guilt for all the room charges. When I think about it now, I can see that I was still recovering from the hyper-awareness I had learned about finances in my first nanny job.

I can't believe how generous these people are. The charges on that bill, combined with the nightly cost of my room, were about as high as one semester's college tuition, and yet Danny didn't bat an eye. I'm still feeling bad about it, but I guess I should accept what he said. It makes me feel good that he seems to think I'm worth it.

I was glad I had my notebook along because I'd been meaning to write a letter to Mandie for a long time. When else would I have time to write an old fashioned letter, but on a long plane ride.

*Dear Mandie,*

*Guess where I've just been. Okay. I'll tell you. Hawaii. And I was there as a nanny! Isn't that a hoot? After my first trip there, I never thought I'd be back in that role. But this was a whole different story. I was with Danny, Rhea and the kids, and it was just GREAT.*

*No, I'm not back in the nanny business, and yes, I'm still going to finish nursing school. They just asked me to fill in, and I was on break anyway, so it seemed like a good idea. Hawaii is a totally different place when you're having fun.*

*Anyway, enough about me. How are you doing, you old married woman? I can't believe you tied the big knot, I still feel like I am not old enough, ok, maybe I'm not mature enough, to make such a big decision. I am assuming with the way you love kids, you'll be having another little adjustment to make, before you know it!*

*Guess what....I have been dating a guy for the last 6 months! Mary, from nanny school set me up, on a blind date, of all things. Anyway, his name is Wes and I REALLY like him. And just in case you're wondering, I'm over my habit of dating bad boys that have A LOT of potential. I know you are cracking up about that little bit of emotional growth I have achieved. Just had to fill you in on my latest 'nanny adventure' it seems like it was eons ago, when we would swap our stories. I wonder what the kids are all like now. Gotta go. The intercom thing is saying it's time to put the tray table up. Miss you, write or call me soon and let me know what is going on with you.*

*Love you,*
*Suzy*

Almost a full year after I had returned home, I told my girlfriends from college that we were all going to the movies on a Saturday night to watch yours truly in my big movie debut in *Jack the Bear,* the film where I worked as an extra in San Francisco. Filing into the movie theater I was thrilled. I felt like a celebrity myself. My excitement grew as the lights went out and the movie started up. There were the credits with the names of the people I'd known on the set. I looked at my friends' faces in the dark as they waited with me in anticipation. Any time now I was going to be bigger than life up there on the silver screen, delivering my four words- "We want the clown!" I knew I'd always remember this moment.

The movie went from scene to scene, and we waited. I was giddy. We waited some more. I was eager to get to my scene, but I told myself to be patient. We waited some more. I started to feel worried and slightly embarrassed. An hour and a half went by. Still no me. Then the credits began to roll. I had not been on the big screen after all. In fact, I had only made it to the tiny frames of film on the cutting room floor. Actually, I'd probably been swept up and put into the garbage by now. My fifteen minutes of shame. *Oh well, I could say I got a paycheck from a movie studio.*

 299

# PART III
## *(alright, enough with the sequels)*

From the moment I started studying to be a nurse; I knew I'd made the right decision. Nursing school flew by, and before I knew it, I had in my hands all I needed. I had earned my Bachelor of Science in Nursing and I was now officially a Registered Nurse. I was excited about pursuing the career that I knew I was meant to do. As a labor and delivery nurse, I would be able to help people through the wonderful and challenging passage of becoming new parents. I was excited about my prospects, even though I hadn't landed a job yet. I went back to Cottage Grove in triumph, ready for a rest before I began the serious search for the job of my dreams.

I'd intended to only be home for a couple of days when I got a call from Whitney, the niece of one of my mom's friends. I really didn't know her well, but she knew me. Since practically the entire town of Cottage Grove had heard my stories from the City of the Stars, this wasn't a big surprise. Whitney, who had just graduated from NNI, my illustrious alma mater, asked if I could help her find a job as a nanny in Southern California. As we talked, it became clear that I could be the biggest help if I would accompany her to LA and show her the ropes.

I must have had an intuition that I needed to go back to Glamour Gulch one more time. My excuse for going south with Whitney was that I needed a break between school and work. Besides, I could be extremely valuable in searching for an agency that could place her. Before we left, I called Rhea and told her I was coming. As always, she was incredibly generous, offering to have my friend and me stay with their family while we were there.

As it turned out, the day that we arrived, Rhea and the children were planning to attend a charity event and she asked us to go with them. It was a fundraiser for the Elizabeth Glacier Foundation for Pediatric AIDS, an organization founded by Paul Michael Glaser (from *Starsky and Hutch*), whose wife, Elizabeth, had died of AIDS. One of the Foundation's highest profile benefactors was, and still is, Magic Johnson.

When we got to the event, which was staged outdoors, Whitney's jaw fell open. The entire event was set up as a carnival, with stars working as carnies, offering kids the chance to win prizes at each station. There was a basketball shoot, a bottle-toss and a chance to sound a gong by hitting a platform with a fake sledgehammer. This was a far cry from the Cottage Grove's annual Bohemia Days, when the carnies' hands were so greasy I was always scared to hand them my ticket because I didn't want to touch their black hands.

The first person we shook hands with was Magic. Celebrity faces were endless. Whitney's personal favorite, Luke Perry, was there along with Mel Gibson. I couldn't get over how different *People's* Sexiest Man Alive (two years running) looked in person. If this guy had walked into Safeway while I was buying groceries, I don't know that I'd even have noticed him; he's so short and ordinary looking. He did graciously have his picture taken with Whitney, and she nearly fainted right there. Perhaps the highlight for her, though, was standing in line to get her picture taken with Jason Priestly from *Beverly Hills 90210*, her favorite TV program.

One head towered over the crowd. I didn't know who he was. I guessed from his build that he was probably a professional basketball player, so I had my picture taken with him. What the heck. Later, I heard the kids call him Shaq. When I got home, my younger sister's current boyfriend was blown away when he saw a picture of me with his hero Shaquille O'Neal. I gave him the photo since he seemed so excited about my brief meeting. This single act of generosity has been brought up to me more than once, by my sweet husband and dear friend Jason, who did not appreciate me giving away the evidence that I touched the NBA super star.

When I had my picture taken with Magic, the photographer joked that he would have to either use a wide-angle lens or stand in the parking lot, to get both of our faces in the picture. As I remember it, the top of my head came to the edge of his pants pocket. I did have enough sense to keep that picture. And come to think of it, I am not going to take any more hazing from Jason about my unfortunate lapse in judgment; he got a picture of the love of his life, Paula Abdul, with Yours Truly.

As we were ambling along gawking at the stars, I remarked, "Oh look, there's Yakov Smirnoff, that Russian comedy guy."

"No, Suzy," said Rhea, who was far less impressed than the two of us. "That's Ringo Starr."

"Oh my, my mom would just die if she were here." I couldn't wait to call her.

Besides raising money, the other purpose of the event was to allow children with AIDS to spend part of the day with big celebrities. I felt a bit sheepish standing in line with these poor children, some of whom were only five and six years old, to get my picture taken. After a couple of hours of milling about and socializing, Rhea wanted to leave. As we began to walk back to the car, my heart nearly stopped and I literally had to work to catch my breath. Standing by the ice cream stand were Grandpa and Grandma Swartz-with two children about the sizes that Amanda and Brandon would have been by then.

I began waving frantically and shrieking, "Mrs. Swartz, Mrs. Swartz! Over here!" I trotted toward them, still waving. Mrs. Swartz craned her neck a little in my direction, no doubt trying to discern who was yelling at her. She squinted as I approached.

"I know you," she said. "Don't tell me now. Your face looks so familiar. Has it been a long time?"

"It's me. Suzy," I said, hoping that that would be enough of a clue.

"Oh my God," she said. "I can't believe it's you, the nanny." She went on to tell me that Steven and Julia had gone to New York and given her and Grandpa the tickets to the event. I was relieved to hear that the Swartz' were out of town and wouldn't be making a surprise entrance any time soon.

Amanda and Brandon stood by, looking patient. They listened to the adult talk like they were taking it all in. I bent down toward them, breathless and grinning. "Do you remember me?" I asked Amanda.

Amanda's face lit up with a smile of her own. "Yes, I do, you were our nanny."

I couldn't believe she remembered me; she wasn't even 5 years old when I left. I did the math. Amanda was almost ten and Brandon was six. I couldn't believe it. They were just as beautiful as ever.

Standing up, I looked back at Mrs. Swartz and asked her if Maria and Concetta were still there, thinking she would tell me they'd left years ago. To my surprise, they were still working for the Swartz'. I don't know why I was surprised. I should've guessed that they would still be there; given their patience and the limited choices they felt they had in making a living.

I remembered my last conversation with Concetta about her pregnancy, so I asked Mrs. Swartz about her baby. She looked genuinely sorry when she said that Concetta had lost the baby. I remembered how excited Concetta had sounded on the phone, and I felt so sad for her. Amanda joined the conversation and said she was really sad for Concetta, too. It seemed as if the children weren't as spoiled and lacking in compassion as I'd feared. Maybe the stability of child-care that Maria, Concetta and the Swartz' provided was giving them what they needed.

"Oh yes," Mrs. Swartz continued, referring to Concetta's pregnancy. "Julia gave her time off. You know how good she's always been with the girls." Of course, I couldn't help but agree with how generous it was of Julia to let her take time off, but I really didn't agree that women of 30 and 45 should be referred to as "girls."

Throughout this entire conversation, Mr. Swartz stood silent. He looked at me pleasantly, but with a tinge of coldness that I suspect meant "shame on you for leaving my son high and dry."

"How's Josh?" I asked while keeping my fingers crossed that early senility had erased the elder Swartz's memory of the "infamous" Butter Incident.

"He's fine. He didn't come with us today because he thought it would be boring."

Out of the blue, Brandon took my hand and asked me to ride with them on the tram back to the car. I nearly teared up when I felt his hand, the hand of a boy and not a baby, in mine. After the brief tram ride we got off the bus together. I asked Amanda if I could give her a hug. When she said yes, my heart grew three sizes. Then Brandon threw his arms around me and squeezed me, too.

If I were to be truly honest with myself, I'd have to say I don't even really know if Brandon remembered me, but for a brief moment, it felt like we were kindred spirits. Maybe I read too much into it, but I could swear that within his hug I felt him saying, *"Thank you, Suzy, for loving me."*

# THAT'S A WRAP

# Postcards
## from the Edge

To: Mandie@montanamail.com
From: Suzy@oregonmail.com

I got your Christmas card yesterday. Can't believe you're having another baby and Jaymes is NINE already. I swear it never fails. Right after you get rid of all the baby stuff, right? I know it's a nice surprise, and you'll love having another little one around. It will be nice to have Jaymes be big enough to help you out. Sometimes I wish mine were a little more than two years apart, I felt like I could barely keep my head above water for awhile. Life has gotten a little easier, now that they are both out of the 'baby' stage.

OK..........So...........when is my body going to get back into shape, I would like to know?

I thought of you yesterday when I saw an interview with one of the supermodels, who had just given birth. She giggled while she explained to the audience of moms——get this little quote, Mandie — "I don't know how I got back into my size 2 jeans so quickly after the baby, the weight just seemed to fall off." Then she giggled.

Ya right! Unfortunately for me I appear to still be packing some of it around, almost 3 years later. It's funny, she didn't happen to mention her work out schedule with her trainer, her chef's schedule or a darn word about the full time childcare she has, so she can concentrate on her own body. It was surprising to me that she left those minor details out of her story. But I am sure she shared them with the studio audience on the commercial break.

While I am on my roll, did you read that article on the cover of one of the women's magazines with that one actress, described as a "one woman show," since she claims, she now raises her children **without** a nanny. Hmmmm...can't imagine there's any more to add to that story.

Mandie, I think I am getting more cynical than ever since I have become a mommy.

The more I read, the more ludicrous it sounded. Ya gotta read it, you will be howling, she said on one film location she was working 12-14 hour days with no nanny. Yeah. Right! Let's see, tending to the needs of three children, meeting with the director, rehearsing lines and having hair and makeup done. I am thinking *somebody* was working very long hours behind the scenes. Maybe it made her feel better, if she didn't call the person a "nanny."

I can't believe this stuff still gets me riled up after all these years, I just don't think it is fair to the average Moms who are probably feeling inadequate by comparison. My gosh, I feel inadequate, because some days I can barely get through with my sanity intact.

I would have to be admitted to the local rehab unit for "mommy exhaustion" if I didn't have my wonderful cleaning lady, turned frequent housekeeper (I would like to turn her into a full-time-live-in- house-manager, except she doesn't like the idea of living in our garage without a bathroom). Fortunately, I have my dear sweet husband so convinced that I can't do it all, that he lets me have her work several days a week. In fact he got a little peeved the other day because he says she has more W-2 income than he does. I always cure that concern by saying; "You don't want to have to come home from a long day of work and worry about cleaning the bathroom do you?"

The only exception to the "hide the nanny rule of Hollywood" that I have ever heard of is Rosie O'Donnell. I was so glad when she gave credit to her nannies and housekeepers on one of her shows. She acknowledged that she spent a lot of time with her kids, but that she shouldn't be compared to the majority of parents out there who do not have the resources to pay people to provide the level of help that most celebrities have. I loved Rosie for saying that and I miss having her show on TV.

All right, off my soap box dear. I have laundry to do now and I have to go to Costco because I am out of detergent.

Hey, I just got an idea. I am going to write a letter about this to Oprah (they have GOT to have some cattle call for the worlds biggest fan *someday*). I will tell her that the moms of wealth are not born with superior multi-tasking genes, as they would lead us to believe, they are just ordinary women with one hell of a great support system.

Just for your own personal laugh at my expense, I am forwarding you this email I sent to all my friends that tells the story of a day in the life of me. I know people would expect more from a former childcare professional, but my friends understand me.

Love you, write me soon,

Suzy

To: Family & Friends List
From: Suzy@oregonmail.com

Dear Friends and Family,

Whenever you are having a bad day, and are feeling mommy guilt cuz you are not doing it all perfectly, just pull up this email and you'll feel like Mother of the Year, by comparison. Before you start reading I'd like to ask you to put on your most non-judgmental attitude and promise not to report me to the health department.

Here's what happened today. And before you call to ask me if I am exaggerating (shocking that I would be known for that) please know, this is EXACTLY what happened.

I took my two darling children out to our new health club and spa for a fun day of swimming. We had a great time, playing in the indoor and outdoor pools for two hours.

Okay, actually I spent at least half of the time chasing after Parker. The problem with that is, I was in a swimsuit in my less than firm postpartum body (I realize that I am pretty much at my time limit with that excuse), and not exactly feeling like a Sports Illustrated Swimsuit model, but that is another email.

When we were done and the kids were dressed, I came up with the brilliant idea to put Parker and Jadyn in the daycare for a short time so I could actually dry myself off, blow dry my hair **and** get dressed without a little person hanging on my body. Then it occurred to me that maybe I could *really* push the envelope and get my eyebrows waxed too, while they were supervised in the 'oh so fun' day care center! I stopped by the spa and made a quick appointment, both kids in tow.

Realizing that they hadn't eaten lunch, I came up with another stroke of genius. So I ran to get them a snack from the little bistro and took it back to the childcare center. I set Parker in a high chair and Jadyn at a small table beside a brother and sister who were eating their lunch. I noticed the siblings had nicely packed lunches in those compartmentalized Tupperware containers. I momentarily paused to reflect...OK, fine, resent the fact that their mom is probably one of those super moms who has it totally together. One of those women who thinks nothing of getting a lunch packed, along with all the swimsuit gear, dry clothes etc. probably along with some educational CD's she has for her perfect kids to listen to. I doubt she finds it **any** kind of ordeal to find shoes *and* jackets for both kids and get them in the car, without having to run back in the house three times for things she has forgotten. *But I digress............*

Returning from the deli counter, I proudly showed off my cache to my precious offspring: two hard-boiled eggs, yogurt and a bottle of water. My eldest child, the self-proclaimed vegetarian, proceeded to only eat the white part of the eggs and discard the yolks. All right! So far, so good. Jadyn was happy. Parker, however, was another story. I offered my darling two-year-old the yogurt and he would have absolutely nothing to do with it.

He started pointing and yelling, "Juice! Juice! Juice," over and over and over. The children of the Martha Stewart-type mother were drinking out of a juice box, Parker having seen their superior beverage, would settle for nothing less.

Thinking only of myself, and not wanting to miss my noon appointment, I have needs too you know. I made another trip back to the counter with Parker on my hip. I couldn't leave him. He was screaming "JUICE" so loudly it was frightening the other kids. Unfortunately, my luck, the bistro didn't have those **exact** juice boxes, just smaller ones that need to be poured into a cup. I grabbed two of those and a straw and headed back to the daycare, with the cashier yelling, "Ma'am, you forgot to sign the slip to put it on your account." I pretended I didn't hear her. I proceeded to explain to my toddler that these are **different** juice containers but a wonderful choice all the same. He was definitely not buying it.

The muffin I brought along didn't go very far in distracting him from the realization that he had a DIFFERENT kind of juice box.

By now, it is one minute to noon and the last three minutes have been spent trying to convince Parker that this juice is great. But he won't even put the straw to his lips. Visibly distraught about his juice situation, he's still pointing to the other, more desirable type of juice box. (Did I mention it was his naptime?)

I proceed to walk over to the little girl who's sitting next to Jadyn. She's just getting up to leave her half-eaten lunch. I pick up her juice box and then her brother's to check which one has more juice left in it. I choose hers. Then I say, "Honey, are you done with this?" She gives me a strange look and says "Yes." I take the straw; turn it upside down in the juice, assuring myself that this child's germs will now be mixed in with the juice, instead of directly touching my darling little boy's lips. I then hand the juice box to my toddler, with one of the daycare busy bodies looking on in horror.

Now, I'm telling you, this child, whose juice I had just pirated, showed no signs of illness. The obviously childless day care worker was looking at me as if I were out of my mind. Parker was now shouting "Cracker, Cracker..." I asked the young lady standing next to me with her mouth hanging open if they happened to have any crackers in the cupboard, she said, "Uh, no Ma'am" So I was left with no choice, I scooped up a handful of the little brothers crackers out of the Tupperware container, and put them on Parker's highchair tray. With that, I turned, my head held high, knowing my children's cuisine longings were satisfied. I walked off to my appointment.

So there you have it. Just another day in the life of Super Mom.
Love,
Suzanne

# THE OUTTAKES

*I wanted to start the book with this story that exemplifies the never ending questions I was asked about being a nanny. But, the editors told me I couldn't and I was too exhausted to put up a fight. Anyway, like any good movie - it ended up in the outtakes.*

## Buford T. Justice in Lukewarm Pursuit

I was watching Taylor, a friend's son (you remember the one from the story whose uncle is Ken Kesey), to make extra money while preparing for nursing school. All was quiet while he was napping and then I heard loud screaming and yelling outside. At first I thought someone was being abducted on the sidewalk, so I ran to the window, but I couldn't see anyone out front. That's when I realized it was coming from the house across the street.

Being the busybody that I am (of course my sister had to nickname me Gladys Kravitz after the nosy neighbor from *Bewitched*); I went out on the porch to see what all the commotion was. I could hear a man and a woman, obviously having a very heated argument. Then I heard sounds of wood breaking and the woman screaming again. I ran inside and dialed 911, thinking this woman was going to be dead in a matter of minutes.

The dispatcher asked for my address. I didn't have a clue what it was, so I told her, "It's Bill Thompson's place, the high school wrestling coach, everyone knows him. Ask around the police station. Someone has got to know where his house is. I don't know the address."

She said, "Uh, Okay," and I waited on the phone with her.

"I can still hear them fighting," I reported to the dispatcher, who was treating me like the routine call that I was. I was thinking of suggesting they send an ambulance too.

Soon, to my relief, I saw a cop car coming into the driveway. I ran out in my bare feet to tell him the story. Immediately I recognized Officer Miller, a fixture at our High School football games where he worked security. He got out of the patrol car slowly. By the time I reached him, I was chattering at full tilt trying to describe the mayhem transpiring at the house across the street.

"First I heard a terrifying scream from a woman," I said spitting the words out as fast as I could, and trying to catch my breath. "Then, he yelled at her," I rambled. "Then I heard this loud crash, like somebody threw a punch bowl at the wall. You've got to get in there right away, Officer Miller." I spoke feverishly and flailed my arms over my head in a panic. "He's going to kill her!"

I expected, as any rational person would, that with my flurry of hysteria, Officer Miller would draw his gun and run to the front door while simultaneously calling for backup. Then he'd rescue the damsel in distress. Instead, he cocked his head in curiosity and asked, "Aren't you one of Craig Hansen's daughters?"

"Yes, I'm the middle daughter," I said in a very irritated voice.

"Aren't you the one that was the nanny to the movie stars?"

"Yes, I was," I said, exasperated. "But the woman over there was screaming like-"

"So what was that like working for those celebrities?" At this point he was leaning against his car opening a pack of cigarettes. I once again tried to tell him that I was sure there was a felony in progress, not really knowing whether spousal abuse is actually a felony. "I heard you met Sylvester Stallone. What was he like?"

After one last attempt to try and get him to investigate the situation, I gave up and muttered, "It was really quite an experience working in Hollywood."

"Now weren't you in my son Tommy's class in school?" he wondered.

"I was a year ahead of him," I said exasperated. The whole conversation was discouraging, but it occurred to me that the screaming had stopped. Either one of them was unconscious, or they'd gone to their corners for a break.

Officer Miller said casually, "Oh, we get calls on them all the time, and wasn't that girl Tammy.....what was her last name? Didn't she work for someone famous too?"

"Uh huh, she did"

I looked over my shoulder and out came the couple (arm in arm, nonetheless), looking like they had been through WWIII, but be-bopping down to the ole grocery store like everything was hunky dory. Great, so the happy couple got to go on their merry little way and I was standing outside with Buford T. Justice for twenty minutes telling him nanny stories. Fortunately, Taylor woke up and I could hear him yelling from in the house, "Soozy, where are you?"

I quickly thanked Officer Miller for coming, apologized for bothering him, walked back into the house and let the screen door slam behind me. I had come to the conclusion that people's curiosity was never going to fade away, and that I'd better resign myself to the fact that I'd be asked about being a Hollywood nanny for the rest of my life. Maybe I should just write a book.

"Taylor honey, did you have a good nap?"